MW00811110

Adolescence
The Sacred Passage

Inspired by the Legend of Parzival

by Betty K. Staley

Rudolf Steiner College Press

Publication of this book was made possible by a grant from the Waldorf Curriculum Fund.

Cover photo: Carrie Hofer
Cover design: Claude Julien and John Wihl

ISBN 0-945803-80-X

Printed by Sierra Copy & Printing, Sacramento, California.

The content of this book represents the view of the author and should not be taken as the official opinion or policy of Rudolf Steiner College or Rudolf Steiner College Press.

Book orders may be made through Rudolf Steiner College Bookstore. Tel: 916-961-8729, Fax: 916-961-3032,
Catalog and online orders: www.steinercollege.edu
E-mail: bookstore@steinercollege.edu.

Rudolf Steiner College Press
9200 Fair Oaks Blvd.
Fair Oaks, CA 95628, U.S.A.

This book is dedicated to all the teenagers I have taught and am teaching now. Each one has presented me with a riddle and challenged me to greater depths in my understanding.

Acknowledgements

Rudolf Steiner College Press publisher Claude Julien encouraged me to write on the theme that has grown into this book. I appreciate his positive support and enthusiasm during the writing process. Jim Staley freely gave of his time in editing and giving important feedback on the first draft. Judy Blatchford of Rudolf Steiner College Press, who continued the editing process, was a great help as we worked through the final draft.

Thanks to Andrea Kane who shared the significant work that is being done by the Campaign to Prevent Teen Pregnancy, keeping me in touch with contemporary research. Thanks to my colleague Brian Gray who has shared many insights over the past decade when we have team-taught a course on Parzival at Rudolf Steiner College.

The insights I have gained into the adolescent process are the result of over thirty years of teaching, mainly at the Sacramento Waldorf School, as well as guest teaching at several other high schools. The insights of Rudolf Steiner were the inspiration for my work, and I thank him for his gift of Waldorf education.

With my colleague Arline Monks, I have been involved in a ten-year project adapting Waldorf methods for students at risk with T. E. Matthews Court and Community School in Marysville, California, a school for juvenile offenders. This work served as a model for designing and carrying out a series of workshops for teachers of at-risk students. Thanks to Ruth Mikkelsen, principal, for her commitment to the project and to teachers Sharon De Simone and Kevin Watts who have so effectively responded to the training and brought creativity and insight to their work. The work with youngsters at risk has added an additional aspect to my understanding of adolescence.

Last of all, I acknowledge the support and love during the writing process from my children Andrea, George, and Sonya.

Contents

Introduction

Setting out on the journey of adolescence is like taking a boat into turbulent waters, not knowing where you will end up. Will the boat capsize or find its bearing? Where is the rudder? Thomas Cole painted four magnificent scenes called *The Voyage of Life*, exhibited in the National Gallery in Washington D.C.

> The first is entitled *Childhood*. A baby sits in a golden boat, guided and protected by an angel. The surroundings are paradisal, full of promise and beauty. The spiritual world is active and present. The gesture is of roundedness and protection.

> The second is *Youth*. A young man (It could just as well be a young woman.) is standing in the boat with arms outstretched, pointing toward a distant castle. The whole gesture is forward looking. The world is beautiful and it can all belong to him.

> The third is *Middle Age*. The rudder on the boat is broken. The boat is lunging toward the rapids. The man is kneeling in the boat, praying. He doesn't know where he is going and whether he will survive the turbulence. The surroundings have become dark.

> The fourth is *Old Age*. The rudder is still broken, but the rapids are gone. Ahead is an angel, barely seen but waiting on the opposite shore to guide the old person into the spiritual world.

In this book we will be exploring the nature of adolescence. However, it is important for us to see it in the context of the whole voyage of life.

Early Adolescence, Middle Adolescence and Late Adolescence

In early adolescence, or puberty (roughly age 11–14), childhood is still present even though the child is going through physical and psychological changes. The child's angel is still present.

Middle adolescence has two stages: 14–16 and 16–18. In the first stage, we have the image of the youth pointing to the castle in the air, full of promise, but not much consciousness. He or she wants to do many things but doesn't yet know how to or what capacities are necessary. At this stage the youth is very unstable. In the second stage of middle adolescence, great changes are happening inwardly. The youth carries the forward motion of pointing toward the castle in the air, but now he is beginning to sense rapids ahead. Danger lurks, but there are also possibilities. In the growing inwardness of middle adolescence (16–18), the world becomes filled with both dark and light. William Blake describes the polarities of adolescence in the following lines:

> Joy and woe are woven fine
> A clothing for the Soul divine:
> Under every grief and pine
> Runs a joy with silken twine.
>
> from *Auguries of Innocence*

What is the rudder? It is the Higher Self or Ego, which will begin to steer the boat when the parents and other guides have said goodbye or been left behind.

During late adolescence (roughly 18–21), there is a peacefulness within the excitement of the journey. Adolescents, or young adults, have a better sense of where the rocks and whirlpools are, where the water is stagnant, where the waterfalls come pouring down in torrents, and where the cool, clear, deep water flows. This knowingness culminates around age 21. The youngster has the rudder and is ready for the next stage of the journey.

I call the journey through these stages of adolescence The Sacred Passage because it is the time of life when the sacred element is expressed in the unfolding of the Higher Self of the young person. No matter how chaotic this period can be, there is a sense of something intangible, mysterious, and divine working through it. The people who guide the teenager, significant meetings, feeling a sense of purpose—all these are also representative of the sacred in life.

So much depends on what surrounds the adolescent—what people, what interests, what books, what music, what images from television and movies, what activities. Where is the golden rope that will become the life line through these rapids? Will it be dance, sports, pottery, an author, a teacher, a coach, a neighbor, a romantic relationship? What will the adolescent grab on to, sometimes in a life struggle, to get to the other side? A rope is made of many strands, just as the adolescent's experiences are many and varied.

As youngsters move into the adolescent journey, they have endless possibilities. Each choice will move them into a new direction or close off other directions. We can only see the network later by standing back and getting distance.

The adolescent lives in a tension between what is given through family and heredity and what the individual freely chooses. This is not a passage adults should ignore, hoping it will soon pass. This is a passage loaded with possibility, with wonder. To be a parent, teacher, or friend of an adolescent is one of the most worthwhile relationships one can have, because one never knows what phrase, activity, or gesture will be remembered and be significant for the young person. Adolescents have multiple antennae— paying attention to the world, sensing all the time. Is this true? Is this person a phony? Does she have her act together? Does he really mean what he says? Is she continuing to grow and change? Is he willing to admit his mistakes? Has she given up on life?

When we adults keep in touch with our own Higher Selves and steer our lives with clarity and purpose, we show adolescents the way forward. They won't choose our way, but they learn that there is a way through the narrow passages of dangerous boulders and rough waters. When we share our passions about a subject, a job, a place, or a relationship, our enthusiasm is contagious and teenagers are inspired. When we demonstrate commitment, we model self-discipline and the staying power needed to work through hard times. We should never underestimate the influence that adult behavior has on adolescents.

The story of Parzival is a medieval legend describing the development of a boy from his very protected childhood to the highest position as King of the Grail. The spiritual truths embedded in this legend are universal and illuminate many aspects of life. When we explore some of the major themes in *Parzival*, such as family relationships, love, reconciliation, betrayal, impulsiveness, and loyalty, we find echoes in our own lives and in the lives of teenagers.

3

The legend is especially helpful in understanding the path from childhood to adulthood with an emphasis on the adolescent years. When we study fairy tales, we learn about life by seeing that each character represents a part of ourselves. It is the same with the legend of Parzival. This is not simply a story about a boy becoming a man in relationship to various significant women. It is the story of the human soul with its masculine and feminine aspects. Opening the pages of Parzival is opening gates to the pathway of human development. Continuing through the legend, we see ways in which we learn life lessons and how we can become bearers of our Higher Self, our true "I"—our Grail—in the journey to wholeness.

The sixteen chapters, or books, guide us in understanding the challenge that the adolescent faces. They show us how the youth's background and ancestry lead to a particular destiny, how love matures from mindless physical action to selflessness. The sacred passage of the journey is expressed in these lines by Rainer Maria Rilke:

> As once the winged energy of delight
> Carried you over childhood's dark abysses,
> Now beyond your own life build the great
> Arch of unimagined bridges.
> Wonders happen if we can succeed
> In passing through the harshest danger;
> But only in a bright and purely granted
> Achievement can we realize the wonder.
> To work with Things in the indescribable
> Relationship is not too hard for us.
> The pattern grows more intricate and subtle,
> And being swept along is not enough.
> Take your practiced powers and stretch them out
> Until they span the chasm between two
> Contradictions . . . For the god
> Wants to know himself in you.

Adolescence: the Sacred Passage is a merging of two of my life-long interests: human development—especially adolescence—and literary imagery. My interest in the relationship of these two areas began when I was a college freshman taking a sociology course in which we had to compare William Faulkner's *Light in August* with a sociological study of life in Mississippi. The subject was made so much richer by the images created in the novel than by graphs and statistics. Combining the two forms of information offered a fuller, more informative, way of interacting with the subject.

Following in this vein, I offer this book—the story of Parzival coupled with themes from adolescent life, hoping that it will form a basis by which adolescent life becomes more richly textured and appreciated.

What is the relationship between Parzival and adolescence?

Fairy tales, myths, and legends have survived for centuries. One reason is that they express deep truths. We can understand them on many different levels. This is also true with the story of Parzival. As we explore Parzival we find many themes which are just as relevant today as they were centuries ago. Of course, there are differences because we live in a different stage of conciousness today. These themes form the body of *Adolescence: The Sacred Passage*. By unpeeling the layers of the story and opening them up for examination, I hope the reader will gain insight into the teenage years.

Puberty is occurring at least two years earlier than it did in the past. Yet emotional maturity is not necessarily happening earlier. Therefore, the gap between early physical maturity and emotional maturity has lengthened. For a longer time, young people are vulnerable to outer influences from popular culture, peer pressure, loss of stable adults in their lives, and to inner influences such as impulsive behavior and lack of perspective. This *vulnerability gap* leaves teenagers open to making mistakes that can take them years to rectify.

The changes that occur during the three stages of adolescence shape the ideas, feelings, and actions of the developing adult. The awakening of the Higher Self which occurs between eighteen and twenty-one sets the foundation for the life-choices the young adult will make in the following decade.

Between sixteen and twenty-one, the teenager may occasionally glimpse something bigger, something beyond an everyday awareness of himself or herself. I am referring to this experience when I use the term Higher Self. It can occur in an instant or in repeated moments, but one thing is sure: the teenager is changed by the experience and, from that time on, lives with a different consciousness. Questions arise such as Who am I really? What am I here for? Awakening to the Higher Self lays the groundwork for a later experience—awakening to the Other.

Not all adolescents make the transition through the Sacred Passage in a smooth way. Becoming seriously involved in addictions (drugs, alcohol, sexual promiscuity, eating disorders, criminal activity) can hinder developing maturity and postpone the transition until the addiction has been overcome, which may take decades. Other hindrances arise when teenagers lack appropriate role models who can guide them, or their basic insecurity creates excessive dependence on others for acceptance. These obstacles can be transformed, but it takes effort and time and the good fortune of being guided by an adult who leads the youth into new experiences and insights.

The Story of Parzival
Summary

*P*arzival's background and childhood
*P*arzival's father, Gahmuret of Anjou, was a brave knight who set out to search for adventure in the East, won great fame among Muslims and Christians, and married the African Queen Belakane of Zazamanc. Although Belakane was carrying their child, Gahmuret grew restless and went on adventures. In France he won a tournament, thus gaining Herzeloyde, Queen of Anjou, as his wife. Despite his protest that he was already married, the fact that Belakane was a pagan nullified his marriage. He came to love Herzeloyde, but when she became pregnant, Gahmuret once again grew restless and went off seeking adventure. Before giving birth, Herzeloyde learned that Gahmuret had been killed in battle. Presently she bore a son whom she named Parzival. She took her newborn son and lived as a recluse in the forest of Soltane, where she reared Parzival in nature, away from all contact with the outside world.

Parzival had an idyllic childhood. He lived a simple protected life. One day, however, he asked his mother, What is God? She replied that God was brighter than the daylight, yet He had taken upon Himself the features of man. Later, Parzival, wandering in the woods, saw knights of King Arthur's court clothed in shining armor. Thinking that they must be God, he knelt before them and decided that he must go to King Arthur's court and become a knight. When Herzeloyde heard of his plan, she hoped that he soon would return home. She furnished him with an old nag, fool's clothes, and advice for his journey. Parzival's leaving was so painful for Herzeloyde, however, that as he rode away, she fainted and died.

Parzival sets out for Arthur's court

As he made his way to King Arthur's court, Parzival came upon Jeschute. Following his mother's advice, when he came upon Jeschute sleeping in a tent, he kissed her, took her ring and brooch, and then left. When her husband returned, he was sure she had encouraged the youth, ripped off her clothing leaving her only with a smock, put her on an unsightly horse, and led her through the countryside in shame.

On went Parzival, oblivious of the death of his mother and the punishment dealt to Jeschute. He came upon a weeping maiden holding a dead knight in her arms. The maiden, Sigune, was actually his cousin, and she recognized him and told him his name. She also told him that the dead knight in her arms, Schianatulander, had died defending Parzival's lands. When Parzival offered to go avenge the knight, she tried to protect him by sending him off in the wrong direction.

When Parzival arrived at King Arthur's court, Lady Cunneware laughed, which meant that although Parzival looked like a fool, he would win honor in life. Sir Kei was so annoyed that he beat her. Parzival realized that she had been hurt because of him.

Parzival naively challenged the renowned hero, Ither the Red Knight. Not knowing the rules of knighthood, he aimed for the eyeslot, sent his spear through the eye and into the brain, thus killing the Red Knight. All Parzival cared about was getting the armor off the dead man, but he didn't know how. A young squire helped arm Parzival and put him on the Red Knight's horse. Parzival told him to let King Arthur know he had completed the task and to tell Lady Cunneware he was sorry she had been beaten.

Parzival learns the rules of knighthood and finds love and a kingdom

Parzival arrived at the castle of the old knight Gurnemanz who recognized nobility in the boy and trained him in knightly behavior. He especially counselled Parzival not to ask so many questions. He asked Parzival to stay at the castle, become a son to him since he had lost his sons in combat, marry his daughter Liaze, and become his heir. Parzival recognized he was not ready for this and left for adventure.

His next adventure involved serving Queen Condwiramur to defend her city of Pelrapeire against Clamide who was trying to force her to marry him. Parzival successfully overcame the enemy; according to custom, that meant he became the queen's husband. He waited three nights to consummate their marriage and developed a deep love for her. He became ruler of all her lands. However, one day he decided he needed to see how his mother was doing, and set out on a journey.

Parzival arrives at the Grail Castle but doesn't ask the question

He found his way across a drawbridge to a great castle within which he saw many wonders. The Lord of the castle, Anfortas, was in great pain, but, remembering Gurnemanz's advice, Parzival did not ask any questions. Anfortas gave Parzival a special sword that would always protect him. In the morning when he awoke, he was alone. As he crossed the drawbridge, it was snapped up as he was barely across. He heard the words shouted: Ride on and bear the hatred of the sun. You are a goose.

Parzival begins to wake up to the results of his deeds
Parzival felt something had gone wrong; somehow he had failed. He wanted to return to the Grail Castle, but he could not find a path. He came upon a weeping maiden holding a dead and embalmed knight in her arms. When Sigune recognized him, learned that he had been to the Grail Castle and had a special sword given to him by the suffering King Anfortas, she assumed he had asked the king why he was suffering. When she realized he had not asked the question, she became furious and cursed him. When he left, he realized that, although he had succeeded in finding a loving a wife and a kingdom, he had failed in a deeper way. He decided he must search for the Grail. Along the way he healed the suffering of Jeschute by proving to her husband Orilus that she was innocent. Parzival sent Orilus to serve King Arthur and to offer his service to Lady Cunneware.

Parzival and Gawain meet
Parzival entered a dark forest. Although it was Spring, a snowfall had covered the ground and three drops of blood left by a wounded wild goose stood out. As Parzival looked at this sight, he went into a trance. All he could see was the white snow, the red blood, and the dark forest, which reminded him of the white skin, the red lips, and the dark hair of his wife Condwiramur. Parzival, unaware of what he was doing, had his lance erect, a sign that he was ready for battle. As he had ventured into the territory of King Arthur's court, a young knight, Segramors, challenged him, and when he came to consciousness, he knocked Segramors from his horse. Then Sir Kei rode out and was dealt a worse blow in which his horse was killed and he broke one arm and leg. Gawain was the next knight to challenge Parzival, but he realized what was happening, covered the blood with a silk scarf, and thus brought Parzival back to consciousness. He offered to bring him to the court of King Arthur, and from then on they became very close friends.

Parzival is cursed by Cundrie and he leaves in shame
Just as King Arthur welcomed Parzival to the Round Table, a strange woman rode into their midst. She had hideous features, black hair as

coarse as a pig's, black eyebrows so long they were braided together, a dog-like nose, rough and hairy skin, two horrible tusks for teeth and claws for hands. She was covered in richly ornate garments and wore a hat with peacock feathers. She was Cundrie the sorceress, a messenger from the Grail. She denounced King Arthur for including Parzival in his court. Then she cursed Parzival because he did not ask the suffering Anfortas the question. She told him he had a half-brother Feirefiz who had greater honor than he did. A guest from the East told Parzival that his half-brother was a powerful king with great wealth, that his skin shone like magpie's feathers, black and white. Cundrie mentioned the Castle of Wonders where noble queens and four hundred maidens were held captive. After Cundrie left, another stranger, Kingrimursel, arrived and accused Gawain of having slain his master. Although Gawain was innocent, by knightly rules he had to fight Kingrimursel. As Gawain left to take up this challenge, he said he hoped God would help him serve Parzival one day. But Parzival denounced God because both he and Gawain had been brought to such disgrace. He said it would be better to trust women than to trust God.

Gawain meets temptation
On the way, Gawain had several adventures. The first one involved Obie, the daughter of Prince Lippaut, who rejected King Meljanz's offer of marriage. Because she insulted him, he took revenge by attacking her father's castle and planning to take her by force. Her younger sister Obilot, still a child, fantasized Gawain as her shining knight and lover. Because Gawain was serving her father in battle, Obilot gives him a silken sleeve to take as a token of her love. Gawain won the battle, and King Meljanz was taken prisoner. Gawain learned that Parzival, now known as the Red Knight, was fighting on the other side and had sent knights he had captured to seek the Grail on his behalf. If that were not possible, they were to go to Queen Condwiramur to assure her of his love. Gawain brought about reconciliation among the opponents, and the war was ended. Gawain had treated the child with the greatest tenderness and respect, but she was in anguish that he was leaving.

His next adventure involves another misunderstanding
Gawain arrived at the castle where he would meet Kingrimursel and try to redeem his honor against the accusation that he had killed Kingrimursel's master. Gawain and the king's sister Antikonie are immediately sexually attracted to each other when an old knight

catches sight of them and sends out an alarm that the slayer of the former king is seducing his daughter. As the king's army responds and wants to capture Gawain, Antikonie leads him to a tower where the unarmed Gawain defends himself with a large bolt torn from the door, while Antikonie throws heavy chess pieces down at them. Kingrimursel arrives during the melee and is horrified that his promise of safe conduct for Gawain has been broken, so he joins in on Gawain's side. There is much confusion, but harmony is restored. Gawain is given the task of seeking the Grail.

Parzival meets his spiritual teacher

Parzival traveled for many years and took part in many battles. The sword given to him by Anfortas had been broken, and he had renewed it at the magic spring. When he rode up to a hermit's cell to ask directions, the woman who lived there turned out to be his cousin Sigune. When she realized that he felt remorse for his misdeed at the Grail Castle, she wanted to help him. She told him that Cundrie brings food to her from the Grail Castle and he might be able to follow her tracks.

On Good Friday, Parzival met a knight and his family on a pilgrimage and acknowledged that he had no trust in God. The knight told him that if God could help, then He might show Parzival's horse the way. Parzival let go of the reins, and the horse led him to the cell of the hermit Trevrizent, where he asked Trevrizent to give him counsel for he had sinned. Trevrizent taught Parzival the history of Cain and Abel, Christ, and the background of the Grail. He explains that Anfortas (who is Trevrizent's brother) received his wound because he had loved a woman sexually against the rules of the Grail knights. Because of the suffering of Anfortas, Trevrizent became a hermit to do penance for his brother's sin. From then on, the Grail knights have lived in hope that, as foretold, a young knight would ask the question, but only a foolish young man had come who did not ask what ailed the king.

When Trevrizent asked about Parzival's family, he realized this young knight was part of the Grail community. After Trevrizent told him that his mother had died when he had left home, and that the Red Knight he had slain was a relative, Parzival felt guilty. After a while, Parzival confessed that he was the young man who had not asked the question. Trevrizent told Parzival he did not have to seek the Grail because only those who were divinely chosen reached it, but he should be a good and honest knight. In the fifteen days Parzival stayed with Trevrizent, he was deeply moved by the teaching about God. When he left, Trevrizent asked Parzival to give his sins to him.

Gawain faces his great challenge

The story moves back to Gawain. When he came upon a woman weeping over a wounded knight, he used his skills to relieve the bleeding. The knight told him he had been attacked by Lischois Gwelljus who had taken his horse. Gawain rode off to set that right. On his way, he saw the city of Logrois with its castle set on the peak, with the road winding around it resembling a spinning top. He encountered a beautiful woman, Orgeluse, the Duchess of Logrois, whom he wished to serve. But she scorned him and heaped insults upon him. When he told her he would accept any treatment she gave him, she gave him tasks, and when he accomplished them, she only scorned him more. He experienced rudeness and trickery from characters he met in her realm. As he looked up at the castle, he saw ladies sitting at the window and wondered about them.

After Gawain triumphed over Lischois Gwelljus, a ferryman invited Gawain to spend the night in his cottage, told him the ruler of this land and of the Castle of Wonders was Clingsor. When Gawain asked about the ladies in the Castle of Wonders, the ferryman was griefstricken and begged Gawain not to ask questions. He gave Gawain a sword and a shield, and advice on how to enter the castle. If Gawain were successful in overcoming the Wonder Bed and facing death, he would become lord of the land and bring happiness to many. Gawain learned Parzival had been nearby a few days earlier.

Gawain made his way into the castle by following the ferryman's advice and found himself in a room with a highly polished floor and beautifully jeweled bed on wheels of red rubies. When Gawain managed to jump into the middle of the bed, it crashed and banged into the walls. A hailstorm of rocks pounded him, then arrows came flying toward him. Only the shield protected him. The bed stopped, and a heavily muscled peasant clad in fishskin and carrying a large club challenged him, followed by a huge lion who nearly killed him with its sharp claws. Gawain cut off one of the lion's legs, and blood covered the floor. Over and over again the lion attacked Gawain, who fortunately was able to plunge the sword into the heart of the lion, killing it.

The ladies of the castle had watched the battle and came to tend Gawain's wounds. Queen Arnive (who was King Arthur's mother), Sangive (Gawain's mother), and Itonje and Cundrie (two sisters of Gawain) had been taken hostage and enchanted by Clingsor. Since Gawain had left his family at a young age to be a page, they did not recognize each other.

After a restless night because of his yearning for Orgeluse, Gawain explored the castle and found a crystal pillar in a tower that reflected the lands for six miles around. Arnive told him the history of the crystal pillar, which had been stolen by Clingsor from Queen Secundille in the East. It could reflect whatever the person wanted to see. In it Gawain saw Orgeluse accompanied by a knight. Despite his wounds, Gawain insisted on taking him on in battle. Using the spear the ferryman had given him, he overcame the knight, known as the Turkoite, but endured more insults from Orgeluse. She gave him another task to test him—to leap over a dangerous chasm and pluck a wreath from a tree guarded by King Gramoflanz. Gawain took a mighty leap with his horse, but the horse fell backwards and was carried downstream by the quickening current. Finally Orgeluse was moved by Gawain's courage and the possibility of his death, and wept. But Gawain grasped an overhanging branch, reached out for his spear which was floating nearby, and was able to save his horse.

Then he climbed the embankment to pluck the wreath. King Gramoflanz challenged Gawain, informing him that Orgeluse had sent him to do this task as a way of gaining revenge. Gramoflanz had killed her husband and then tried to force her into marriage, but she had scorned him. Now Gramoflanz would exact a penalty from Gawain for taking the wreath. Since Gramoflanz never fought with fewer than two opponents, he decided to ask Gawain to do him a favor. He had fallen in love, sight unseen, with Itonje, and asked Gawain to act as a go-between and deliver a ring as a love token to her. He announced that the only knight he would fight alone would be Gawain, and furthermore, Gawain's father King Lot had killed his father in battle. When Gawain identified himself, the two agreed to meet in battle in eight days' time.

Orgeluse now offered her love to Gawain. When he presented the wreath to her, he chided her never to behave in a scornful manner to any other knight. Orgeluse explained the root of her behavior in Gramoflanz's killing of her beloved husband. In order to get even with him, she had asked Anfortas to take revenge for her. The land and its castle had fallen under the possession of Clingsor who used black magic to wound Anfortas and cause him unending suffering. She also mentioned a Red Knight who had recently been in the kingdom. When she had offered him her love, he had rejected her in preference for a wife whom he loved.

Gawain sent a messenger to King Arthur to tell him of the battle that would take place between himself and King Gramoflanz and to invite him to bring the entire court of the Round Table to support him in this difficult struggle.

13

Gawain is lord of the Castle of Wonders

By successfully undergoing trials, Gawain had broken the spell of Clingsor and become master of the Castle of Wonders and the realm of Logrois, with Orgeluse as his Queen. The next series of events were filled with intrigue. Gawain delivered the ring to Itonje, not revealing that he was her brother. From Arnive he learned that Clingsor had resorted to black magic as a way of gaining power over others after being castrated by the King of Sicily for having an affair with his wife. It was Gawain's task to bring harmony into the ordering of affairs on earth, and he set about doing so.

More intrigue and mystery followed. Gawain's army arrived but was not identified and was challenged by Orgeluse's army. The enchanted ladies were reunited with their relatives—Arthur with his mother Arnive, his sister Sangive, and his two nieces, Itonje, and Cundrie. He also met and welcomed Orgeluse. Gawain left early one morning to practice for the big battle, but a knight approached him with spear erect. Because the knight was wearing a wreath, Gawain assumed he was Gramoflanz and met the challenge head-on. Meanwhile, Arthur sent a messenger to Gramoflanz asking him to cancel the joust. Gramoflanz, however, was anxious to show his prowess in front of Itonje and refused.

On the way back, the messengers saw Gawain weakened and in great danger, and called out his name. When the stranger knight heard that this was Gawain, he called out, "It is myself I have vanquished," and identified himself as Parzival. Upon Gramoflanz's arrival at the scene, he postponed the battle until the next day so Gawain could rest and be a match for him. Parzival offered to take Gawain's place, but Gawain refused. Parzival was much relieved to be welcomed to King Arthur's court, because the last time he had been there, he had been humiliated by Cundrie's curse.

The next morning Gramoflanz rode out early. When a knight armored and ready appeared, he assumed it was Gawain, but Gawain was back at camp, attending Mass and preparing for the big day. When he arrived on the field, he found Gramoflanz losing the battle. Gawain postponed their battle until the next day. Itonje learned that Gawain was her brother. Thus, whether Gawain or her beloved won the battle, she would suffer. She pleads with Arthur to call off the fight. Orgeluse is persuaded to give up her hatred of Gramoflanz, and Itonje convinced Gramoflanz that his love for her would be endangered if he killed her brother. Thus the battle was cancelled, reconciliation triumphed, and

Arthur gave Itonje in marriage to Gramoflanz. During the great festivities that followed, Parzival rode off alone to continue his quest.

Brother meets brother

On his way, Parzival met a richly attired knight ready for battle. The two fought bravely, neither one unhorsing the other. Finally they fought hand-to-hand on the ground. Parzival, gaining advantage over the stranger, brought his sword down on the other's helmet and the sword broke. The stranger, a heathen from the East, seeing his opponent had no weapon, called for a truce because he would not fight an uneven battle. As they learned each other's identity, they discovered they were half-brothers. Feirefiz, half black and half white, was searching for his father. Parzival informed him that his father—their father—was dead. They acknowledged that they were part of each other. They returned to Arthur's camp and were welcomed. Cundrie appeared to tell them Parzival's name has been revealed as the Lord of the Grail. Also Condwiramur and their two sons were on their way to meet Parzival. When Cundrie told Parzival he had to choose a companion to go with him to the Grail Castle, he chose Feirefiz.

Parzival becomes Lord of the Grail

Parzival and Feirefiz made their way to the Grail Castle, and Parzival asked the question, "Uncle, what ails thee?" Anfortas was healed and made young again, and Parzival became King of the Grail. He visited Trevrizent and told him Anfortas was healed, and then he was led to his wife's tent. Parzival was reunited with Condwiramur and embraced his two young sons, Kardeis who would become king of Parzival's domains, and Lohengrin who would become a future King of the Grail.

When Parzival went to visit Sigune once again, he found that she had died. He placed her in the coffin alongside her lover Schianatulander. Parzival and Feirefiz arrived in the evening at the Grail Castle and feasted. But Feirefiz could not see the Grail because he had not been baptized. He is mesmerized by the beauty of Repanse de Schoye and agrees to be baptized if that will win her love. A wedding follows. It is with relief that when Feirefiz and Repanse make their way to the harbor where his boats were waiting, they get the news that his wife Queen Secundille had died. The story goes that Feirefiz and Repanse have a child in Italy, Prester John, who established Christianity in the East.

The story ends with an account of Parzival's son Lohengrin who was brought by a swan to help a young princess. He became her husband but only on the agreement that she would not ask his identity. Unfortunately, she demanded to know his secret; the swan appeared, and he was taken back to the Grail castle. He left behind a sword, a horn, and a ring, and he became the inspirer of a new culture.

Chapter 1

The Role of the Family in Childhood and Adolescence

Book I. *Gahmuret gains fame in battle*

*P*arzival's father, Gahmuret, was a second son. By custom, his older brother, Galoes, inherited the lands and wealth from their father. Galoes was gracious and honored his younger brother, offering to share the inheritance with him. However, Gahmuret has other ideas. He wants to see the world, to make his own mark. Although he is grateful for his brother's offer, he is off to seek adventure. He accepts only what will help him on his journey—five excellent horses, a boat, and bars of gold. His brother happily consents to give him this small portion of their possessions. His mother also gives him chests filled with precious silks. So, the warrior takes his leave with treasures given by his family.

Gahmuret admires his older brother's skill in battle and his way with women. Although Gahmuret is a person of moderation, modesty, and honor, he chooses to serve the most powerful ruler on earth, the Baruch of Baghdad, as a way of making his own reputation. Rather than accepting his father's coat of arms, Gahmuret chooses his own—a white anchor on a field of green. Gahmuret proves to be a man of courage, yet he is restless and does not find any place in which to settle.

Years pass and Gahmuret has gained fame and honor. His ship is caught in a storm and he is shipwrecked off the coast of Africa in the Kingdom of the Moorish queen Belakane. There he finds a most unusual circumstance, all based on poor communication which leads to tragedy. Isenhart was Queen Belakane's lover, who dies trying to prove his love by fighting against her enemies. Belakane was brokenhearted. Because she had friends on both sides of the battle, eight groups of white Christians were fighting eight groups of black Moors, and she is under siege from two sides. Gahmuret falls in love, decides to fight for her, defeats both armies re-establishing harmony and peace, and wins her love.

Once the fighting is over, however, Gahmuret becomes bored and longs for adventure. Belakane is dearer to him than his own life and she is carrying their child. Nevertheless, Gahmuret steals away in the night, leaving her a letter telling her that he might not have left if she had been baptized. In the letter, he tells her of his ancestry and mentions that the men of his line have been knights, most of whom died in battle. Queen Belakane later gives birth to their child, Feirefiz, who is described as black and white.

Establishing the Home Ground

The treasures that Gahmuret's family gave him for his journey carry him to the next stage of life. In time he will need to win his own treasures. The homeground of all our lives is the family. Wherever we are, whatever our age, we carry the family treasures and burdens with us. There we first experience love and nurturing; there our eyes lovingly connect with the eyes of our parents and siblings. There we experience attention or lack of attention, joy and sorrow. However, as we come into adolescence, we need to find a new relationship to our family.

Teenagers may separate themselves, consider their families useless and old-fashioned, reject their parents' values, and fight bitterly against expectations and family rules. Yet they need their families as a ground of support during this rocky time.

While many movies and television programs depict parents as dumb, misguided, and the last people to be sought out for advice, more and more studies are confirming that teenagers value what their parents say and do and count on them for guidance. It is in the family that the child establishes an identity. In the family the child experiences the influences of biological influences, family structure, and environment.

Biological Influences, Race and Ethnicity, Religion, and Economic Situations

First there are the genetic influences that the child has gained from the family. A teenaged boy is worried about his height. While he is fretting that he is one of the shorter boys in the class, he is somewhat comforted by the fact that all the men in his family matured late and all became taller than 5'10". Another short boy is

ones along to the movies or initiate them into wearing certain clothing, smoking, drinking, or taking drugs. If the older one is more rule-abiding, the second-born may strike out in the opposite direction just to be different.

It is not surprising in high school to experience the youngest child in a family expecting to get away with breaking rules and doing less and poorer quality work. Youngest children are very conscious of the way their older siblings went through adolescence and how the parents feel about that. One younger student commented, "My parents messed up with my older brother, and they want to make sure they don't make the same mistakes with me."

The only child
The teenager who has been an only child has been the recipient of a great deal of attention, has grown up in an adult environment, and may tend to be a loner. The only child with two parents has a completely different experience from that of the only child living with one parent. The bond with the single parent is stronger as the two must fulfill many of each other's social and emotional needs. The only child has to figure out how to play alone, often developing imaginary companions. When other children come to visit, the only child has to learn how to share. Only children can be like little adults, self-reliant, and conscientious, used to being the center of attention. As they grow older, they may feel that they are special, but they may also feel that they have missed something by not having other children to play with, not learning the rough and tumble of sibling activity. They have not had to cope with arguments, defend themselves, or go on the offensive, and always be aware of the other children in the family. The special challenge for parents of only children is to be sure to give them opportunities to socialize, to learn give-and-take, and to find out they are not the center of the world.

Adoption
Adolescence is often a time when adopted children want to find their birth parents. With easy access to the Internet, it has become more common for this to happen. However, finding birth parents and relating to them in a positive way can be completely different. What is the situation of the birth parent today? Does his or her spouse know of this child's existence? Does the birth parent want a

25

relationship with the child? There are so many unknowns that the teenager has to deal with in this situation, including the possibility of being rejected a second time by the birth parent. Yet adolescence is a time when finding out who one is becomes critical. As one teenager said, "How can I find out who I am if I don't know who my biological parents are?"

Illegitimacy is not as big a burden today as it was in the past nor as it is in some other cultures. It has become far more common for a single woman to decide to have a child without a husband, or for a couple not to marry but still have children together. Even so, the teenager has to figure out a way to be comfortable with the situation and find a way to answer the question, Who is your father? or Where is your father? Similar stress is put on teenagers who have gay or lesbian parents. Having contact with other teenagers in the same situation can be a source of strength during this time when the adolescent is struggling to figure out his or her identity.

Divorce
Adolescence is a time when whatever happened to change the family structure is raised again. Teenagers want the skeletons to come out of the closet, and they want the truth to be told. As children, they were unable to understand the subtlety of family problems and were dealing more with security, insecurity issues. Because teenagers are developing their own romantic and sexual relationships, they look at their parents differently from the way they did when they were children. They are more attuned to the quality of the relationship between the divorced parents and may be concerned that they themselves will not be able to sustain a successful relationship.

For children of divorce, the feeling of being divided in half never really goes away, although, as teenagers, they may find new aspects of each parent to relate to. The complexity of life in high school can put more stress on the divorced parents' needs to continue custodial visitation. Vacations can be particularly stressful times for the teenager who is being asked to divide time between parents when he or she may prefer to spend time with friends.

Yet the teenager is very aware of the support or lack of it that parents exhibit—whether or not they show up at events such as parent conferences, sporting events, theater productions, or graduation. Teenagers of divorced parents carry a wound that can never be completely healed as they try to satisfy needs and expectations of both parents. Occasions that are supposed to be happy can be made miserable by the tension between divorced parents. It is no longer a simple situation to ask the question after a school break, How was your vacation? What one hears is a torrent of frustrating replies of how the teenager tried to keep both divorced parents happy, and, in the end, nobody was satisfied.

If divorce occurs during the children's adolescence, teenagers often feel that they are somehow the cause of it. It is very painful for them to have to take sides and support only one of the parents. They are often caught in the middle. Jeremy had to help his father move his clothes from the family home to his father's new apartment. He hated doing it but felt he couldn't refuse. He felt he was assisting in the break-up of his family. Rita sat on a bench, weeping, because she couldn't figure out what she had done to contribute to the tension that led to her parents' divorce. Peter had to go to court to testify which parent he preferred to live with. He felt that no matter which parent he satisfied, he would displease the other.

If the divorce happened years earlier, living patterns are usually well-established by adolescence. However, teenagers will often want to have some choice about the living situation in the present. If a girl has not had a close relationship with her father for many years, she may have been fantasizing about him for a long time and now wants to go live with him. In many cases, the reality of their relationship turns out to be quite a shock. Whether she is joining a newly formed family through her father's remarriage, or whether she joins him in the apartment in which he lives alone, there will be a readjustment in store for both daughter and father. Illusions will be shattered, and it will take hard work and patience for the new relationship to prosper. However, if the father has been pursuing having his daughter come and live with him, that can be more positive.

Step-families
Teenagers are affected by the remarriage of one or both parents. They are not only dealing with the relationship of their parents, now divorced, but of relating to the new wife or husband as well as new step-brothers or sisters. Even when the situation is harmonious, the teenager's identity is affected. The teenager is always aware of something that once was, is now broken and which has been rebuilt in a different configuration.

Of course, the quality of the experience is affected by the age of the adolescent when the step-family was created and by the interaction between step-parent and teenager. There are many situations that work out surprisingly well. The main issue, however, is that the teenager internalizes a sense of identity that is complex. There is almost always an underlying tension having to do with belonging.

Fatherless families

In most cases in which only one parent is rearing the child, it is the mother. The loss of the father in most teenagers' lives is significant. The reason the father is absent has a great deal to do with how the teenager lives with his absence.

If the father has died, the teenager can build up an image of him that can be romanticized. The father did not choose to leave; either illness or tragedy took him away.

If the father committed suicide, this is one of the most debilitating experiences for a teenager. Why didn't he stay? Did he not love me enough? What caused him to do this? The long-term effects of a father's having committed suicide is one of the most damaging to the adolescent's sense of self.

If the father abandons the family, the teenager may live with the hope that one day he will return. There is also the feeling that, somehow, the child was not worthy for him to stay. Because there is no closure on the relationship, as there usually is with death, teenagers may attempt to find their fathers.

In other situations, the father has not abandoned the family, but because of divorce, he gradually drops out of the picture. This is a great loss for the teenager who has an emptiness in his or her soul life. Particularly for boys, the loss of a father is a very serious situation. He desperately needs and yearns for a relationship with his father. Without it, he does not really know who he is, nor does he have a model of manhood to follow. The girl who grows up without her father may idealize men or may expect men in her life to leave at some point.

Family history

Family history plays an active role in establishing the background. This includes the myths and tales that permeate the family culture—the accomplishments, the skeletons in the closet, the odd uncle, the explorer three generations back. All these memories that are cultivated contribute to the adolescent's sense of self.

Adolescents live with the results of parents' decisions—where the family lives, with whom, in what part of town, what schools are chosen, what professions the parents are in. All these factors influence the teenager's development of identity. Each teenager experiences these factors differently. In each case, the journey of the adolescent through these critical years opens up possibilities for development.

If we think back to this chapter in Parzival, we see the individuality of Gahmuret with his striking contradictions. He is moderate, but he chooses to fight for the most powerful ruler in the world. He is honorable in battle, yet he sneaks out and leaves his wife. He is restless, yet he chooses an anchor as his coat of arms. Where will he find peace? Where will he settle down? Will he?

These contradictions also live in teenagers. They are noble yet obnoxious, idealistic but cynical, helpful but lazy, fun but sullen, and dependable yet risk-taking. Contradictions are a part of real life. One of the signs of maturity is the recognition that none of us is completely consistent, and we have contradictions in our personalities.

As we continue the story of Parzival, we will experience many aspects of adolescent development which illuminate the path to Selfhood.

Chapter 2

Relationships, Expectations, and Boundaries in Adolescence

Book II. *Parzival's father and mother meet*

*T*he action takes place in Spain, the meeting place of East and West during the Middle Ages. Gahmuret has gone to Toledo to see his cousin Kaylet, King of Castile. When he arrives, he finds that Kaylet has just left on a knightly expedition to Waleis, so Gahmuret decides to catch up with him. He has one hundred spears and silk banners with white anchors made to be carried by his cousin's men.

The Queen of Waleis, Herzeloyde, has proclaimed a tournament, offering two countries and herself as prize to the winner. She is a strong-willed woman who takes hold of her own destiny and decides the means by which she will be married. Many knights fight for the prize and lose. Gahmuret rides into the city, displaying the wealth he has won in the East. Rumors of his fine manners, his heathen attendants, and his noble bearing create a stir. Who is this fair knight of great wealth?

When his cousin learns that Gahmuret is nearby, his heart leaps with joy. He is also glad to have Gahmuret's strength against a king who has been challenging him. They catch up on family news. This is the first time that we hear that King Arthur's mother has gone off with a cleric who spoke magic spells, and that Arthur is riding to catch up with him. Present at the tournament are Arthur's brother-in-law, King Lot, and Lot's young son Gawain. Many of the characters we will meet later in the book are at the tournament. (Gurnemanz, Cidegast, Brandelidelin, Lehelin.)

The Queen of France, Ampflise, had been a childhood sweetheart of Gahmuret's. When he was in knightly training, he had chosen her as his ideal. When she becomes aware of his presence in Waleis, she sends him a letter with her ring enclosed as a token of her love, and she asks him to become her husband and the ruler of her land. Gahmuret agrees to do her bidding and to fight on her behalf in the tournament.

In the Vesper games which are set up as practice sessions, Gahmuret knocks some of the strongest knights off their horses. He is so impressive in battle and so clearly the winner that the other knights do not feel that they need to have the games the next day. Queen Herzeloyde is happy to hear that he is declared the winner because he has already won her heart with his knightly courage and manly beauty. At the same time, representatives from the Queen of France arrive and press their claim that he become her husband, especially because she knew him earlier, because she loves him more than the others do, and because he has agreed to fight in her name. As Herzeloyde listens, she realizes this needs to be decided in the highest court in the land.

Gahmuret speaks of his love for his wife, commenting that others may think her inferior because of her black color, but to him she shines like the sun. However, she was overprotective and didn't want him leaving her to fight. He had thought that he could calm his restlessness by engaging in knightly battle and then return to her. Now he has fought and won, and although he is tempted by the beauty of Queen Herzeloyde, he should return to Belakane. Gahmuret also learns of the death of his brother, and, filled with grief, he retreats to his tent. Gahmuret is filled with double sorrow, the death of his brother, and the possible loss of his wife Belakane.

When Herzeloyde comes to claim him as her prize, he protests that he already has a wife whom he loves as much as his own life. He also protests that he only fought in the Vesper games, and since the tournament was called off, his victories do not count. However, the judge rules in favor of Herzeloyde, dismissing the fact that Belakane is already his wife because she is a heathen and has not been baptized. Under the rules of chivalry, Gahmuret has to accept the decision. However, his heart is pulled in three directions—the love for his wife Belakane, the love for Queen Ampflise who educated him in chivalry when he was a youth, and his new arrangement with Herzeloyde. Nevertheless, the customs of the time prevail.

Gahmuret settles down as the husband of Herzeloyde, king of her lands, and soon after, the father of their child. After Gahmuret explains to Herzeloyde that one of the reasons he left Belakane was that she kept him from participating in tournaments, she agrees that he may leave to fight once a month. As time passes, he fights many a battle, always returning to his queen with whom he comes to share much love. However, when he learns that his lord the Baruch is in trouble in the East, Gahmuret leaves to join him and is killed in battle.

For six months, Herzeloyde waits for his return, and then, pregnant with his child, she has a nightmarish dream. Just at that moment the news arrives of Gahmuret's death. She is overcome with grief and wants to die, but she realizes that if she dies, her child within will also die, and it would be like a second death of Gahmuret. Two weeks later, she gives birth to a son whose size almost kills her. She loves the child and nurses him as she recalls Mary nursed the infant Jesus.

Relationships, Expectations, and Boundaries

We are now familiar with Parzival's parents—his mother whose name Herzeloyde means "heart's sorrow" and his noble, restless father, Gahmuret.

Restlessness and Stability

Gahmuret is modest, humble, beautiful, courageous, and noble. Such a description would fit many of our adolescents as they go out to seek adventure in the world. They go with the best of intentions, as Gahmuret himself did. Yet they find themselves in complex situations that challenge commitments they have made. Are they dishonest? Are they out to use people? Gahmuret chooses the image of the anchor for his shield. He is searching for some stability to find a place to land. When he weds Herzeloyde, he replaces the anchor with a panther from his father's shield. The restlessness of the adolescent comes to mind here as the tension between settling down and seeking adventure is expressed.

Teenage relationships
Some teens develop intimate relationships early in high school. Together the two youngsters learn about life and mature. Yet, often, these relationships are torn apart by infidelity. Although from our adult perspective, we may condemn the unfaithful partner, it may also be the case that he or she is not ready to settle down. This in no way belittles what has been gained from the relationship. Very important capacities of intimacy and sharing have been awakened,

and are ready to be tempered further in relationships to come. The grief that accompanies the ending of the relationship is real, and adults can empathize with the teenager. Yet we adults must also be careful not to label the errant partner with unflattering names. There are lessons to be learned, and we can help by supporting each of the pair, listening to them, helping them to gain perspective on the positive aspects of what they shared, rather than taking sides and either condemning or finding excuses to justify whatever happened.

The medieval knights and ladies lived according to strict rules of chivalry that they learned as they grew up. Every act was governed by rules, whether it was the kiss of greeting, the rules of combat, or the rules of courtship and marriage. Honor was the highest value of the time. Young people learned through apprenticeships in which they absorbed standards of behavior, clear expectations, and stress on quality.

Ambivalence toward authority
We are living in a time when rules of behavior are questioned. Perhaps out of their own upbringing and societal changes, many parents have difficulty insisting that rules be followed. Instead, every rule can be negotiated according to many teenagers. Many young people question whether rules have any validity at all. In our time of freedom, rules are looked at as mere conventions. We have seen a breakdown in rules of dress, of behavior at sporting events and at the theater. There is an aversion to anything that is considered authoritarian. This is a great loss for our adolescents who yearn for guidelines at the same time as they fight against them. Of course, there are parents who hold a standard of behavior for themselves and their children. They experience frustration as they fight against the tide of relativism that expresses itself in many areas of behavior.

Boys need physical activity. The rules of chivalry recognized this need and channeled it into proper knightly behavior. A modern analogy to these rules might be in the realm of sports: You can't step over this line. You can't touch the other person above the waist. You can only dribble in a particular way. The umpire has the last word. Recognizing such rules, the adolescent boy or girl has to put aside individual feelings and obey the coach or umpire or referee. There is no middle way; they are either in or out, right or wrong. Arguing gets them into trouble. To go further, in the world of basketball (and other sports), the coach also has to live in this black and white world. If the coach begins to act like an adolescent, the referee can throw him or her out of the game also. Teenagers learn these rules and play by them without questioning their validity. However, when rules are placed on social behavior, the teenager often takes exception.

Of course, rules need to be sensible. In our litigious society, parents can be as difficult to deal with as teenagers are. In these cases they may approach school policies with a legal eye rather than focusing on how the policies will contribute to the growth of the students. Many parents question rules, especially when their own sons and daughters are being punished for disobeying them.

When I first began teaching, the rule book in our school was only a few pages long. As the years went on and the school had occasion to discipline students, some parents insisted on knowing exactly where and in what detail the rule was stated in writing. So more and more rules were written down, and the rule book became thicker and thicker. As I have discussed this with teachers in other schools, I have found they had similar concerns—parents putting pressure on teachers to change grades, to change discipline policies, to give their children preferential treatment. It is not unusual in a parent meeting at school to experience this gap between parents who carry an anti-authoritarian attitude toward rules and those who consider rules important as a framework.

It may seem as if I'm being overly critical of parents, but I am trying to sound a wake-up call. However, I have found that in the last forty years more and more parents lack respect for rules or high expectations of social behavior. They are willing to sign notes stating that their sons or daughters were home ill when it isn't true. They put pressure on their children to get high grades regardless of how they get them, instead of asking them to do their best. Severe measures have had to be taken at sporting events to create a civilized atmosphere. One high school recently made parents, coaches, and students come to a behavior workshop. They had to complete it and pass it before they would be allowed in the gym. We see a similar lack of respect for rules in the poor language which students and adults use, whether it is a matter of vulgarity or of proper English syntax.

Behavioral Expectations

In many high schools, students dress as if they were going to the beach, cleaning the yard, or parading in a Miss America contest. Fashions such as those shown on MTV so dominate the market that it is even difficult to find clothes that do not follow the latest trend. Some schools have gone to uniforms to simplify questions of dress because they can't rely on the students' or parents' judgment of appropriate dress, or they want to avoid the pressure on children to wear a particular brand. In some schools, the requirement to wear uniforms avoids the problem of gang-affiliated colors.

Over the past year, I have heard a number of news reports related to the change in the way people dress. One survey asked Americans what they considered appropriate dress for particular occasions. The responses showed that a large number did not know what characterized casual or formal dress, nor did they differentiate between them. There didn't seem to be a sense of appropriateness of what to wear on particular occasions. One report described the change of dress among church goers, especially at Easter. Gone are the days of the Easter outfits, complete with hat and gloves. Jeans have become common dress for any occasion. Another report expressed frustration at the sloppiness and casualness of opera goers.

Does it make a difference how people dress for special occasions? Does it represent a breaking down of a system of expectations? Is it a liberation not to feel obligated to dress in a prescribed way? Had we gone too far in requiring specific kinds of dress and now we are leaving it completely up to the children and parents?

Clothes are just one example of changing rules and tastes. What kinds of rules do teenagers need to help them develop appropriate behavior? We can start out by establishing sensible rules of behavior in the classroom. It is amazing that one has to spell these out: respect for whoever is speaking, honoring people who express different points of view, not calling out, not sleeping, not eating or throwing food, not writing on furniture, not getting up and walking around, coming to class on time with the needed supplies, doing the required homework and handing it in. Yet these seemingly obvious rules have to be taught and reinforced..

Over the past twenty-five years, I have accompanied high school students to theatrical performances in San Francisco. These matinees were especially for high school groups in northern

California. Before each performance, the stage manager would address the young people, telling them something about the production and expressing hopes that they would enjoy the play. About fifteen years ago, a most astonishing change happened. The stage manager told the students, "This is a theatrical production, not television. These are real actors and actresses on stage. If you throw things at them, it will affect their performance. If you eat and talk, you will distract the performers from concentrating on their parts." Teachers accompanying the students had to discipline students to keep them in line. A basic sense of how to behave in the theater was gone.

Similar problems in behavior are experienced in school assemblies and at graduations in schools across the country. Hooting, shouting, hissing, and general rudeness affect the tone of these gatherings. This is another example of a coarseness that is coming into American culture. One has only to attend high school or college graduations, assemblies, or sporting events to see how standards of behavior have changed.

Legislators in California are considering drastic measures to control violent outbursts among sports fans and participants. Up to twelve hours of anger-management classes would be part of any penalty for assaulting an official or participant during a game. In addition to a growing lack of courtesy, parents place heavy pressure on their children to win at all costs in order to gain college scholarship. This kind of rudeness is learned behavior, which means not only that it has come about by changes in society, but that it can also be overcome by effort and commitment to civility. It is not a matter of blaming teenagers. They imitate what is around them. It is a matter of setting a new standard of courtesy and respect that can infuse our society. Civility has become out of fashion, but that doesn't mean that it cannot come back into fashion.

Whereas the code of chivalry of Parzival and Gawain and Arthur may not have worked all the time and with all people, nevertheless there was a general sense in society at large that it was appropriate to have particular expectations, to honor a person's word, and to control oneself in public arenas.

Chapter 3

The Path of Childhood

Book III. *Parzival's childhood. He hears the call and sets out on adventure. Learning the rules of knighthood.*

*I*n despair over her husband Gahmuret's death, Herzeloyde renounces the world and, with her child Parzival, she withdraws into the forest of Soltane. She requires that peasants who work her fields never mention anything about knights to her young son. The only aspect of Parzival's royal background is a bow and the arrows that he whittled himself.

He is deeply moved by the sweetness of the birdsong. However, whenever he shoots a bird whose song is too loud, he weeps and tears his hair. It awakens deep sorrow in him, but, as is often the case with children, he cannot explain this to his mother. When Herzeloyde realizes the birds are the cause of his sorrow, she has her plowman and fieldhands kill the birds. Some, however, escape and continue singing. When Parzival questions why the birds are being killed, Herzeloyde herself wonders aloud why she is changing God's creation. This prompts the child to ask, "O, what is God, Mother?" Herzeloyde responds, "He is brighter than the daylight, yet He took upon Himself the features of man. Son, mark this wisdom and pray to Him when in trouble, for his fidelity has ever offered help to the world. But there is one called the Master of Hell, and he is black and faithlessness is his mark. From him turn your thought away, and also away from inconstant wavering!"

As Parzival matures, he learns to hunt, and he kills many deer, carrying the carcasses home, even though they would be a heavy load even for a mule.

Parzival hears the call

One day while hunting, Parzival hears the sound of hoofbeats. Because his heart had been stirred by his mother's mention of the devil, he prepares himself to fight. "I would stand up to him for sure." In his state of excitement, he sees not the devil but three beautiful knights covered in armor riding by, their armor shining in the sun. Soon behind them comes a fourth knight. The knights are chasing two other knights who had abducted a woman. At first Parzival thinks that the knights must be the devil and he will fight them. The fourth knight—the prince—asks Parzival if he has seen two knights and a lady ride past, but Parzival is overwhelmed by the shining brightness of the knights' armor and thinks they must be God. The knight says they are not God but knights of King Arthur. Parzival looks at the knight's metal mail and asks, "What are these rings? Why do you wear them?" The knight explains they are for protection.

Parzival is so enthralled by this experience, that he tells his mother about knights. Herzeloyde is filled with fear because she had tried so hard to keep her son from knowing about knighthood, and now her worst nightmare is coming true. Upon hearing his words, she collapses. When she comes to, she asks him how he knows about knights and Parzival tells her. He is anxious to get going to King Arthur's castle and begs her for a horse. She realizes that she cannot hold him back but gives him fool's clothing, hoping that people will mock him, and that he'll return home to her. Herzeloyde also gives her son the following advice:

1. Beware of dark fords. Ride boldly only into those that are shallow and clear.

2. Be polite and give people your greeting.

3. If a man grey with age is willing to teach you behavior, follow him willingly.

4. If you can win a good woman's ring and greeting, take them. Make haste to kiss her and clasp her tightly in your embrace. This brings her happiness.

She also tells him that he is the inheritor of two lands that have been taken away from him. Parzival responds, "I will avenge those who took them, Mother." Not looking back, Parzival sets out. Herzeloyde collapses and dies from heartbreak.

Embarking on the journey—separating
Parzival comes to a dark ford, but doesn't cross until he finds a fine, clear ford just as his mother told him. On the other side is a meadow and a splendid tent. Sleeping inside is Jeschute, wife of Duke Orilus. Parzival enters the tent, takes her ring, kisses her forcefully, and takes her brooch. Then he realizes that he is hungry and eats and drinks. Jeschute asks him to give back the ring and brooch, but he refuses. He kisses her again and leaves.

Jeschute's husband, Orilus, returns and thinks that his wife has been entertaining a lover. She protests, but he doesn't believe her. Orilus tells her that their companionship is over. They will not eat together or share a bed. Moreover, she will be humiliated by wearing ripped clothing. Of course, Parzival is oblivious to the pain he has caused.

Parzival learns his name

Continuing on his way, Parzival encounters a woman with the corpse of a knight lying across her lap. She is Sigune, whom Parzival will meet three times on his journey, and the knight is Schianatulander.

Parzival impulsively asks, "Who killed him? I'll get him." Sigune asks his name, but he answers, "Bon fils, cher fils, beau fils." By the French expressions, Sigune realizes who he is. "In truth your name is Parzival, meaning right through the middle. Your mother is my aunt."

Sigune tells him his name and ancestry. "Your father was an Angevin. You were born a man of Waleis on your mother's side, at Kanvoleis. You are King of Norgals. Some day you will bear the crown. The dead prince, Schianatulander, was slain for your sake because he defended your lands." Sigune also tells Parzival about the two brothers, Orilus and Lehelin, who have taken his land. It is Orilus (husband of Jeschute) who has killed Schianatulander as well as Parzival's uncle. Schianatulander had served Sigune when she was Herzeloyde's ward.

Parzival is eager for battle and wants to avenge Schianatulander's death. When he asks Sigune for directions, she protects him by sending him off in the wrong direction. He heads off in the direction of Arthur's castle, greeting everyone along the way, saying, "This is what my mother told me to do."

Evening comes. Parzival sees a house. He is hungry and hopes for a meal and a good night's sleep. He asks for food, but the greedy owner, a fisherman replies, "I don't care about anybody but myself, and after that my children." The owner will take Parzival in only if he has money or valuables. Parzival offers Lady Jeschute's brooch, and the owner changes his tone and gladly invites him in for food and to spend the night.

Parzival meets the Red Knight

In the morning, the innkeeper shows him the way. As Parzival continues, he sees a warrior dressed in red armor coming his way. This is Ither of Gaheviez, King of Cumberland and a cousin of Arthur, a knight of very high reputation. Ither is known as the Red Knight. The Red

Knight is partial owner of Arthur's land. According to custom, a knight claims possession of his kingdom by riding into Arthur's tent and scooping up Arthur's goblet. However, Ither unintentionally spilled the wine in Guinevere's lap. Now he is out in the field waiting for Arthur or a representative of the Round Table to challenge him.

The Red Knight is very pleasant to Parzival. He sees right through his foolish clothes and recognizes a beautiful young man who will have a difficult life. He says, "Grief will wear you down. You will bring sorrow to many women." The Red Knight asks Parzival to tell King Arthur and all his men that the he has not run away and will wait for anyone who wants to joust with him. Parzival agrees and rides away. As he approaches the court, a crowd gathers around him. He responds, "God keep you, as my mother told me to say before I left her house. I see many Arthurs here; which one will make me a knight?"

A squire leads Parzival into the hall of the Round Table. "I don't know which of you is the king," says Parzival. He relays the message from the Red Knight. "I think he wants to fight. Also he says he's sorry he spilled wine on the queen. I will go and fight him."

Arthur can see that Parzival is inexperienced and rather simple, and he is reluctant to let him go fight such an experienced knight, but Sir Kei urges him to let the youth go, and Arthur gives in. As Parzival leaves the hall, Lady Cunneware laughs at him. The proud and fair Lady Cunneware was never to laugh until she had looked at one who had won, or was to win, supreme honor. Sir Kei cannot understand how she can see nobility in such a foolish young man, and he is so upset that he beats her. Then the fool Antinor speaks. He would speak only when Lady Cunneware laughed. Sir Kei then beats Antinor. Parzival sees this and feels distressed that these two have suffered on his account. This is Parzival's first awakening to the thought that his actions affect other people.

Parzival meets the Red Knight the second time

Parzival goes out to fight Ither, the Red Knight. The Red Knight realizes that he is dealing with a boy untutored in knightly conventions. He tries to avoid direct confrontation, knowing Parzival will be hurt. He knocks Parzival off his pony, but Parzival reacts furiously, goes against the rules of knighthood, and throws his hunting spear, which strikes the Red Knight in the opening in his visor and kills him.

Once the Red Knight is on the ground, Parzival tries to take off the armor so he can put it on and feel that he is a knight, but he doesn't know how. He completely disregards the body inside the armor as he pushes it around trying to take the armor off. A young squire has to show him what to do. Once the armor is off the corpse, Parzival sends the squire back to Arthur's court with the goblet he has taken from Ither, puts the armor on top of the clothes his mother had given him, and is ready to live the life of a knight. He now is known as The Red Knight.

Parzival learns the rules

The squire tells Parzival how to find Gurnemanz, an old knight who will teach him the art of knighthood. Parzival remembers, "My mother told me to listen to gray-haired old men." He rides off to the castle of Gurnemanz where he learns the rules of knighthood. Gurnemanz tells him, "You talk like a little child. Why not stop talking about your mother and think of other things? Follow my advice."

1. Know the value of a sense of shame. Over time one learns to recognize quite painfully each time one's speech or deed has become unworthy.

2. Show compassion for the poor and needy.

3. Be both poor and rich appropriately.

4. Leave bad manners to their own quarrel.

5. Do not ask too many questions.

6. Give thoughtful answers to questions and let your senses— sight, taste, and smell—guide you to wisdom.

7. Let mercy go along with daring, and do not kill defeated opponents.

8. Wash well after removing your armor so your beauty can be seen.

9. Be manly and cheerful of spirit.

10. Let women be dear to you and do not lie to them for that can never serve love.

11. Husband and wife are as one as the sun. Strive to understand what marriage means.

Parzival learns well and serves his teacher in battle

Gurnemanz comes to rely on Parzival to help defend his castle. As time goes on, Gurnemanz hopes that Parzival will develop a relationship with his pure and sweet daughter Liaze. In fact, Gurnemanz would like

Parzival to wed Liaze and join his household. He has received good fortune by having Parzival come to his aid. Gurnemanz instructs Liaze to let Parzival kiss her and to do him honor. Shy though he is, he kisses Liaze. She serves him his food and cares for him. She does her father's will with grace for the next two weeks. But Parzival feels that he needs to excel more at battle before enjoying "the warmth of a lady's arms." Although he is attracted to Liaze, he realizes that he is not ready to settle down.

One morning Parzival asks permission to leave Gurnemanz's castle. Gurnemanz rides with him to the castle gate and tells him how he has lost three sons. Since Parzival has become like a son to him, he has now lost a fourth son. Parzival realizes the deep sorrow Gurnemanz has suffered and tells him, "Sir, I am not wise, but if I ever win knightly fame so that I am fit to ask for love, you shall give me Liaze your daughter, the lovely maid. You have told me too much sorrow. If I can relieve it then, I will not let you bear so great a burden of it."

The Path of Child Development

Teenagers don't cross the threshold from childhood to adolescence empty-handed; they come filled with experiences and memories. They come with joys and sorrows, with wounds healed and unhealed. They come with their pleading eyes—trusting, suspicious, yearning, loving, and fearing. They want to believe that they belong somewhere, but they aren't sure where. They want to feel that their childhood has meaning.

In order to understand adolescents entrusted to our care, we need to step back and immerse ourselves in the world of childhood. This chapter will be longer than all the others and could stand on its own as an overview of child development. However, I find it necessary to include it because it is such a significant part of moving from childhood through adolescence to adulthood—traversing the sacred passage.

A child is a gift of the universe. All that will occur spiritually, biologically, socially, intellectually, and emotionally lie in potential in the birth of each child. Each child is a celebration of life, of dreams, of possibility. Each child poses questions to us: Will you welcome me into the world of human beings and teach me what it is to develop fully? Will you recognize that I have come from the spiritual world with a task to accomplish?

In turn, we pose questions to each child: Who are you? What will you become? How can we help you become what you have come here to be and do?

The relationship between parent and child implies an agreement between what has been, what is, and what will become—between matter, soul, and spirit—between human beings and an unseen higher power. The child has to find his or her way from the world of spirit into the world of physical existence. Step by step, we adults need to support this process. This process takes twenty-one years, a longer time of childhood and youth than for any other creature on earth.

We parents never know what the incoming child will ask of us, what capacities will be stretched, what interests will be awakened, what sacrifices will be necessary, what joys will be experienced. Each time we welcome a child into our family we do so on the basis of trust and hope that we are up to the task. Consciously or unconsciously, we rely on the unfolding intelligence of the child, and we rely on our own strength and vision that we will fulfill the unspoken promise we have made to honor the developmental process.

Birth to Three

Every child has physical needs—food, clothing, shelter, clean air and water, rest and exercise. These are necessary for healthy growth. Every child has emotional needs—to be lovingly cared for, to have a sense of belonging, a feeling of protection, joy and happiness, and ways of communicating. The child hungers for emotional nourishment as well as for physical food.

The first three years of life are extraordinary. The child learns to master his or her body—crawling, turning, sitting, standing, and walking. The child is in constant movement—movement without consciousness. When the child lifts himself or herself into an upright position and steps freely, what a moment of joy! Being able to walk independently is also a ticket to greater exploration. Soon to come are running, hopping, and jumping. The hands are free for stirring, patting, pushing, holding, clapping and waving.

The child learns to speak—from words to phrases to sentences. Each spoken word elicits an image that in turn becomes enriched through repetition. The amazing experience of expressing thoughts unfolds during this time. The child learns to think—to pretend, to problem-solve, to identify, to meet the world, and to respond to it. The child joins the social interaction of the human community. Communicating with adults is a necessary part of this period. As mother, father, or other caretakers speak and respond to the child, a precious dialogue arises. It is expressed in eye contact and smiling, in gooing and cooing, in statements, and in conversation. Through this dialogue, the child is filled with a sense of security, of belonging, of trust.

The dialogue between adult and child has been carried through daily conversation and in storytelling. As these experiences occur, the child builds internal images that will form the basis for all later thinking. The quality of interaction influences brain development and sets the stage of later learning.

The emotional warmth of the dialogue carries over to the thinking process so that the child associates support and love with particular images. This encourages the child to relate these images to a wider experience of thought. As the child feels confidence and pleasure in the adult world, he or she expands the interaction, reaching out to encompass new words, new phrases, new thoughts, new ideas. Emotions and thoughts interact. Through positive emotional interactions, the child experiences physical well-being. Thereby, a threefold relationship of body, soul, and spirit is harmonized and through this process the child's sense of self develops.

One of the most harmful influences of television on the young child is that it interferes with this process. Television entertains by producing images rather than allowing the child to create his or her own images. Interactive conversation and play are the greatest aids to a healthy development of internal imagery and are necessary for the next step of development. Television impoverishes this experience.

As the child begins to say No, he or she experiences a boundary between the self and the outer world. The child stands straighter and stronger by declaring No! It is a sign that the child is forming a new relationship to the world and is experiencing a sense of power in the self. Thus begins a period of stubbornness. It, too, will pass, but in the meantime parents become exasperated. It is necessary to acknowledge it is just a phase and keep perspective.

From Three to Five

The child has language and movement. A new stage of development expresses itself in play. Instead of playing side by side with other children of the same age, the child now begins to imagine situations and act them out. Who is the mommy? Who is the doctor? What kind of dinner will we have? Is the baby sick? Will two trucks crash?

Play is the child's work. The child imitates movements of the people he observes. Watching adults carrying, hammering, sewing, cooking, driving, planting, shopping, etc. forms the child's textbook. The child becomes what she sees, what he drinks in. He or she orders the world according to what has become the norm. What is allowed or not allowed? May I have a cookie? Is it ok to do that? The child learns to navigate within the boundaries. Play creates the context for language development and is the source for internalizing life experience and learning about the world.

It is at this phase that the great question *why?* greets the adult at every turn. Along with Why? and How? comes the word, *because*. Children of this age are trying to relate cause and effect in physical experiences, such as in the statement, I'm drawing a picture because I'm waiting for dinner.

These children yearn to know about the world. Everything interests them. (Are you better, grandma? How do you get better?) They begin to problem-solve verbally (You could do this, or you could do that), building confidence with each new insight.. (Daddy's car broke down. It was a small problem, just the motor.) They also begin to joke and get silly, distinguishing this behavior from serious behavior.

Language blossoms, as the child plays with new words, phrases, and sentences. This is a time of rich creative imagination. The child begins to transform the world. Cloths become dress-ups, blocks become forts, chairs become airplanes or ships, acorns become potatoes, and a puddle becomes an ocean. The child moves in and out between imagination and reality, easily passing from one to the other and knowing the difference between pretend and real. The feeling life is developing in polarities—sadness and joy, crying and laughing. Great joy is expressed through reciting nursery rhymes and singing songs. The child is becoming a citizen of the earth, connecting his or her thoughts with the thoughts of others. Ideas and actions begin to interconnect.

Between Five and Seven

Today's children often are rushed through these experiences as many people believe formal learning should be pressed down into an earlier and earlier age, accelerating learning of skills and thus ignoring the key experiences that the child really needs at this time.

By age five, children have developed a complex inner world of images and are now able to take hold of stories in a different way, especially if the stories are repeated many times. As children internalize a strong interconnection between word and image, they then can act out the story, and incorporate it into the play. If stories follow each other in quick succession without an opportunity to be deeply embedded, there is little time for digestion and creative interaction. Their eagerness to learn can mislead one to think that we should be offering them a feast of stimulation rather than a few stimulating experiences that can be more deeply processed.

Five- and six-year-olds need to play out the experiences they observe in the outer world. That is how these experiences are made their own. If they see firemen pulling a long hose and aiming it at a fire, they will find some object that can become the hose and play at being fireman. Rather than imitation being the stimulus, children now create a scene in their minds. Play offers the opportunity for a next phase in thinking. Children acting as firefighters may imagine a difficult fire where the hose isn't long enough. They problem-solve the situation and out of their imagination work out a solution. When a younger child imitates using the hose to put out the fire, the experience stops with the activity, and does not move into problem solving. Movement and imitation were satisfying enough. But the imaginative world of four-, five-, and six-year-olds is far more complicated.

During this time, the child develops a conscious will, directing his or her energy toward doing, making, and other purposeful activity. Adults who can do things are highly respected and invite imitation. Children of this age need a warm and loving environment that is open-ended, with opportunities to discover, play with others, explore, move about, hear stories, sing, garden, climb, and be engaged in active experiences. This is a time for children to feel enthusiasm, security, and joy, a time for their bodies to grow, their eyes to mature, their hearts to be nurtured. The three Rs for this age group are rhythm, repetition, and routine. With the frantic pace of modern life, it is even more important that children at this age feel calm and peaceful, supported and warm—a chance to be children. They need an environment in which they learn through hands-on experiences, using their limbs, their hearts, and their minds to explore. The richness of language in storytelling, poetry, and songs stimulates their vocabulary and their ability to comprehend meaning much more than filling in blanks on a paper worksheet does.

Children of this age need space, blank paper on which to draw or paint, simple toys that can be changed through their own imaginations, and unstructured time for imaginative play—all these experiences call upon the child to use his or her activity to fill the space. Of course, teachers or parents should tell a story, sing, and so on. The key point, however, is that children need an opportunity to respond to the story through their own activity, rather than in a pre-packaged form. All healthy cognition begins in action.

Expecting children to perform abstract thinking at this time stresses them because they are not yet at that stage in their thinking. At this age children are developing in many areas—physically, socially, emotionally, and intellectually—and they need time.

Between Seven and Twelve

Around the age of seven, the child's body has reached a certain maturity. This is marked by the loss of the first teeth and the arrival of the second teeth. Children now approach life mainly through language. Although movement was earlier based on imitation, it now becomes rhythmical, as in childhood ball games and jump rope.

> Teddy bear, teddy bear,
> Turn around, round, round.
> Teddy bear, teddy bear
> Touch the ground, ground, ground.

Movement and language become integrated as the child turns around while jumping, touching the ground, and running under the rope. The child is gaining mastery over his or her body.

Earlier when a child heard a sentence such as, The prince rode quickly through the forest, he or she felt the need to act it out. But now, the movement goes inward, and the child creates an image in his or her mind and is able to change it at will. If the child does not make this transition and continues to make movement outward, problems usually occur at school, and he or she may be labeled hyperactive.

During this period, children are waking up to their feelings. This is a time to reach children through the arts. When they are engaged in music, drawing, painting, or drama, they are active and participatory in the creative process. Through stories that evoke feelings, the child builds thoughts based on lively inner pictures that work on the senses and activate the imagination. If we only focus on the child's accomplishing a goal, focusing on a product, and miss connecting with the child's feelings, we miss an important opportunity to engage the child in the learning process.

In addition to connecting with their feelings, children of this age are still closely connected with the spiritual world. Their consciousness is poetic and dreamlike. Because of this connection, they benefit from a relationship with nature that is experiential and imaginative. Their feelings, their connection with the spiritual world, and with nature are strengthened.

Separation—the ninth year change

The period between eight and ten is a sensitive time. The children's feeling of oneness with the outer world is weakening, and they develop a deeper sense of an inner world. From now on, they will not imitate unconsciously, but imitate by following directions of someone they admire. They are finding that they can make things happen out of their own activity, rather than relying on others. Thus they test limits to see how far they can go. It is as if they have built their own inner house, and now they are figuring out how to occupy the rooms. They are searching for adults who can teach them how to behave and how to do things. Necessarily the changes during this time influence the child's relationship to the parents.

As youngsters at this stage become more lonely, they also become critical. Boys and girls generally express their feelings in different ways. Boys tend to turn outward to affect the outer world, testing limits, aggressively expressing anger and frustration, and testing themselves. Girls tend to turn inward, becoming moody, self-critical, and overly conscious of how they fit into groups. Boys and girls need to learn the world of peers, of friends who approve or disapprove, and who include or exclude, what it means to be welcomed into a tribe or not. They also are learning to figure out expectations between themselves and their parents. When they test boundaries, they learn what happens if they cross a line between what is acceptable or not, and they learn what kind of behavior affects each parent in a particular way. They are learning to read, and the text is the world of inter-relationships.

For many children, nature becomes their mentor as they relate to the seasons: to the hot summer sun, when they enjoy swimming, making sand castles, or cultivate a garden; to autumn's brilliant colors, when they harvest cucumbers and tomatoes, carve pumpkins, rake leaves; to winter, when they make snow igloos, ice skate, ski, or sled; to spring, when they walk in puddles of spring rain, dig beds, plant seeds, build tree forts. As they are embedded in nature, they are extending their sense of home beyond the family place to Mother Earth. In cities, too, children can relate to the seasons—even though nature is not as accessible—to the winds that blow the autumn leaves, to the heaps of snow along the streets, to the changing games they play on the street, to the time spent in parks, and to the pools that open for summer swimming.

The boy's development of self-esteem centers on doing. If he meets his challenges well, he feels good about himself. If not, he feels worthless. What he craves most of all is gaining a sense of satisfaction from doing things, especially with his father or another male. He needs to know what the rules are, who is in charge, and what happens if he breaks the rules. He is concerned about issues of fairness and justice.

The girl's development of self-esteem is based on relationships. Girls of this age can be very hard on each other with betrayal, exclusion, snubbing, and insults. The girl often whines, talks back, is stubborn and argumentative, especially with her mother. She wants to grow up at the same time as she wants to remain dependent. She is especially vulnerable to pressure from friends and from media. The girl is attuned to subtlety between people more than the boys are. She interprets everything she hears as a judgment on herself.

When children pass through the ninth-year-change, they are ready for the next stage of childhood. How they pass through this change will influence the years to come. Have they gained self-confidence or do they consider themselves unworthy? Does life feel good to them or do they continually have to be on guard against danger? Are they trying to act like teenagers they see in the movies, in magazines, or in their neighborhood or are they content to be children for a few more years?

The next stage falls between the coming in of the second teeth and the arrival of puberty. Generally this is a healthy time in a child's development. Children are light on their feet, have abundant energy, and gradually master their limbs. Emotional needs vary, depending on whether the child is able to deal with disappointment and delay or whether he or she is insecure and unable to handle change—in other words, whether the child's sense of self is integrated or fragile.

A child with an integrated sense of self can adapt to situations, understand priorities, and wait to have reward. As children learn what other people like and don't like, they are able to incorporate that into their feelings. They don't always have to have their own way. They can come up with strategies for solving problems. They can express sadness or frustration without giving up. As they begin to take hold of themselves, they feel power. On the other hand, the child with a fragile self often feels impotent, a victim, and doesn't know how to gain power in an appropriate way. Such children have difficulty waiting for a result and become frustrated and angry if they can't have what they want right away. They react aggressively or give up trying.

Nine to Eleven—the heart of childhood

The child has come through the ninth-year change and now enters a period of harmony. What a wonderful stage this is! The child's physical development is at a place of balance and health. The child's emotional life is filled with rich feelings, making it a time for laughter and a time for tears, a time for exploration of new interests and a time for developing new skills. A musical quality fills this time of childhood. Children walk with swinging arms and rhythmic stride; they run with grace, memorize long stanzas of poetry, and sing their hearts out. It is a good time for them to be involved in playing an instrument (although this certainly can begin earlier). A balance has been reached between breathing in and breathing out, both physically and emotionally. Children at this age are creative and open to new ideas.

One of the most important needs of this age is to develop wonder and reverence toward life. These qualities help stabilize the youngster's idealism as the age of criticism, and even cynicism, begins to emerge. Even as adults, we can look back to that carefree time when the world was filled with unending possibility and joy, when sorrows came and darkened our sky and then the sun shone once again.

Nature is the great teacher of this age
Working with animals—caring for them, raising and training them, admiring their beauty and strength—develops self-discipline and responsibility. This can occur in a city apartment as well as in the countryside. Often a child will tell his or her animal about cares and worries that can't be shared with people.

Much can also be learned from caring for plants, raising seeds, cultivating a garden in one's own space or in a community garden, making jam or jelly, drying fruit, making juice, gathering wildflowers for pressing, drying plants, gathering plants for dyeing wool or fabric, drying herbs, or roasting sunflower seeds.

Fishing, hiking, orienteering, skiing, swimming, flying kites, and boating are some of the other ways children deepen their relationship to nature as they learn to work with natural laws expressed through wind, water, mountains, forest trails, and topography. Children of this age often like to collect minerals, identify them, learn about volcanoes and earthquakes, and memorize capitals of countries. They are grasping geography and geology in a new way.

Another way children connect with nature is through arts and crafts. Working with clay, wood, stone, wool, paint, pastels, and pencils stirs creative juices. All these activities take time. To benefit the child, new skills need to be cultivated because they do not arise merely through rote learning or quick sessions. Creative experiences are focused on process rather than on product. It is a very different experience for the child to do an instant project where all parts are pre-cut and ready to be put together in a day rather than gathering materials, measuring, and developing a skill.

Thinking changes from imitation to imagination
During this period the child's thought process goes through a significant change. The earlier phase of imitation is passing over into an imaginative one. The child is dreamy and thinks in pictures, in imagery filled with feeling. What may seem factual to an adult is not so cut and dried for the child. His or her thinking is affected by imagination. The child's inner needs are often met with the great myths and legends that come from diverse cultures, whose images feed the soul-longing to know about the world of heroes, adventure, good and evil, compassion and transformation. The child reaches out through feeling-filled thinking to understand the inner world. At the same time, the child is trying to find a relationship to the outer world. This is done through finding a personal connection with what is taught because learning is subjective. Stories of nature, vivid descriptions of animals and human beings in nature, captivate the child's imagination. The child becomes interested in the learning if it has something to do with his or her life.

Examples of how feeling-filled thinking affects the youngster at this age can be seen in the way children evaluate life. Catastrophes, unfortunate circumstances, and illnesses are exaggerated. For example, if a child hears that a burglar is in the neighborhood, he or she is convinced that the burglar is coming into his or her house. Rumors abound. I remember from my own childhood, a rumor that a girl had developed leukemia because she only ate mustard and bread. That seemed reasonable in my child-brain, and I cautiously stayed away from mustard and bread. Because children of this age are vulnerable to sensational images, it helps if matter of fact descriptions are given of safety precautions or health issues, without alarming them and creating fear or feelings of helplessness.

Children are tremendously concerned with appearance. Boys see pictures of men in an unrealistic body form, and they become dissatisfied with the way they look. That means that even before his body begins to change, a boy has a preconceived idea of what he wants it to look like. Anything less will be inadequate. The typical boy worries about whether he's strong enough to withstand intimidation by other boys, whether he's attractive to girls, whether he's too scrawny, too short, too fat, too thin, and whether he has achieved masculinity in his own eyes.

Puberty: Eleven- and twelve-year-olds try to find a relationship to the world

I see something in the dark.
What it is I do not know.
A shape against the snow.
I knew it was a foe.
Lurking dark and low.
But soon I find it in front of me.
Hurt and torn.
A monstrous beast.
I took him home to help his wounds.
Along the way he turns a path.
Now I know what he is,
A helping hand,
A
Loyal
Friend.

Louisa Kane
11 years old

As differences between boys and girls begin to become stronger, the period from eleven to twelve can also be seen as the first stage of adolescence. I will focus more on the gender differences in the next chapter. Here I will focus on some of the issues boys and girls experience during this 11–12 age period and the challenges to healthy development.

Changes in thinking: From imagination to concept
Around eleven or twelve, another change occurs as thinking becomes more abstract, more conceptual. The child begins to understand cause and effect. Because interest shifts from mythology to history, biographies of great people stir the child's inner life. The child begins to be interested in ideas of morality, ethics, and

meaning. Free of emotions, the intellect starts to bloom. The child becomes more objective about what he or she is learning. Thought becomes separated from the object or experience. Thus the child stands apart from the world and begins to see how he or she can learn about, deal with, and overcome or gain control of knowledge.

This change in thinking is crucial for moral development. The child needs meaningful material to understand stories from history, to understand problems of life in which moral considerations apply. This stage is marked by a neurological growth spurt. Skills such as playing a musical instrument or learning a language before the age of eleven are easier to acquire. On the other hand, it takes more effort to develop new capacities that are not built upon earlier experiences.

Appearance and identity
Girls have a particular interest in how they look and are vulnerable to societal pressures in this area. They are aware of other girls and wonder if they are attractive enough. They absorb messages from the mass culture that tell them to focus on appearance and popularity rather than on being smart. They are more subtle than boys in their ability to pick up cues from the surrounding culture. In fact, the smarter they are, the more they sense double standards, sexualization of females, violence connected with sex, and what a girl has to do to be accepted in certain groups—all this despite the feminist revolution.

Girls focus on relationships. They speak with sophistication about feelings, have a large emotional vocabulary, and often give the impression they are more mature than they actually are. They tend to speak with each other and listen carefully. They ask themselves, "Do I like her or not?" "Does she accept me?" "Do I want to be seen with her?" They have left behind the world of fantasy and need to join the big, outside world that is both exciting and frightening. They are broadening their interests.

Boys, on the other hand, find their identity in action. They tend toward quick solutions, one-upmanship, rituals of domination, and physical aggression. The boy releases stress quickly, perhaps by kicking the table and cursing it. He seldom asks for help or wants to involve another person. He tries to solve problems by himself. His concern when he plays a game is the rules, the penalties, and who's in control. Boys of this age also have many concerns that they don't speak about—disease, fears about being successful, looks, and embarrassing parents.

Need for perspective
As the inner life of the child grows stronger, there is a tendency to become more self-centered. A reversal starts to take place. In general, boys tend to withdraw and become more introspective, and girls tend to go outward. They need help in putting things in perspective.

Boys and girls try to figure things out based on their own life experiences, which sometimes can be quite limiting. During the summer I turned twelve, I sat at the side of a country road day after day, looking at cars passing by. Since my family did not have a car, I didn't know anything about yearly registration of license plates. As I observed these cars, I noticed that the old cars and new cars all had the same year on the license plates. I puzzled over this for weeks and did not have an answer until several years later. A simple question to an adult would have solved the puzzle, but I never thought about asking.

Another aspect of this lack of perspective is fear of the unknown. Youngsters of this age may spend sleepless nights wondering, worrying, and thinking about problems at school or home. It is helpful to encourage them to ask adults about these issues.

The child's inner world is different during this period from the balance and harmony of the nine- and ten-year-old. Youngsters can feel very lonely as they experience changes in their bodies and in their feelings. Sometimes this results in breaking up with childhood friends and reaching out for something new in friendship.

Shift in bonding from parents to peers
Eleven- and twelve-year-olds are trying to work out their relationships with parents. In saying "My friends can do all kinds of things you won't let me do," they are trying to figure out how much responsibility they can have, how much freedom they should have. As their bonds with friends becomes stronger, they move out from the protective home structure and test boundaries, demanding space for their likes and dislikes. They find out that their parents' friends have different ideas about what is allowed and not allowed, and they realize that not all parents expect the same thing from their children. They also begin to realize the limitations of their parents' knowledge and experience.

How often parents have said, "If my youngster is going to be difficult, I'd rather it be at home." It is not surprising for parents to hear how cooperative their child is at someone else's house or at school, when at home the child tests boundaries, demanding more privileges, and balking at family traditions. They are trying to gain control over their lives. They want to make more of their own decisions, not having their parents make all the rules for them. They may tell their parents, "Don't kiss me in front of my friends." Or "Why do you always embarrass me?" Friends are now setting the standards of what is normal or "cool."

They are also changing in their relationship to peers. They challenge each other in games of skill, use the sharpness of their power of thinking to compete, manipulate, put down, humiliate. Girls become more underhanded and secretive in their power over others, while boys are more direct, proving their strength or courage. This is also the time of "cutting," "dissing," telling sick jokes or gossiping. Now they challenge each other and gain power by using language rather than brute strength.

Justice is a big issue for eleven- and twelve-year-olds. They see through outer appearances, what is phony or authentic, and they want fairness and consistency. Yet they lack experience to judge authenticity unless they have experienced it in their environment. Particularly if there is a lack of strong parental guidance, they are often overwhelmed by the glut of images surrounding them, taking advantage of their vulnerable self-image, and by the unlimited access they have to musical lyrics, R- rated movies, videos, and magazines.

Developmental Compression—the changing life of
eight to twelve year-olds
An expression in current use to describe the pressures asserted on the child's healthy development is developmental compression. For many children, childhood is ended prematurely around eight, and the period between eight and twelve, is called "tweens" by marketers. These youngsters are still children, yet the way they dress and behave is more like the sixteen-year-olds they emulate.

The contrast between what is healthy for eight-to-twelve-year-olds and what they actually experience in our culture is dramatic. If we were not speaking about the same age group, the reader might think I had gotten my chapters mixed up. The changes that teenagers go through are challenging enough, but when we speak about pressures on eight- nine- ten- eleven- and twelve- year-olds, we can feel quite helpless.

Retail marketers have zeroed in on this age group, pushing music, videos and video games, television programs, magazines, fashion, and food. These tweens consider themselves as sophisticated as sixteen-year-olds and as clear about the image they wish to adopt. They also have the disposable income to buy the products that fit the image.

Early awareness of bodily image causes tweens to avoid wholesome foods or to skip eating altogether, so they will have bodies that match those on MTV or in magazines. Eating disorders are on the rise with youngsters. Fashion-conscious pre-adolescents, insecure about their bodies, look up to models who represent what they feel they should look like.

Early awareness of bodily appearance is causing tweens to choose their clothing based on sexual allure rather than how comfortable or how fitting for particular activities it is. The "tween" mentality results in girls of eight and nine dressing like prostitutes, wearing heavy makeup, and wanting to be sure that, whatever they are wearing, it is sexy.

Such focus on one's body creates anxiety, nervousness, and insecurity at an age when children should be exploring physical activities such as biking, gymnastics, playing tag and ball games, climbing, running, skipping, hiking, and fishing. For many children experiencing "developmental compression," these wholesome activities are not considered "cool." Evidence that "tweens" do not see themselves as children shows up in reports from toy retailers who find that toys, dolls, and games that were popular with eight-to-ten-year-olds no longer bring in many dollars. New lines of sophisticated makeup, clothing, and electronics are what sell best. Girls of eight and nine know what is "cool" and they have no interest in having their parents go shopping with them.

Whereas children need a time of carefree exploration, of feeling that endless possibilities lie ahead, of gradually developing maturity, they are being pushed into a pressure cooker environment, cutting short the time allowed for healthy development. The behaviors we think of as adolescent are also making their way down in age. These include juvenile crime, shoplifting, suicide, bullying, sexual activity (especially oral sex), pregnancy, and increased use of drugs and alcohol. For movies and magazines to sell in the under-twelve market, they must include sex, violence, and sensationalism.

What is causing this earlier awakening of children into teen behavior? Some would consider that children are reaching puberty at earlier ages. Although the average age at which girls begin to menstruate has fallen from 13 to between 11 and 12½ today, this doesn't seem a strong enough reason to explain this behavior. Most thirteen-year-olds do not try to act as sixteen-year-olds and wait to express themselves sexually. In fact, in many cases today the children who are trying to behave like sixteen-year-olds have not even completed puberty. So what is going on?

Two factors that many child psychologists and educators agree on are a sexualized and glitzy media-driven marketplace and absentee parents. Children rely on other children for guidance. Since parents are either absent or preoccupied, youngsters are left to their own devices. Parents have less and less authority over their children as they leave them alone more and more. These children seem competent enough to take care of themselves after school, but the reality is that they need adults around to balance the powerful influence of media and peers. Many children spend hours at home without adults—whether it be "pop-in-the toaster breakfasts" or stopping by the coffee shop and then returning home to frozen dinners they put in the microwave. They often eat alone in front of the TV, without being engaged in conversation or having any feeling of belonging in a family.

Some tweens brag about how their parents are never there and don't care or know what they do, while others feel lonely and don't want to go home to an empty house. They take advantage of after-school activities or just hang around. In the absence of adults, children rely on peers who seem to know what is going on.

It takes a supreme effort to arrange situations where children can be with other adults or in school activities while the parent is at work during the after-school hours. Despite parents' attempts to keep in touch with cell phones, we can't escape from the fact that many children spend hours and hours alone. Some feel abandoned. Some feel afraid but try to be brave. Others become skillful at lying to appease their parents' guilt. "Everything is fine. I'm doing my homework. No one else is here," when this is not the case. Parents don't really know what their children are doing.

Some of the child's peers at school impose strict guidelines on the child's taste and performance, bullying children who don't wear the "right" clothes or carry the "right" backpacks. In an article describing the harm that heavily loaded backpacks are doing to schoolchildrens' shoulders, boys interviewed said they'd never push a backpack on wheels, as some girls do, because "it isn't cool."

There is much concern about American cultural values becoming empty and trivialized, consumer-driven, and materialistic. This situation is particularly threatening to us all because, if moral development is not encouraged during this age of childhood, it will not be a strong presence in adulthood.

Where are the parents?

So we come down to the consciousness of parents. Many frustrated parents are fighting these trends, trying to keep connected to their children, giving in on some things, while holding firm on others, compensating for having to be at work during the day by being very present in the evening, being firm about clothing and media choices, and looking to schools to help them require firmer guidelines. They often feel as if they are being swallowed by a tidal wave that they cannot control. Some change their children's schools, some homeschool; they do the best they can.

Unfortunately, other parents not only ignore what their children are doing, but encourage the cuteness of it. Parents spend sums on the latest fads, on clothing styles the children insist on, and give in rather than making a big issue of it. "After all, these are just fads. We all had them in our own childhood and adolescence, and we came out fine." Or "These are small ways for me to make sure that my child knows I care."

Television producers tell us that they aim their programs for the ten- year-old mentality, that sex, violence, vulgarity, and sensationalism are what sells. Some parents are not sure how to be parents because they haven't let go of their own adolescence. To them, little girls dressed in spandex pants and midriffs are cute little sex objects and little tough guys in their baggy pants are just being boys.

It isn't only in the area of dress that parents need to become stronger. A Kaiser Family Foundation Study in March 2005 says that young people today live media-saturated lives, spending an average of nearly $6^{1}/_{2}$ hours a day with media.

Children who grow up in a media-oriented home spend more time watching TV and playing video games and less time reading. The time of watching increases by 1½ hours a day if the youngster also has a TV in his or her bedroom. The majority of young people say their parents don't impose any rules regarding their use of TV, video games, music, or computers, but if the parents did impose rules, it would cut down on their involvement in media, even up to two hours a day. How can parents become stronger authorities in dealing with their children? They can set rules about how long they can use the computer, how long they can play video games, how much TV they can watch, what they can do on the computer, what kind of music they can listen to, and which TV shows or video games they can engage in.

Where can we look to for change? How can the many parents who are consciously trying to bring sanity to our society effect change? They are doing it in small ways in many places, gathering in parent organizations, giving each other support in being firm with their children, organizing support groups to talk about these issues, working with teachers and administrators to change the atmosphere in a school. They are trying hard and they need our support.

Where are the schools?
Schools are also struggling, often turning to uniforms, strict behavior rules, and specific disciplinary actions for specific infractions. They often have to fight parents to gain support in enforcing these rules. Teachers are often blamed for not protecting children against bullies. The schools struggle to find a balance between being too strict and too loose. Faculty members have long, contentious meetings discussing how strict to be, often with swords drawn between generations.

Consumerism and glitzy sexuality also pervade school buildings with soda machines, advertising in the gyms and on notebook covers, films and videos that use some of the same methods as advertisers to entice children with the message, "Learning is cool." They flatter children into thinking that they know more and are capable of making better decisions than adults. The image on the screen becomes the ultimate authority, whether it is to sell a product or sell an attitude.

Teachers complain of behavior at school that would never have been accepted by parents in the past—feet on the desk, throwing food, talking back. When teachers call parents to complain of this behavior, it is not unusual for the teacher to get attacked for being too fussy, too restrictive, or too weak to control the class.

Many parents are afraid of their children. They are afraid to insist on rules of behavior, on appropriate dress, on courtesy. A strong anti-authoritarian attitude prevails among some parents, influencing the whole style of modern life. It isn't only parents. Many teachers and psychologists celebrate the individualism of a child who doesn't automatically obey the rules or conform to "middle-class" behavior. Looking over ads for schools for children with drug problems, obesity, or eating disorders, I see ones for the "defiant" child—a new disorder.

As with any change society goes through, we have to find a middle way. Each generation is often battling the wars of a past generation. While the Sixties was a time of new ideas, of fighting against a conformity-obsessed generation, it also opened the floodgates to an attitude of "anything goes." As parents, we need to understand the influences on our own lives so that we can become clearer about the way we are rearing our children and why.

In the past, the pressures I have described might be part of a chapter on early adolescence, on the twelve-to-fifteen-year-olds, but in fact they are pressures today on eight-, nine-, ten-, eleven-, and twelve-year-olds, children who have not yet developed a sense of who they are, nor have they arrived at a capacity of thinking that will nourish their morality. At this young age, they form their sense of identity from what others say they should be and promote certain behavior. In the past, it was often parents and teachers and other caring adults who stimulated and encouraged social behavior and responsibility, thus influencing their sense of identity. The media and peer values have taken their place. The forces working against the child's healthy development have forced their way into the home, into the minds of children and adults, and have overpowered common sense. William Blake painted a picture entitled, "The Good and Bad Angel Fighting for the Soul of the Child." He prophetically pointed to the battle for the soul of childhood that is going on in our midst.

Gratitude, Wonder, and Responsibility
The spiritual guidance of the child

Let us look once again at Parzival's early years. What can we modern parents learn from Parzival's childhood? What has Herzeloyde done that we ourselves might want to emulate or avoid as parents? And what can we learn about the needs of the young child as we contemplate Parzival?

What treasures does the child gather during childhood?
Parzival had the bow and arrows that he had whittled himself. He shoots birds whose songs are too loud, but then he weeps. His soul is disturbed by his actions. He cannot explain his pain. His mother's response when she realizes the cause of his pain is to eliminate the cause. She responded to the fear of her son's becoming a knight in the future by trying to control his environment. Her love for her child is so mixed up with fear that she will do anything to keep him from waking up to the dangerous world outside.

The expressions of a mother's love
Herzeloyde is the archetype of mother. Having carried her child within her womb for nine months, she has cradled him in her arms, suckled him at her breast, felt her heart beating in rhythm with his heart. She is no longer one, but two in one. Her child is part of her and she is a part of him. Although her mind knows that one day he will grow into a man and leave her, she will do anything to postpone the separation. She wants to protect him from any pain or sorrow that life will bring him. Thus she is in inner conflict—between her head and her heart. Her actions may not seem rational. However, her attempts to spare him pain and her fear that he will be hurt create in her a desire to protect him, to build a high wall around her beloved child. Despite the torment in her heart, Herzeloyde gives Parzival the best guidance she can, as she has done from the moment she first held him in her arms. She has given Parzival three great gifts in his childhood.

First, she has cared for his physical and emotional needs; day and night she was pouring her life's energy into his well-being. The child has been the center around which all action occurred, and he has grown strong and healthy under her protective shield.

The second gift has been to have the natural world as his playground. He has drunk deeply of nature's offerings. Whereas she could have lived in a castle, attended tournaments, been the center of court, possibly found a royal husband, she has given up all of that for a life of seclusion, a life in the forest. Many mothers and fathers sacrifice to provide their children with a healthy environment, perhaps giving up professional advancement or financial benefit to move to a better neighborhood, be near a park where the child can play amidst trees, brooks, and meadows, or move to be near a particular school.

The third gift Herzeloyde has given Parzival is spiritual guidance. This love represents the great outpouring of spirit, sacrificing all. It is the same unceasing love of Mother Earth yielding her bounty so that animals and human beings can have life. The child does not analyze this love of the parent and the words of guidance. They just are. They are the water of life pouring forth from a mother. She has taught him right from wrong; she has been a model of caring and sacrifice. She has been the representative of God's love.

These three gifts are expressions of a mother's love. When Parzival leaves, he takes these gifts with him. He is healthy and strong. He is comfortable in the world of nature. He has been taught that there is good and evil in the world and that God brings goodness. Wherever Parzival goes, people comment that he is beautiful. They see that there is something more to this young man than his mere outward appearance.

Herzeloyde also gives her son a description of God. She tells him of the greatness of God and the darkness of the Devil. She places faithfulness against inconstancy. The wisdom of this scene is that in spite of the overprotectiveness, in spite of her desire to keep him from entering the journey, she gives him a key that he will be able to take with him, a way of recognizing good and evil.

Every child also has spiritual needs such as the need to belong, the need to find meaning in life, the need to feel a connection with a reality bigger than that of everyday life. Children ask questions that point to their spiritual needs. Why are we here? Why is the world the way it is? Why should I do that? Where did grandpa go when he died? Are all the people since Adam and Eve still in Heaven?

The world from which the child comes is spirit. Anyone who has been present at the birth of a human being is filled with a sense of otherworldliness. One of the secrets of early childhood is that physical needs are also spiritual needs. The mother is the representative of God, caring for all the child's needs and surrounding the child with love. The young child is a complete sense organ, soaking up everything in the environment—and imitating it—trusting in the world with complete receptivity and devotion. The child's trust is a religious experience, uniting herself with the parent. The parent's task is to be worthy of this trust. The moral experiences of small children arise from learning what is right and wrong. Family life is the center of the young child's life and should satisfy the spiritual need of the child for a long time. In developing the spiritual life of the child, parents have two tasks: to guide the child into life on earth and to help the child keep a connection with the spiritual world.

The main attitude toward life that children need to develop during the first seven years is *gratitude*. If we can help the child feel gratitude out of the experience of customs and rituals, bedtime routines, story-times, meal times, festival life, and other family experiences, then the seeds have been sown for a healthy childhood and for the first secure steps on the spiritual journey. The parents' actions become the model of spiritual love for the child. For example, if the mother or father visits a sick neighbor or family member, perhaps bringing flowers and fruit, this tells the child that caring for other human beings is an act of love. If the parents help someone in need, this is a deep moral lesson for the children of how human beings can be selfless.

From ages seven to twelve, the child takes the next step in his or her spiritual life through developing a *sense of wonder*. The feeling of protection that the small child felt fades, and the older child often experiences loneliness. What happened to those wonderful days of running through leaves, climbing rocks, and imagining that they were mountains, feeling one with the world? The child's eyes are opened, and he sees the contradictions and imperfections of people close to him. The child is left feeling empty and often alone. The child doesn't understand these feelings but may express discomfort through moodiness and dissatisfaction.

This is a time when helping the child to feel at home on the earth has special meaning. A close relationship to nature can compensate for much of the loss that the child feels inwardly. But that is not enough. Nature itself needs to be imbued with wonder. Wonder is the connecting thread to the spiritual world at a time when the connection is becoming tenuous. Listening to and reading stories of great persons who have served the right and conquered the wrong helps the child develop a strong sense of values.

Parzival played in the forest. He learned the ways of the animals. He learned to hunt, to occupy himself, whistling through a leaf as he wandered the pathways. So the world of nature gives our children self-confidence. It is the natural next step away from being cloistered in the family. Life in the natural world offers many opportunities—time to run around with friends and hide behind trees and boulders, pick berries, climb trees, hike, build forts or treehouses, dig tunnels, swim in streams or lakes, gaze at the stars in the evening sky. Likewise, organized activities through clubs such as the Y, the Scouts, 4-H, and family experiences—camping, backpacking, orienteering, fishing, identifying animal tracks, identifying birds, identifying constellations, gardening, raising animals—help children feel close to nature.

Learning to be comfortable in nature marks a shift from the matrix of human-mother to the matrix of earth-mother. Nature is a place to gain courage, overcome fears, learn skills, expand one's imagination. Whether one lives in the city, suburbia, or a rural community, possibilities exist for the child to explore this connection to nature. This shift is not a loss but an expansion, an enlargement of the world that nurtures, protects, and amazes. The child takes hold of his or her physical body, directing it, challenging it, experiencing strength, finding ways to use the body to make an impression on the physical world—whittling a branch, building a snow house, constructing a dam, sharpening a stone, making trails, and so on.

Being in nature is a special experience for children where they can experience purpose, beauty, and wholeness. For example, learning to sail or to canoe calls for being able to read the winds and the water; backpacking involves map reading and independence; farming includes understanding the soil, plants, animals, weather. Teenagers gain strength and self-confidence in their experiences with nature; they gain a sense of reverence and serenity from the beauty of the natural world.

Parents should decide what kind of *worship*, if any, they wish to include in the family's life. However, the spiritual needs of the child are more than Friday, Saturday, or Sunday events. They are daily and continuous. As the family chooses and practices a form of religious life, the child experiences it as an anchor, a place of calm in the busyness of life (until he decides to question it.)

To develop *interest in and compassion for others*, school-aged children need to do things for other people: special favors or visits with old people, fixing broken things for a neighbor, making things for friends and relatives. When the child is quiet and alone, he may feel that there is something higher living within himself. He becomes more aware of his sense of right and wrong, of the divine and the earthly. However, he still needs help in developing behavior that is worthy.

As they get older, especially around ages 13 or 14, youngsters often make fun of family customs and don't want to participate. On one hand, they reject them and on the other hand, they secretly yearn for them. It is very helpful if there are younger children at home to involve the older ones in carrying out customs or rituals, thus finding an appropriate role by which to participate. The older child may take on some of the responsibilities the parents had formerly held. Artie was uninterested when his parents discussed preparations for Easter morning. "This is stupid. I know you're putting out the eggs. Why do we have to pretend?" However, when his parents asked if he wanted to be the one to hide the eggs, he agreed with a bored, "I guess so." He actually had a good time deciding where to hide them, and he especially enjoyed watching his little sister's eyes sparkle as she gathered the eggs the Easter Bunny had hidden.

From ages 14 to 18, youths have different needs in developing their spiritual life. There is a Chinese saying that the young are in "the house of tomorrow." They carry the future within themselves. During this time, young people have different needs—a greater need for privacy, a need for heroes, and a need to respect adults and be respected by them. As the adults consider the adolescent years laden with minefields, the biggest concern is whether the young person will arrive at his or her right destination. Will teenagers be fired with youthful idealism or focused only on themselves?

Teenagers have a deep interest in truth. Profound questions arise. Who am I? Why am I here? A help in cultivating the spiritual life of teenagers includes the study of world religions and interest in and respect for all people. They also need opportunities to help other people, to serve those in need. It is important to speak of spiritual issues without being dogmatic. Adolescents hunger for the divine but are often put off by dogmatism or an authoritarian approach. They want their freedom of thought respected so they can come to their own conclusions.

Developing Responsibility

Issues of Protection: Holding on and Letting Go

Herzeloyde represents every mother who fears her child's journey into the dangerous world of adolescence. Every parent faces this worry at some point during the child's life. The pain of letting go occurs at many different stages—the child's first day at school, attending sleep-away camp, the first time the child spends a night at a friend's house, attending a first school dance, allowing the child to choose which movie to attend, deciding whether or not to allow the child to have a telephone or television or computer in his or her room.

During the sixth, seventh, and eighth grade years, these questions begin to intensify. As the child pushes for more and more freedom, the parent struggles to maintain control. The parent feels: How far should I stretch? How much should I give in? The child feels: I need independence. I need to make my own decisions. How much more freedom can I get from my parents? The parent confronts fears of the child's getting hurt, of not having the maturity to make wise decisions, of losing the child to stronger external influences. Is the child ready? Can I trust the world to be kind to my child?

The response, I believe, always has to do with the stage of development of the child. Understanding how the child thinks and the child's stage of emotional maturity can guide the parent. In any case, releasing the child to the influences of the world is a gradual process. The intrusion of popular culture into our homes is powerful and very difficult to hide from. At the same time, it is our responsibility as parents to decide which values we want emphasized in our children's lives.

This means the parent has to exert some control over what comes in through media, through friends, through school. However, it is not just a matter of keeping influences out, but of strengthening what is within. It means that the parents have to create a strong family culture, with moral guidance, a sense of belonging, activities that channel youthful energy, and community relationships. Family life needs to be filled with joy, excitement, and opportunities for challenge and accomplishment. This is the treasure that the youngster will hold in his or her heart when it is time to leave.

Popular culture sends powerful messages, urging the child to grow up quickly and enter the adolescent world long before he or she is ready to cope with it. Parents should become familiar with these messages by listening to music, reading teen magazines, seeing an occasional MTV program or movie. Why? Because even if children do not receive direct impressions from these sources, images make their way into the children's psyches. Believing that we can shut our children away from all harmful influences can be as naïve as Parzival's mother's thinking that she could get rid of anything that might hurt her child or that she could keep his world pure.

The younger the child, the more control we need to exert over the environment. Until around age nine, the child is particularly sensitive as the forces of imitation are especially strong, and there is a lack of discernment on the child's part as to what is or is not healthy. Parzival's mother tried to control who came into the forest, she tried to eliminate anything that would give her child pain. When our children are young, this is completely appropriate. The question is always, When is the right time to soften the protection? From nine until puberty the challenge is great. Children at this age can fool us, seeming to be older than they are emotionally and mentally. They need to have their world expanded, but at the same time they still need protection.

Overprotectiveness
Parzival's situation is also a common experience of today's children. His father is absent—in this case because he is dead—and his mother is fearful of losing her son to the same fate. To assure that he will not leave her, she withdraws and tries to keep the world far away. Unfortunately, he gains a glimpse of the world in the

presence of the knights who happen to ride by. He is fascinated by their shining armor and relates that to the image of God whom his mother had described as brighter than the daylight.

Many of our teenagers are growing up in single-parent homes today. As with Parzival, the majority of these homes have a mother, and the father's presence is minimal, or totally absent. We have two situations here: the loss of the father and the overprotectiveness of the mother. Because several of the main characters in the story grow up without fathers, I will deal with this theme later. For now, let us concentrate on the issue of overprotectiveness.

As a starting point, let us be clear that the following comments are not made to be judgmental but to shed light on a contemporary situation. It is understandable that a mother in pain and fear of losing her child would choose to protect him or her in whatever way possible. Yet there are repercussions when it goes too far.

Being concerned about the dangers which our children face is understandable and appropriate. Whereas in past generations parents felt that they were doing their duty by preparing their children to join society, today the situation is different. There are many threats facing children as they make their way into society. These include physical dangers such as kidnapping, violence, drugs, alcohol, and sexual abuse. In many neighborhoods, children cannot play safely outside, so they are relegated to being babysat by the television set. Instead of physical harm, they are exposed to violence and brutality through the images on the screen. The recent explosion of cell phone connections between parents and children is another example of staying connected in the face of danger. The cell phone extends parental supervision over their children and may give them peace of mind.

There is protectiveness and overprotectiveness. Each parent has to evaluate his or her behavior in relation to this. There are reasons to be protective of children, both for the dangers threatening from without and the dangers coming from overexposure to popular culture through the media, video games, and computers. Where is the line beyond which the parent becomes overly protective? Being protective with an eight-year-old is very different from being protective with a fifteen-year-old. It is appropriate to try to create a safe, nurturing world for young children, whereas teenagers need more space to make decisions. They need support and guidance. They need to learn responsibility when they are yearning for freedom.

71

Many single mothers have worked out a healthy balance with their sons. They are protective without becoming overprotective. They cultivate adult relationships so that they do not have to burden the sons with being the mothers' confidants. They seek male role models in the family and community so their sons experience what it is to be a man. They love and honor their sons, and at the same time, they are clear that if their sons run into difficulties, they will support them in learning their lessons.

However, some single mothers struggle with their relationships to their sons. Lacking an adult male in the home, a single mother may rely on her son for that relationship. The boy experiences a double burden. On one hand, his mother looks to him as the man of the family. He knows more about her life than he is capable of handling. She leans on him and makes him prematurely responsible. On the other hand, she protects him from the consequences of his behavior out in the world. For example, if he gets into trouble in school, she rises to his defense and makes excuses for him. What message does the boy get? I'll keep you from facing the results of your behavior. I'll lie if I have to, but I don't want any authority out there (usually male) making you feel bad.

When this happens over and over again, the boy has trouble recognizing that there are boundaries to his behavior. He can do what he wants, and Mom will get him out of any fix. The boy remains immature during the very time he should be learning to face consequences and deal with them. He will still have to do so, but it will probably happen later. When he leaves home to go to college or get a job, he will be unprepared to be responsible. He may return to the safe nest that his mother has provided instead of stepping out into the world. He may lose job after job because he expects the world to cater to him. It may mean that he comes up against strong authority figures who have no tolerance for babying him, such as in the military.

Ralph stole an item from a store while on a class trip. When the school authorities found him and called his mother, she went on the attack. Her poor darling had been embarrassed enough by being caught and didn't need any more punishment. She was very angry when the school did put him on probation and made him do community service, and she did her best to spread rumors about the unfairness of the teachers. When Ralph did not get top grades, which he thought he deserved, she took his part and claimed that the teachers were punishing him because of the shoplifting incident. Ralph felt invincible. He felt excused from having to do his best because his mother would excuse the results and blame the teachers. When Ralph went off to college, his mother's protective screen was gone, and he had to face the world by himself. He had a very hard time and got into serious drug use. For several years, his mother was in denial about her son's difficulties. Only when Ralph hit bottom and friends no longer shielded her or him, did she begin to wake up to the fact that he needed help.

Overprotectiveness isn't a problem for single-parent families only, however. Overprotectiveness can also be part of a family dynamic when the husband is present but very dominating. The wife may protect her son from his father by pretending that everything is fine.

John was taking drugs and his schoolwork growing worse and worse. The teachers saw this pattern and heard about the drug use from other students. When the teachers spoke to John's mother about the situation, her main concern was that the teachers should not tell the father about it. Kept in the dark, John's father did not know about his son's drug use and blamed the school for not teaching his son well. Unfortunately, the teachers had agreed to abide by the mother's request and did not tell John's father. This was a dreadful mistake with terrible consequences.

John's father (who was not very observant or was denying his son's problems) took the boy out of the "incompetent" school and placed him elsewhere. John continued to take drugs and have problems. His life ended when he drove a car into a tree under the influence of drugs. Under the pressure of this tragedy, the father realized that he had not been in close contact with his son and he went through an agonizing period in admitting that he had blamed the teachers instead of realizing what was really going on. The teachers realized that they had played a part by agreeing to keep the information from John's father.

Although many overprotective situations occur between mothers and sons, they also occur between parents with daughters. Even in this modern era of liberation, there is still a double standard in many families regarding how much freedom sons or daughters have. Each family has to figure out what restrictions are appropriate for each age. Overprotectiveness can take the form of not allowing a young teenager to attend school functions, to invite friends home, to go shopping with friends. It may include not allowing a seventeen-year-old daughter to date, or requiring that she not be alone at any time with her date. Expectations which are completely appropriate to a pre-teen may become overprotectiveness when applied to a teenager, especially to one over sixteen.

It is not only a situation created by overprotective single mothers; baby boomer parents have difficulty letting their children learn and handle consequences. many colleges are having to deal with "helicopter parents" who hover over their children by exerting their pressure on counselors, teachers, dormitory advisors, and college nurses.

Appropriate protectiveness
Being overly protective is one thing. Being conscious and cautious is another. Parents who are cautious, who check to be sure that chaperones are present at parties, who want to know where their daughter or son is going and with whom, are being appropriately protective. In fact, they are doing their job of supporting, yet ensuring the safety of their child.

Lily answered the phone. Her friends were inviting her to a party down at the beach. She knew there would be beer and maybe marijuana. She signaled to her mother not to let her go. Then she said to her friend, "My mother's so tight. She won't let me go. Maybe next time." Lily was happy to be able to use her mother as a shield to prevent her from getting into a situation she didn't welcome. She wasn't ready to tell her friend she didn't want to go.

Underprotectiveness
The opposite problem is failing to be protective when it is needed. This can be a result of a philosophical attitude, or it can be neglect. Some mothers and fathers may be concerned that their children will not like them if they set strong boundaries or make specific rules as to behavior. Or they may simply not want the hassle that comes when limits are placed on teenagers' behavior. These youngsters grow up without a sense of what is appropriate. Having to fend for themselves, they may be fortunate to have another adult whom they admire and who has good sense and sets a good example. Some teenagers in this situation have a strong moral sense and are able to set their own boundaries. In general, however, parental

authority, when it is clear and supportive, benefits teenagers in their development. This means, of course, that there will be conflicts and times of misunderstanding.

Teenagers are trying to find their relationship to freedom (Which decisions can I make? How can I figure out my own rules?) and there are bound to be times when parental guidance or expectations irritate them or even challenge them to lie or manipulate in order to achieve a sense of freedom. How they deal with these situations says a great deal about their character. It is understandable that they will make mistakes along the way.

In most healthy parent-teenager relationships, there will be clear boundaries, expectations that are appropriate, and times when tension arises due to different definitions of freedom and responsibility. If the parents' love and support for their sons or daughters are clear and fair, and they have a clear sense of their responsibility as parents, they will all get through this period in a positive way. The main learning during this time has to do with figuring out how much and when to give over responsibility to the teenager. If parents had a hard time holding boundaries when their children were younger, the issues only compound in adolescence. Children will naturally push and try to gain more freedom than they can handle, especially around ten and eleven years of age. Whether parents are able to stand up to this pressure or whether they cave in when their children argue with them or accuse them of being unfair will affect the kind of communication they have during the teenage years.

No matter whether parents are overprotective, underprotective, or "just right," the day comes when they must let their children go—to make mistakes, experience pain, and leave a trail behind them of broken hearts, missed opportunities, and wounds that must be healed.

Parental advice

What is Herzeloyde's intention when she gives Parzival her advice? Perhaps her son will come home, because people will mock him in his funny clothes and sad-looking horse. Does she hope for this? She tells him to be polite and give people his greeting. But Parzival is so naïve that he takes her literally.

Her advice is not to force himself on a woman. She tells him that first he has to win a woman's ring and greetings, but she doesn't tell him how to do this. What he hears is the next part of the advice, "Take them (the ring and the greeting). Make haste to kiss her and clasp her tight in your embrace." Parzival doesn't understand any of this. Lying down on the woman is no different from eating or drinking. He doesn't understand what he is doing. It may be that Herzeloyde's advice is so fragmentary and unhelpful because emotionally she cannot let go of him and therefore is unable to prepare him for the next stage of his life.

Parzival needs a man to give him guidance about women. What Parzival does grasp from his mother's advice is to fight for the right, to avenge those who have taken away his land. This gives him a reason to be brave and make things right.

The Calling and the Awakener
Sigune proves to be the awakener for Parsival's higher self. At first he is impulsive and wants to kill the murderers of Schianatulander wherever they are hiding, and that is before he even knows his own or their names. It is significant that once he learns his own name and situation, he asks for directions. He doesn't just wander. However, Sigune, like Herzeloyde, recognizes his vulnerability and wishes to protect him, so she sends him off in the wrong direction, towards Arthur's castle rather than toward Orilus and Lehelin. Parzival doesn't realize how she is caring for him. He takes each situation at its face value.

Children have many goals (I want to be an astronaut!), yet they have no idea of what it would take to get there. They want their goals achieved now!

Parzival has no idea of the danger that is inherent in fighting the Red Knight. Yet he is ready to take up the challenge. Is this bravery or foolhardiness? Parzival doesn't know the rules of the game—of knighthood. He is entering the challenge unprepared.

Learning the rules to be able to participate in social life
Rules of games are very important in the lives of children after the age of eleven, especially for boys. Research has shown (see *Raising Boys*) that by age nine boys and girls relate to rules in games differently. Boys want to know three things: who is in charge; what are the rules; what are the consequences if I break the rules. You often hear on the playground, "That's not fair! You broke the rules. You're out." With girls, the situation is different. They are not so concerned about the rules, but they are concerned with the quality

of relationships. They will break the rules to keep peace in a friendship (I'm choosing Beth on my team because I don't want here to feel left out).

Games are not just good entertainment for children; they are a valuable part of childhood. Whether they are playground games or board games, children learn that there are boundaries, that there is order, and that rewards come to those who follow the rules.

One of the reasons that sports have such an allure for pubescent children is the clarity of rules. At the same time as they are resisting and challenging rules set by their parents, they embrace the rules of the game. All sports have boundaries and rules. So does life. Learning to play inside the lines is a life skill. For example, in a particular sport, either you can't step inside a line or you must hit the ball within the lines. The rule is clear. It is not left up to the players to decide in each situation. An umpire or referee makes the judgment. Whether the players agree or not, they have to obey the decision.

In medieval times the rules were set out in terms of preparing for an occupation. In the world of knights, there were steps to ascend: page, squire, knight. Each had its rules and necessary skills to acquire. In the trades, there were the levels of apprentice, journeyman, master. Each stage was a rite of passage.

Parzival sees only the outer appearance of the Red Knight. He does not know the rules. He doesn't care about rules. He only knows what he wants. His thinking is concrete. He has a goal, he seeks the goal, he gains the goal. That's it. There is no area of consideration, dealing with change of circumstances.

On the other hand, the Red Knight knows the rules. He is able to distinguish this boy from a serious threat. He sees the contrast between the silly clothing Parzival is wearing and the nobility that shines through him. He tries to push Parzival off his horse in a way that will not hurt him, but Parzival knows only that he has been hit and wants to fight back. He knows how to use a spear from his time in the forest. He aims straight for the eyespace, which is against the rules of knighthood. Out of his impulsiveness, he kills the Red Knight.

It is our task as adults to see beyond the clothing of teenagers. Who is it that really lives within those outrageous outfits? Can we uphold the rules even when teenagers are looking to break them? Or are we adults still rebelling against authority and break the rules ourselves.

Deena was having a party at her house. When the word got out that there would be a keg at this tenth grade party, Mr. Lowell, one of Deena's teachers, called her mother to ask her if it were true. Her mother replied, "Sure, the kids will have a good time." Mr. Lowell reminded her that it was illegal to serve alcohol to minors and that she would be responsible for any accidents that might happen when students drove home. Deena's mother told Mr. Lowell it was not his business. The best that Mr. Lowell could do was to alert other parents in the class that the party was not a school function and to be aware of what rules Deena's mother was enforcing.

Another example of Parzival's immaturity is the way he deals with the body of the dead Red Knight. He does not even see him as a person, only that here is a costume he has been wanting. He has no idea how to take off the armor. He is like a little child in the way he treats the body. There is no awareness of what he has done nor any remorse. He is centered in his desires.

Was Parzival culpable? Did he understand what he was doing? The connection between cause and effect does not really take hold until a youth is past sixteen or seventeen, and even then it is not completely understood.

Once Gurnemanz teaches Parzival the rules of knighthood, Parzival begins to take responsibility for his actions. He learns what is appropriate and what is not. Now that he knows this, he can try to live his life within the rules. However, he takes everything that Gurnemanz says literally. This is what will get him into trouble. He doesn't yet understand the essence of what Gurnemanz is telling him; he can't consider the advice within a context. He is still at the stage of concrete thinking. At least, now he does know how to handle himself; he knows what is allowed, what is not allowed. This represents the consciousness of the early adolescent. Every teenager needs a Gurnemanz to give him or her the rules of social life. For many boys, it is the father who prepares them to enter society. For others it is a surrogate father, a teacher, a coach, an uncle, or other significant male.

Chapter 4

Adolescents and the Awakening of Sexuality

Book IV. *Parzival meets Condwiramur.*
His heart is opened.

*P*arzival leaves Gurnemanz's castle and the sweet Liaze and makes his way now as a knight, with knightly manners and skills. No longer simple, he has experienced the beauty of friendship with Liaze, and his thoughts focus on her. He is so filled with longing that he lets his horse choose the way across many trackless paths and unknown hills and valleys.

He arrives at a city that is in distress, surrounded by armies, with battle raging from both sides. The shouts of Go back! Go back! frighten his horse who refuses to step onto the swaying drawbridge. Parzival dismounts and leads the horse across the bridge to a battlefield where many men lie dead. He knocks on the gate of the great hall, and a young woman comes to ask him whether he is an enemy. He answers, "Lady, you see here a man who will serve you, and if I can, your greeting shall be my reward. I am eager to do your service."

The army behind the castle walls has been reduced to starvation. The queen, Condwiramur, is extremely beautiful, even outshining the sweet Liaze. Parzival now has grace and manners, thanks to Gurnemanz's teaching, so he does not ask questions but is silent. The queen interprets his silence as scorn for her and decides that, since she is the host, she needs to start the conversation. It turns out that Condwiramur and Liaze are cousins. Food arrives for the starving people, a scanty meal is shared, and Parzival is led to his bed.

During the night, Condwiramur comes to his bed, not for love, but for help and a friend's advice. She weeps and needs consolation. He offers her his bed, and she agrees to lie beside him as long as he does not "wrestle with her." She tells him her sad story of how King Clamide has destroyed her father's castle and land, leaving her a poor orphan, and how he wants her for his wife. She is ready to kill herself before giving herself to this man who has killed one of Liaze's brothers. Parzival pledges to serve her and defend her against Clamide's seneschal Kingrun, who would come to take her away.

The next morning, Parzival fights his first swordfight with Kingrun, and Kingrun offers his surrender. Parzival sends him to the court of King Arthur to present his oath of surrender to Lady Cunneware.

Parzival treats Condwiramur with honor as they share their bed that night, and although he leaves her still a maiden, she thinks that she is his wife. Her heart is given to him, as well as her castles and country. On the third night, they consummate their relationship.

Clamide, determined to gain Condwiramur for his bride, meets Parzival, now known as the Red Knight, on the battlefield. After slashing and attacking, Parzival holds Clamide's life in his hand and could easily end it. Now, he faces his first test, bestowing mercy on his enemy. Instead of killing him, Parzival also sends Clamide to Arthur's court to pledge service to Lady Cunneware.

The love that Parzival and Condwiramur have for one another is strong and beautiful. Each finds unwavering devotion to the other in the next fifteen months or so that they are together. One morning he asks her permission to make a journey to find out how his mother is; he would also like to have some adventure. She grants him permission, and he sets out on his journey.

Parzival enjoyed the friendship of Liaze, and she became his first love. His longing for her awakens him to developing a relationship with Condwiramur, in which he acts more consciously and more maturely. The boy is becoming a man. In this scene, we see examples of a boy or girl coming to terms with intimacy and behaving honorably and maturely. Parzival offers his service to Condwiramur without hope for reward. He honors Condwiramur's request that he respect her and not make sexual advances when she comes for advice. Parzival is still struggling to respond appropriately, but Condwiramur is confused by his silence and interprets it as scorn or rejection of her. Girls often blame themselves when they don't understand a boy's reactions. Parzival pledges to defend Condwiramur against Clamide. He is successful and sends Clamide to Arthur's court. He is showing mercy on his enemy.

Parzival and Condwiramur experience the innocence of their love, which by the third night is consummated. Condwiramur interprets their relationship as marriage and takes on the role of wife even though no formal ceremony has taken place. Parzival discovers his love for Condwiramur and honors her as his wife. He accepts the responsibilities of becoming king of her lands and of being a loyal husband. In time, Parzival realizes he has not thought of his mother for a long time and goes off to seek her. Condwiramur honors his request and gives him freedom to do what he needs to do.

Puberty, Adolescence, and the Awakening of Sexuality

As youngsters come into puberty, their emotional life undergoes change as well. Power struggles increase, mood swings erupt, new desires awaken. The youngster is vulnerable to all that the world pours in on him or her. This is the time when physiological changes, especially hormonal changes, significantly influence behavior.

Girls struggle to hold on to their assertive, confident selves. They often split into two: they want to be smart and they want to be sexy. They want to be treated with kindness, but they can be cruel to peers. They try on new roles, think their families are boring, don't want to be embarrassed by parents, fantasize about having freedom, test limits, are obsessed with their bodies, want to grow up, want to stay young. Appearance strongly defines social acceptability. They talk a lot with friends and become secretive with adults. The big question is: Am I normal? They constantly compare themselves with others.

Boys are very insecure about changes in puberty and seldom talk about it. They are watching their bodies change, feeling confused about ejaculation, spontaneous erections, masturbation, and wet dreams. They have many fears based on labels (nerd, macho, fag) and fears about their abilities. They can be sharp with words as they tell sick jokes or cut each other down. At the same time, they are very sensitive to criticism. They are clumsy and awkward, sensitive to comments about their growth and about whether they are strong. Although boys go through this stage about two years later than girls do, the quality of the change is similar in terms of vulnerability, confusion, and struggle to understand what is happening.

Their thinking is still concrete, and they have difficulty thinking through the possibilities that will result from their decisions. This is especially true in relation to their sexual activity. They may have sexual feelings, but they aren't sure what to do about them. If they find themselves in situations where they can be sexually active, they haven't planned for it, don't anticipate the consequences, and lack the intellectual ability to set limits. Because of their concrete thinking, they have problems in making sound judgments about their sexual behavior.

The combination of sexually stimulating movies, videos, and music puts tremendous pressure on young adolescents who are not emotionally or intellectually capable of dealing with them. They have a hard enough time understanding their own needs, and they have an even more difficult time perceiving a situation from another person's perspective. Empathy does not usually develop until middle adolescence, around 16 or 17 years of age. One of the problems of children in early adolescence is that once their feelings are aroused, they feel pressure to act, and everything gets out of control. If we add to this the presence of alcohol, the youngster is in a dangerous situation.

One child psychiatrist commented that to ask an early adolescent boy to connect the idea of relationship with sexual experience is to miss the point. He is not there yet. His problem is what to do with his penis, not what to do with a girl's feelings.

Cultural Influences and Sexuality

Cultural influences certainly play their part in the way teenagers express their sexuality. In American society, there is a combination of earlier biological maturity, later emotional maturity, later marriages, heavy emphasis on sex in the media and in the culture at large, and dangers in relation to sex such as AIDS, sexually transmitted diseases, and teenage pregnancy.

How does the longer period of biological maturity put girls at risk?
Around 1900, a middle-class girl began menstruating at age fifteen or sixteen, finished formal school at about the same age, and married in her early twenties. Today girls menstruate at twelve, finish

high school at eighteen, and don't marry until about twenty-five. This means that there is a longer time in which girls are vulnerable to pregnancy, unwed motherhood, sexually transmitted diseases, and quitting school. Unwed mothers are less likely to finish their education and are more likely to end up on welfare and to experience poverty than women who give birth after their teen years.

Girls are less protected by the society, yet the imagery in popular culture encourages them to become sexually active. They are encouraged to dress in a sexually provocative way, and to project themselves as sex objects. Appearance is everything. With the increased amount of disposable income that teens have, they are able to buy clothes, tapes, and CDs, to fulfill the image. Even adults have given in, accepting this image. (J.C.Penney had to withdraw an ad in which they showed a mother encouraging her daughter to dress provocatively—with her blouse pulled up and her skirt pulled down to reveal her belly button and hips.) The clothing industry emphasizes this image all the way down to tots' clothing, particularly aiming at the seven- to eight-year-old girls' market—to stimulate sexual fantasy in figure-hugging outfits, advertising young girls posing alluringly, and broadcasting provocative scenes of teeny-boppers on MTV.

How do they get away with this? They play on a combination of insecurities that girls in this culture experience, the fact that girls (and women) are more likely to turn to media for advice on their clothing, cosmetics, exercise routines, ways of speaking and gesturing than boys (and men) do, and on the girls' romantic attitudes towards sex. Because girls are hypersensitive about their bodies and their appearance, pre-teen girls already experience themselves as sex objects even before they begin developing physically. By the time girls arrive at puberty, they have internalized the Barbie image which their own body does not and usually could not replicate. This creates dissatisfaction with their own bodies.

In addition to this flood of images confronting the girl, social attitudes have changed. Being a virgin today is no longer considered highly desirable. Girls are expected to be sophisticated about sexual issues, even if they choose not to indulge. It is not unusual today for the mother of a middle-school-aged boy to complain about the girls who pursue her son with telephone calls, e-mail, or sexually provocative notes. The pressure on girls to be sexually precocious is affecting their emotional as well as their physical health.

Girls have varying degrees of protection from their families. No longer are many fathers insisting on being old-fashioned in knowing where their daughters are going at night, with whom, and what they will be doing. This lack of supervision and support from adults is leaving teenaged girls open to early sexual activity. The resulting behavior includes emotional distress, depression, suicide, eating disorders, substance use and abuse, sexual abuse and victimization, and unwanted sex. They are having sex at younger age than in the past. Even if they are not actually having intercourse, they have to think about sex and worry about sex when they are younger. The early development of breasts seems to act as a signal to certain males that these girls are good targets for sexual teasing and harassment, and unwanted sexual attention from older boys and even men.

Girls tend to link sexual intimacy with emotional intimacy and commitment. Disappointment and emotional distress is often associated with early sexual activity. Even when girls consent, many experience feelings of emptiness and loss after their first sexual intercourse. If they are sexually active, they expect their partner to be part of a couple, part of their social life, and not a secret lover.

Boys and sexuality
Boys have a different relationship to sexuality from that of girls. Male energy is forceful, willful, and is testosterone-driven in a rhythm of tension and release. At about age twenty, they feel a sense of power and invincibility, aggression and dominance. They are impulsive, risk taking, and competitive. Boys like to test limits and challenge authority. They have a strong biological urge toward sexual activity, yet they need to be taught the skills of emotional intimacy and maintaining relationship. As Kindlon says (p. 193) "the boy must make the journey from the simplicity of sex to the complexity of relationship, and that is the challenge for every boy— and for many men who continue to struggle to move beyond the lonely satisfaction of heartless sex to the rewards of an intimate relationship."

The boy's energy must be shaped by the culture. Adult men need to teach boys how to take responsibility in sex with compassion and love. Boys in our culture must deal with the sensational messages coming from the media messages, which encourage violence, woman-hating, and objectification of women.

In the transition between early adolescence and later adolescence, the boy is torn between desire for sexual experience and anxiety about his performance. He may want sex, he may want to show his manliness, but he is concerned that he will be rejected or hurt. He doesn't want to show his peers that he has doubts. So he may act cool despite feeling worried.

There are usually three stages in the development of an adolescent boy's sexual life. From twelve to fourteen, his challenge is to find a way to live in a body that is often out of control. His feet are growing, his face is breaking out. His voice is changing, he is experiencing his first ejaculation. He may be sneaking looks at erotic magazines to stimulate his sexual fantasy. This is a very unstable time, and it can be very awkward as he tries to take hold of new sensations.

During the next phase—fifteen to sixteen—he often has an active fantasy life. He may be sexually involved with a girl, exploring various aspects of the relationship.

As the boy moves into the next phase—sixteen to seventeen—he is filling out; his genitals have fully matured. He is more sexually aroused by real life experiences: dancing, hugging, spending time with a girl, music. His social life has become an important part of his exploration. His emotional life is awakening, and he may be wanting a deeper relationship than he did earlier.

Since puberty is starting earlier, he, too, has a longer time in which he has to channel his sexual energy. In addition, the fact that young people marry later affects the boy as well as the girl. Add to all this, the pressure from the society to "score," and we can see that the boy does not have an easy time dealing with his sexual awakening. He needs to be fully advised about pregnancy, birth control, sexually transmitted diseases, and AIDS.

A teen-aged boy often has sex on his mind. Being surrounded by so many tantalizing visual images adds to the temptations. One of his big challenges is to accurately read social and sexual cues from girls. Boys need to be taught to be sensitive to a girl's feelings, to respect the word "no," not to aggressively force himself on a girl, and never to use his penis as a weapon. This advice could have helped several of the characters in *Parzival*. If a boy has had a troubled youth, it is harder for him to be sensitive to the feelings of others, and he is more vulnerable to images that carry a brutalizing effect in the depiction of violence.

Many fairy tales portray the journey of the male as an outward gesture. He strikes out on his own, meets challenges, has to be strong to overcome obstacles, deals with fear, and eventually wins the prize. He tests the woman's promise to be faithful to him despite the fact that he is in another form, often animal-like, or that she cannot ask him a question about his identity. He challenges her pride and haughtiness. To succeed, he has to cultivate feminine qualities such as nurturing, empathy, and concern for the community.

Growing toward relationship
The girl's journey is more inward. Because she associates sex with relationship, she imagines a boy who pays attention to her sexually is interested in having a relationship with her. She has to learn to determine whether a boy's attention toward her is due to his desire for sex or because he is attracted to her personality. Her active imagination often links them as a couple long before there is a reason to do so. She interprets his actions (and, of course, discusses them with her girlfriends) and tries to understand his emotions based on her own way of feeling.

The girl does not need to prove herself outwardly in the same way that the boy does. Instead, she struggles with inner qualities of patience, sacrifice, loyalty, and devotion. She often analyzes her own behavior in terms of these qualities. (Do I have to give up what I want to do so I can please him? Do I have to agree with him so he will accept me, or can I say what my ideas are? Should I pretend I don't know something so he can feel good about explaining it to me? If I'm too smart, will he still like me?)

Her emotional life is tied in with her physical desires, and if she is going to be sexually active, she wants to be reassured that he loves her and will take care of her. She expects him to be faithful to her and is devastated if he is not. She may be intimidated by a boy's anger or use of power and has to cultivate masculine qualities of courage and strength to keep from being overwhelmed. Often she has to learn that beauty is not enough, that she has to pay attention to her inner qualities. When a boy is respectful and true, she gives her heart to him.

In many stories there is some sort of enchantment, challenging the hero or heroine to act in a way that releases a spell so that the true self can shine through. Very often the hero can find his true self only with the help of a female character. We see several of these situations in *Parzival*.

An adolescent boy has to learn to differentiate friendship from a more intimate relationship. Condwiramur is clear when she comes to Parzival in the night for advice. This is a temptation for some adolescent boys; can they respect a girl when she is clear about her intentions and not press her further. Also, can the girl be clear about her intentions, or does she give mixed messages to the boy.

The adolescent girl, on the other hand, needs to develop clarity about her wants and intentions. Too often, she gives in to sexual demands when she does not really want to. She wants to be liked. She wants to be approved of. Yet, giving in seldom leads to being liked. More often, she is hurt by such actions.

A 2001 poll by the National Campaign to Prevent Teen Pregnancy found much agreement across groups defined by gender, race, income, and geography that teen pregnancy was a serious problem. The majority said that teens should not be sexually active, but teens who are should have access to birth control. One of the most surprising aspects of the poll had to do with influence. While media certainly influence teenagers' behavior, teens said that it was parents who had the greatest influence on their decisions about becoming sexually active.

Teens say that adults should give a strong message to teenagers to abstain from sex until they are at least out of high school. Most surveyed wished they had waited longer. Many said that the main reason teens do not use birth control is because of drinking or using drugs or because their partners don't want to. Surprisingly, teen boys and girls agree that pressure from their partners is one of the main reasons that teens fail to use birth control.

To help teenagers deal with this issue, the following suggestions were made to adults:

1. Be clear about your own sexual values and attitudes.
2. Talk with your children early and often about sex, and be specific.
3. Supervise and monitor your children and adolescents.
4. Know your children's friends and their families.
5. Discourage early, frequent, and steady dating.

6. Take a strong stand against your daughter dating a boy significantly older than she is. And don't allow your son to develop an intense relationship with a girl much younger than he is.
7. Help your teenager to have options for the future that are more attractive than early pregnancy and parenthood.
8. Let your kids know that you value education highly.
9. Know what your kid are watching, reading, and listening to.
10. These first nine tips for helping your children avoid teen pregnancy work best when they occur as part of strong, close relationships with your children that are built from an early age.

Ten Tips for Parents to Help Their
Children Avoid Teen Pregnancy
published in 1998 by
Campaign to Prevent Teen Pregnancy

Friendships between adolescent boys and girls are a helpful practice and preparation for intimacy. When we think of what is involved in friendship—sharing, trusting, giving and taking, facing criticism from a trusted friend, giving of oneself without asking for any reward in return—these qualities need to be learned before sexuality becomes enmeshed in the relationship and the teenagers are unable to untangle themselves. Some wonderful friendships are ruined because a line is crossed and the teenagers cannot return to their previous friendship.

Taking time to bring sex into relationship
Another interesting aspect of Book IV of *Parzival* is that Condwiramur considers that she and Parzival are married. Why? Because she is grateful he respected her request "not to wrestle with her." She is moved by what she interprets as his sensitivity. It's not clear that he was being sensitive, but perhaps he has no clue what else to do. She gives herself and all her possessions to him. Only after all that do they consummate the relationship. She has in her imagination created them as a couple before he even thinks about it. How often girls romanticize a relationship, already imagining their future husband's last name as their own—or at least hyphenated—the home they will have, their children. The boy is unaware

of this and would find it surprising to know that this is going on in the girl's mind. The love that they develop for each other takes time and becomes tender and strong. Their relationship takes fifteen months to mature, and it is only after the flowering of their relationship that Parzival feels that he can leave.

Comparing this relationship to Parzival's father's relationship with Belakane, we see radical differences. Gahmuret was led by his passion, Parzival takes time. Gahmuret steals away in the night, leaving a "Dear Belakane" letter behind. Parzival asks Condwiramur for permission to go see his mother. This shows that Parzival has reached a stage of development that is more mature than his father's. This bodes well for Parzival's life. Overcoming impulsiveness and disregard for another person is an important stage in the boy's maturation.

Boys and their mothers

Parzival's decision to go find his mother is an important point in his development. Until now he has not thought to do this. Why not? He is not ready. First he had to find a male mentor who could teach him the rules of life. Then he had to find the woman he could love. Only then, with those two parts of his life intact, can he leave to reclaim the maternal part of himself. He can return as a man. He has fought nobly, not naively as when he molested Jeschute or fought the Red Knight. He has gained enough maturity to return to his mother with a sense of who he is.

A boy's relation with his mother is full of contradictions; he longs for connections and he needs to pull away. Parzival pulled away, but he never faced his mother and worked it out. He didn't have a father to help him understand that there was a different world to emulate. The glimpse of the knight was enough to beckon him to leave the forest, but he did not know where he was going. He still carried his mother with him, in the fact that he wore the clothes she had given him under the Red Knight's armor, in the way he greeted strangers (My mother told me to . . .), and in the way he took her advice literally. Parzival has now arrived at a different place in his relationship with his mother. He has become a man of the world, and he is ready to go back and clear things up before he can go forward.

It seems to me that in an unconscious way Parzival understands a deep truth here. We cannot pursue our own destiny until we can resolve issues with our parents. No matter what age we are, unresolved relationships with our parents haunt us and limit us. We need to go back and take care of those before we can go forward. If our parents have died, then we have to find another way, perhaps through meditation, through inner speaking with the parent, through forgiveness. When Parzival decides to find his mother, he has to go across the threshold to the spiritual world; he is led to the Grail Castle. Through that experience he learns his main task in life—to find the Grail.

Changes during Adolescence: No—Maybe—Yes

As they absorb the popular culture, teenagers want to spend more time with friends rather than with family. Friends become the most important people in their lives, and often they change friends during this time, as many long-term friendships weaken. ("I'm much more mature than Elizabeth."or "Those boys are such babies. They're pathetic. I don't know why I spent any time with them.") Their focus becomes not only who their friends are, but to which group they belong.

In middle adolescence (16–18), boys and girls go through a major change in their thinking, as concrete thinking gives way to the capacity for abstract thought. No longer at the whim of cause and effect, they begin to grasp concepts. Although they are still self-centered, there are moments when they begin to perceive other people's needs, feelings, and actions. Their energy is beginning to move from their sexual organs to their heart.

The years between sixteen and eighteen are focused mainly on pushing aside the old and finding a map through this new world of relationships. Disappointed with the lack of perfection in the world, young adolescents often become angry and negative. Between sixteen and seventeen, their *No!* shifts to a middle stance, into the more conditional word, *Maybe!* This shift allows the youngster more room to consider the world outside without reacting immediately.

Their sense of their own importance grows strong. They may feel invulnerable, omnipotent, omniscient, and invincible. They are the center of the world, and nothing bad can happen to them, despite the risks they take.

Toward the latter part of this stage, teenagers begin to look at themselves more objectively. Earlier they were focused outward and saw the world as messed up, but now they can own their problems. They realize what they are good at, what they can and cannot do well, what they feel is important, and where they choose to apply their energy. They are able to make choices and be self-critical. However, as the focus on their inner life becomes more real and they begin to weigh their abilities as to success and failure, they may lose confidence in themselves and become depressed. This is a dangerous, anxiety-ridden age with possibilities for deeper psychological problems such as eating disorder, depression, and suicide. Being turned down for a date can be seen as catastrophic. Life is not worth living. Doing poorly on a school assignment can bring the world crashing down.

At this time the focus on sexuality intensifies. Middle adolescents may long for intimate relationships, experiment with sexual behavior, question their orientation, and explore emotional and physical contacts. Love becomes the center of their emotional life. (What is love? Am I in love?) They long for the idealized form of the other; this is the time of the crush, their first real love. As idealized longing gives way to reality, the adolescent learns something of compassion and humility.

Even though this is a very difficult time, teenagers are now back on course. They regain their footing, are more willing to relate to adults, are open to examining their behavior, and are able to compromise. One girl said, "I am so grateful for my parents and teachers who were like rocks that anchored me during this shaky time."

Physical development is mostly complete by eighteen. Boys and girls feel as if they now inhabit their bodies. I often experience the contrast between younger teenagers and those around sixteen or seventeen years old when I attend basketball games. The Junior Varsity, mostly made up of younger players, seem like puppies. Their bodies are directing them, rather than the other way around. Legs sprout, shoulders and torsos are thin and round, limbs get in the way, they fall over themselves. Watching the Varsity boys and girls play is a different experience. They have filled out their bodies, and they control their movements right to their fingertips and toes, anticipating movements of others, and expressing their skills in the way they handle the ball and pass to each other.

The *maybe* stage that usually occurs between sixteen and eighteen is very important as it allows teenager time and opportunity to live in the inner world, make sense of the outer world, and set clear and obtainable goals. As they become seventeen or eighteen years old, thinking becomes a stronger force to organize behavior and allow feelings to show. As they become slowly wise, they begin to integrate their thinking, feeling, and willing so that their Self can shine through. Their ability to think abstractly reaches another level as they now have the capacity to analyze and synthesize their thoughts. Their attitude shifts from *maybe* to *yes*.

During the nineteenth or twentieth year, teenagers often have a sense of what they want to do with their lives. Even though they may follow another course of action in the following decades, in later years as adults they may return to that earlier sense of purpose and reconnect with it. By age 21, teenagers have completed the cycle and are ready to begin their adult years.

Chapter 5

Adolescence Is a Dangerous Time

Book V. *The Grail Castle:*
Why didn't he ask the question?

*P*arzival rides out to seek his mother, but thoughts of Condwiramur trouble him. Letting his horse lead him, he rides through rugged lands, over fallen trees, and through marshes. At evening, he comes to a lake where a fisherman apparelled in rich finery sits in a boat. Parzival inquires where he might find lodging for the night. The fisherman tells him that there is nothing for thirty miles around except one house nearby where he would have to cross the moat to enter. He, himself, would be the young knight's host. He urges caution because the roads lead to no one knows where. Parzival follows the fisherman's directions and approaches not an ordinary house, but a great castle. Upon telling the gatekeeper that the fisherman has sent him, he is welcomed and treated hospitably. Once inside, the squires care for his horse, help him remove his armor, give him water to wash off the rust, and give him a silk garment of the queen's until his own clothes will be made for him. They lead him into the great hall.

Everything is most splendorous; the walls are covered with tapestries portraying every human activity. "A hundred chandeliers all aglow with candles gave light from above" to the gathering assembled there. At the far end of the hall, the lord of the castle (who was the fisherman at the lake) reclines on a couch facing the central fireplace. Even though there are three great fireplaces with fires burning in them, the lord is clothed in rich furs as if icicles hung on the walls. Next to him is an empty seat. The lord, Anfortas, bids Parzival enter and welcomes him graciously to sit beside him. He is the epitome of courtesy.

Then comes a moment of great sorrow as a youth, bearing a bleeding lance, comes through the door. Blood seeps from the point, past the shaft, and runs into his sleeve. The guests, who are reminded of a great sorrow that has taken place, are weeping and wailing, filling the castle hall with the sound of moaning. Maidens enter in beautiful gowns of brown silk with wreaths of flowers in their hair. One group follows another, carrying ivory stools, candles, and a table-top carved from a single garnet, all of which is placed before the lord Anfortas.

Queen Repanse follows them, carrying the Grail. The person who carries the Grail has to be pure and truthful, but Parzival gazes at her, thinking only that it is her cloak he is wearing. She is the essence of beauty. One steward enters for every group of four knights, carrying a gold basin, followed by a page carrying a towel. A hundred tables are brought into the hall, set with white cloths. The knights wash their hands and dry them on silk towels. Squires carve meat at each table and bring drink. A hundred squires bring bread, drink, and other food that has been blessed before the Grail.

Parzival notices all of this, but for courtesy's sake he refrains from questions. He remembers that Gurnemanz has told him not to ask too many questions. Anfortas presents him with a jeweled sword and sheath that will help him in any battle. Still Parzival does not ask the question.

The feast ends, the hall is emptied of all tables and dishes; the maidens leave after bowing to the king and to Parzival. As they are walking out, Parzival glimpses a beautiful old man reclining on a couch. Still he does not ask any questions. The king bids him good night and Parzival is brought to a beautiful bed covered in silk. In the candlelit room, pages undress Parzival but when maidens come in, and he realizes he is naked, he jumps under the cover and peeks out.

After offering him a soothing drink, the maidens leave. Parzival has a restless night, filled with suffering and agony. When he awakes, there is no one there to help him dress, although his clothes have been laid out and his horse is ready. In his anxiety, he runs around the castle feeling both angry and grief-stricken. As he rides over the drawbridge, he hears a voice calling, "Ride on and bear the hatred of the sun. You are a goose. If you had only moved your jaws and asked your host the question."

As Parzival follows the tracks, he thinks about his new life as a warrior. He remembers that he has the wondrous sword that Anfortas has given him, but because he had not earned it, he might be considered a coward. As he is thinking these things, he sees that the tracks grow fainter and fainter until he cannot see the way to go. Suddenly, he hears a woman's voice, crying in sorrow. When he comes upon the woman he sees that she is embracing a dead and embalmed knight. Parzival does not recognize that she is his cousin Sigune, but he sees that she is suffering and offers her his service. She thanks him but tells him that this region is too wild. When he tells her he has spent the night in a wondrous castle, she chides him for lying. She tells him that if a person seeks for it, he will not find it. The only way to enter the castle is to come upon it unawares.

Sigune tells him the history of the Grail Castle, and the sorrow of Anfortas, King of the Grail Castle. If he had truly gone there, he could have ended the king's suffering. When they recognize each other, Parzival is surprised at how pale and weak she has become since he last saw her. Then she recognizes the sword from the Grail Castle and assumes that he has asked the question. Sigune instructs him in the special qualities of the sword: The sword will withstand the first blow; at the second it will shatter. If he dips it in a particular spring before dawn, it will become whole again. If he has asked the question, that will not only give her great joy, he will become the noblest and richest man on earth. Parzival tells her, "I did not ask."

Hearing those words, Sigune becomes furious and curses him, "You have the fangs of a venomous wolf!" Parzival asks her to go gently with him. If he's done anything wrong, he will atone for it. But she will speak no further with him.

At this point Parzival feels a deep sense of remorse and self-reproach. He starts to sweat and seeks some cool air. As he walks away, he sees a woman riding on a horse so lean that it looks as if it has no flesh on its body. Its eyes are sunken and sad. The woman's ripped and ragged clothing are knotted to cover her naked body, although not completely. The woman is Jeschute. When she catches sight of Parzival, she recognizes him as the youth who has brought all her troubles to her. He apologizes and tells her that since he has learned the ways of chivalry he has not shamed anyone. But as he experiences her sobbing, he feels deep pity for her with all his heart. He offers to serve her and tries to cover her with his coat, but she wants him to get away before her husband Orilus comes and kills him. Parzival, with his sense of knightly honor, will not run away.

Her husband appears and the two men engage in a furious and well-matched joust—one man fighting because he was unsuccessful in protecting his wife against assault, the other because he wants to convince the husband of his wife's virtue. The older knight is not used to losing, but Parzival's strength and skill work for him and he throws Orilus off his horse and pins him over a fallen tree. He tries to force Orilus to forgive Jeschute, but Orilus says that he would rather die. He bargains for his life by offering Parzival two lands as ransom, which Parzival refuses. Parzival tells Orilus to go and give service to Lady Cunneware; he then convinces Orilus that if he doesn't reconcile with Jeschute, he will not live.

Since Orilus does not want to lose his life, he gives in and the two reconcile. Then they ride together to the cave of the hermit Trevrizent where Parzival swears an oath upon a holy casket that Jeschute was innocent. Parzival says, "I was a fool then, not a man, and not yet grown to wisdom." Parzival returns the ring which he snatched from Jeschute back in the tent. At this point, Orilus truly accepts that his wife was innocent and gently covers her with his cloak. He takes responsibility for having left her alone that day and admits that he has done her a great wrong because of jealousy.

Parzival takes away a brightly colored spear that lies across the casket, and they all go separate ways. After Orilus and Jeschute have bathed and dressed in fine clothes, they arrive at King Arthur's court. Orilus pledges service to Lady Cunneware, but to his surprise, she recognizes him as one of her two brothers, and cannot accept service from him. He identifies himself and begs her to honor his pledge so that he might fulfill what he has promised. She does and thereby sets him free. The knights and ladies of the Round Table then receive Orilus and Jeschute with a warm welcome and King Arthur rejoices in their reconciliation.

Adolescence is a Dangerous Time

The Boy's Journey

Parzival is tested, but he is not ready
Parzival has gone to seek his mother, but she has died. Crossing the drawbridge to the spiritual world, he doesn't really know where he is going. He is in another consciousness where he glimpses another world. The clothing which the squires give him is not his own, it belongs to the Queen of the Grail. He has not yet earned his own clothing. The knights expect him to ask Anfortas why he is suffering, but Parzival is not ready. When one of the courtiers testily jokes with him, Parzival impulsively clenches his fist. If he had had his sword, he would have used it (or a gun in modern times). The courtier takes back the comment, as if to say, "Just joking. Don't be angry." Here we have the impulsiveness of some adolescent boys, rushing to meet insult with violence.

In the great hall, Parzival glimpses a world beyond the earthly, of what sometimes is called "the astral world," where soul forces of purity, suffering, misuse of love, innocence, sacrifice, sorrow, masculine and feminine nobility and beauty, and unrealistic expectations all flow together. What has happened? Parzival has been tested but he is not ready to understand the depth of human suffering. He is overwhelmed by the whole experience, and the only thing he can think of is Gurnemanz' advice: Don't ask too many questions.

Like Parzival, the young adolescent struggles to discern cause and effect. He is not yet mature enough to connect emotions with thought. In a way, he is still being cared for by the feminine (the Queen's clothing), and he is not yet a man. Something is stirring in him as seen in his restless night. But his response in the morning is truer to his self-centered stage of development. He was so well taken care of when he first entered the castle that, when he awakens and no one is there to help him, he runs through the halls, shouting, "Where are they? Why aren't they serving *me*?" He feels grief and anger, but he can't sort out the reasons.

Although Parzival is still centered on himself, grief is a powerful awakener. Something is moving in Parzifal's soul life even though he doesn't yet understand it. Before youths can come to understanding, they must experience sorrow and recognize what it is. Being called a goose confuses Parzival; he really doesn't understand what is happening. However, he has come to some self-reflection when he says, "I wear the sword unearned." This is an important step in Parzival's development. Although he has not found his mother, he is finding himself.

Parents or teachers may be frustrated at times when a boy behaves insensitively, refusing to acknowledge or take responsibility for the results of his actions. Yet it is always important to remember that even in extreme cases such as when a boy may ridicule an adult's expectation of proper behavior, deep down he wants to do the right thing. However, he needs an environment in which the adults believe in his better self, where they are willing to be both loving and firm.

Parzival's emotional development awakens at a deeper level when he sees Sigune and perceives how Sigune has suffered since he saw her last. His heart fills with grief for her, and he pledges his service. This is a very different response from their first meeting when he wanted to go off and challenge the knight who had killed Schianatulander.

97

Sigune's role is significant here. She faces him with what he has done. Only then can he wake up. When she yells at him, he tells her to go easy, that he'll make up for it. Can't we hear our teenaged boys speaking to us: Take it easy. Don't make such a big deal of it. I'll fix it.

Sigune challenges Parzival on three levels. She introduces him to his physical identity by giving him the history of his family. By calling him a venomous wolf, she challenges his soul and awakens remorse for his behavior at the Grail castle. She challenges his spiritual life, his morality, so that he owns his misdeed when he says, "I did not ask."

Even though Parzival has not not asked the question, he has learned something even more important for now: that he has to earn what he gets, that it cannot just be given to him. He is being given images—Anfortas's sorrow and Sigune's sorrow—to take into his soul life. Through Sigune's words, he has taken responsibility for his actions and awakened his moral sense. The door is opened, and he will never be the same. In this way, he prepares for the journey he has to make towards maturity.

As in Parzival's experience, a boy needs to go through the process of perceiving other people's feelings through their voice, facial expression or gesture, and realizing the cause of them. Often, as boys try to be tough, they do not recognize other people's feelings or their own. Parzival needed to make a connection between his perception that Sigune was distressed and weeping over his failure to ask the question and his own feeling of remorse. That he began to reproach himself shows us that he is starting to make these connections.

When boys learn early in their lives to hide feelings and cover up their fears, they separate themselves from their own inner life. They can become confused about what they really feel and what is a mask they wear to show they can handle anything. Rather than acknowledging feelings, they deny them and thus deny themselves access to their essential being. Boys need adults who are comfortable acknowledging their own feelings and who accept and encourage them to do so also. As the boy develops this capacity, he is preparing himself to enter sensitive and meaningful adult relationships.

The adolescent boy's journey is a long one, with many ups and downs. It is a dangerous journey filled with misunderstandings, poor judgment, and misuse of others. It was Sigune, acting as Parzival's guardian, who earlier told him his name. Now she warns him, "It is not wise for anyone to venture a journey into this wild region. Grave harm can befall a stranger here. I have heard and also seen how many have lost their lives here and found their death in combat. Turn back."

Such is the world of adolescence. Parzival cannot turn back to childhood again; he has crossed the bridge. He has now left his mother in another realm. When he had ridden off to King Arthur's court, he had separated from her physically. When he longs to see her, he connects with her spiritually through his thoughts. He looks to a spiritual mother, the Grail Queen, whose clothing he is wearing, who carries the Grail which will give anything he or she wants. The Grail Queen does not judge him. She will wait until he is ready.

Here we have a picture of the rite of passage that every boy must go through. He must cross the great divide and leave his mother. In many ancient cultures an elder would come and forcibly take the boy away from his mother into a man's world. Everything Parzival's mother has taught him he carries as a treasure in his heart, but he must find his way without her before he can return and face her as a man. After Parzival marries Condwiramur, he knows that he is not worthy of her until he goes back and finds a new relationship to his mother. Because she is in the spiritual world, that is where he must go.

The wild region of adolescence is truly dangerous. There are all kinds of temptations waiting to lure the youngster. It is not a world of clear reason, but is filled with emotional whirlpools, wild winds, uncontrollable desires, false steps, illusion, and struggles with power. Go back! But the adolescent cannot go back. This is the Sacred Passage which very adolescent must traverse to become a whole human being. Parzival's journey is really just beginning.

Boys usually settle problems through physical action
Having been awakened by Sigune's anger, Parzival must encounter Jeschute on her emaciated horse. Let us put this scene into present day life. Can we not imagine a similar situation where an adolescent boy aggressively forces himself onto a girl, despite her protests. Her boyfriend then blames her for enticing the other boy and treats her badly. The girl would say to the aggressor, "Stay

away from me. You caused me nothing but trouble, my boyfriend is furious with me." The aggressive boy apologizes and says, "Look, I didn't know any better then, but now I wouldn't behave like that. I'm really sorry."

She just wants him to go, but he feels tenderness for her; his heart is moved, and he wants to make it up to her. The once-aggressive boy wants to face her boyfriend and make him see the girl is innocent. The way he does this is by fighting. The boy's way of settling this with another boy is through physical aggression.

A boy judges his masculinity by looking at everything through a lens of strength or weakness. If he is strong, he is worthy. If he is weak, he is worthless. Even if he doesn't want to fight, he has to be willing to do it. Otherwise, he has no self-respect. Even if he is a boy of small build, or a boy who is more interested in intellectual pursuits than brawny ones, there may come a time when he will have to prove himself in a fight.

When Parzival finally gets Orilus to pay attention, Orilus begrudgingly accepts that he has misjudged Jeschute. But it is Parzival's ability to go further, after he has proven his strength and mastered Orilus, that moves Orilus to change his ways. Parzival takes an oath, returns the ring, insists that Jeschute was not at fault, and admits that he had acted like a fool. It is at this point that Orilus accepts his explanation and takes responsibility for his own actions. In other words, nothing can happen until the adolescent (or the man—Orilus, in this case) recognizes his role and takes responsibility for it.

Parzival's two-fold action in this scene is a good example of the transition between early adolescence and later adolescence. It is only when the boy develops objectivity and can understand other people's perspectives that he realizes physical action is not the only way to solve problems. It is only through willingness to admit his own mistake and show his own vulnerability that change can come about. Think about how many conflicts in the world could be solved through understanding and empathy with the "enemy" instead of with bullets and rockets. Self-pride and hurt feelings perpetuate early adolescent behavior, no matter what age the person is.

The people in the Grail Castle are frozen in time. Their sorrow wells up when the healing question is not asked. They are like the people frozen in Sleeping Beauty's castle. The princess is asleep; everyone is waiting for the prince who will cut through the thorny fence, slash his way in, kiss her, and free everyone. Our Parzival prince is not yet ready to do this. The frozen people in the castle will have to wait. The boy must grow up. He is a goose!

The power of the sword
Sigune teaches Parzival about the power of his newly gained sword. It can be restored in a magic spring. He must place it in the water at the source, beneath the rock, before the light of day has shone upon it. If you join the parts together, the sword will become whole again, the joining of the edges stronger than before.

The sword is the source of Parzival's power. How does a boy renew his power? He has to go to the source of his strength, in the inner world which is dark (before the sun shines upon it) and hidden away. If his power breaks in outer struggles, he can renew it by becoming connected with his inner self again.

The change from earlier to later adolescence is marked by the way the boy uses his sword. When he moves from being a knight, ready to take on any challenger to a knight who keeps the peace through reconciliation, he has made the transformation. The sword has been transformed into word. He then becomes a warrior for peace. A mature man has made this transformation. An example of someone who modeled this transformation in a powerful way is Nelson Mandela when he established the Commission for Truth and Reconciliation in South Africa rather than expressing revenge against those who had committed crimes under apartheid.

The Girl's Journey

The girl comes into her selfhood earlier and through a different path. To understand the girl's journey we need to penetrate the nature of a female.

While a boy's development requires separation, a girl weaves an ever more complex network of relationships—i.e., connectedness—as the fabric of her maturing self. The girl awakens to her sense of self earlier and in a more differentiated way than a boy does. She is a keen observer, watching the way people relate, focusing on gesture, nuance, and subtlety. She cares for others as well as for her own physical and emotional needs. She is more attuned to her own feelings, and she develops empathy sooner than a boy does.

Girls find their identities connected with intimacy. Girls are not as keen on independence as they are concerned with relationships. Being able to participate in relationship is what gives them a sense of self-worth. They are more interested in power *with* others than in power *over* others. Becoming isolated or separated is threatening for girls.

Girls have a broad vocabulary of emotional expressions and talk through their experiences either with someone else or even with themselves. They wake to their own thoughts through the process of talking, relating, and hearing their own process of discovery and problem solving.

As girls come into puberty, even outgoing girls tend to go through periods of moodiness and become unreachable. They are confused about all the changes going on and withdraw for a while. For a time they may relate more closely to another woman such as a teacher or coach than to their mothers.

In general, girls are not as comfortable with competition, but prefer to work together as a team. Because girls are more tuned in to emotional subtlety, they tend to recognize the price that both males and females pay through aggressive competition. They may choose to engage in it and do well, but, given a choice, they will more likely do something that supports the aims of the group or that enhances relationships. However, because girls are more attuned to the comments or gestures of the other girls on a team, rivalries within the team or a falling out with another girl can create serious problems for a team. Boys, on the other hand, tend to pay less attention to emotional subtleties within the team and have a stronger feeling for teamwork, which includes a strong sense of team loyalty. The boys' feelings of rivalry are more directed to the other team, not to teammates.

In this chapter of *Parzival*, we see Sigune sitting with her dead knight. Even in death, she is completely faithful to him. Because she longs to end Anfortas's suffering, she is concerned with Parzival's deed. Her emphasis in conversation with Parzival is that he become more perceptive and respond to the needs of others. She wakes him up to this necessity, and only out of his inner wakefulness is he able to heal what he has destroyed. Girls have a concern about the suffering of others as well as their own. They evaluate whether an action will hurt someone and prefer to give it up if the social price is too steep.

The girl does not have to separate from her mother to find a female model. Her imitative capacity unites her with her mother and other females in her environment, and so she learns what it is to be a woman. At times, she may feel too similar to her mother and may want to stress differences, or she may feel embarrassed by her mother and want to create space. But this is often temporary. She goes through a stage where she needs to define herself and set her own course, but she does not have to physically separate to do this. The boy can only learn what it is to be a man by leaving his mother's environment and basking in a man's world.

In her relationship with her mother, the girl develops feminine qualities of caring, giving, sensitivity to people's feelings, and nurturing. Conversations about relationships tune her in to the subtleties of people's intentions, motivations, and needs. Within the relationship of the girl and her mother, she needs to find her own voice and have the courage to speak what she thinks is true. Once a girl is able to do this, she can have a mutually supportive connection with her mother. If she is not able to find her own voice, she feels overwhelmed or suffocated in the relationship, and she may spend years trying to get her mother to accept her or approve of her.

In addition to the relationship with her mother, the girl must establish a relationship with her father. In her relationship with her father, she develops what are usually seen as masculine qualities that will give her the confidence to strike out on her own, set goals, problem solve how to achieve them, and feel her inner strength. Where her father is absent or their relationship is dysfunctional, the girl may enter into relationships with boys that are challenging. She will be looking for a father figure, or she might accept abusive behavior because that is what she expects in a male-female relationship.

There is a shadow side to girls' strength in relationship. Rather than talking directly to another person about issues, she will often talk around the subject, manipulating the situation, talking behind people's backs, and using her power to control the situation in a subtle way. Girls may become smothering and controlling. Establishing a healthy relationship is a challenge for a girl. If she becomes either too independent or too dependent, she suffers consequences to her psyche.

When girls insist on being too independent, they are ignoring their need for relationship. This often leads to depression and loneliness. They look as if they should be happy because they are independent, but actually they are longing to be part of a relationship. Conversely, if they become too dependent, they may give themselves away rather than risk ending an unhealthy relationship. They will suffer through difficult situations and build up resentment against the other person or even against themselves. Self-sacrifice taken to an extreme creates serious emotional problems. The balance between independence and dependence is a challenge in the girl's journey.

The power of the word
When a boy is angry or frustrated, he tends to use weapons (his fists or a gun) to establish power over another person. The girl often uses words to express her frustration or anger, and to feel powerful. When she goes into a rage, she can become a spitfire shrew. She can use words skillfully to deceive or manipulate. Both boys and girls who react in ways that hurt other people are handling their power in an immature way. When they use words carefully and in consideration of the other person, they move into later adolescence.

When a girl feels that society threatens her safety, sees her as a sex object, denies her intelligence, or limits her possibilities, those feelings quickly turn to anger. Her anger is valid, but she must find a way to articulate the problem and stimulate change. A girl's sense of being a second-class citizen often sensitizes her to the plight of the poor, the homeless, the disabled, and other populations denied access and power.

Adolescence is dangerous for girls because they often mold themselves to popular images, downgrade their own capabilities, and fail to realize their potential.

The Sacred Passage

Adolescence is a perilous journey during which the young person must quickly acquire critical skills. The transitions from early to middle to later adolescence are the stepping stones of adolescent development. Learning to be flexible in response, learning to see the bigger picture, discovering that there are greater and lesser values, experiencing adult role models who guide them through this turbulent time—all of these elements help the adolescent on this perilous journey.

But there is something even more important that occurs at this time. I call it the Sacred Passage because of the awakening of a spiritual quality, an awareness that something greater is happening. This is expressed through the adolescent's search for meaning, in awakening to ideals, in responding to higher values, and in making decisions that will guide his or her destiny for decades.

Chapter 6

It Is Hard for Adolescents to Wake Up and Face the Truth

Book VI. *Parzival meets Gawain*

*I*t is the eighth day of King Arthur's search for the Red Knight (Parzival) to invite him to join the Round Table. Arthur demands of his knights a pledge not to joust without his permission. He tells them, however, that he will help them if they get into trouble because of this oath.

Where is Parzival? Although it is May, fresh snow has fallen during the night. Arthur's falconers have ridden out in the evening for hawking and have lost their best falcon, which has stayed in the woods all night, as did Parzival. In the morning, Parzival rides out to the meadow and the falcon follows along. There are perhaps a thousand geese cackling there. The falcon darts among them and strikes one so it can no longer fly. From its wounds three red drops of blood fall upon the snow. The white of the snow reminds Parzival of the skin of Condwiramur, and the red drops remind him of her lips, and he stares at the drops of blood and falls into a trance.

When the knights learn that a strange knight is nearby in armor and with spear erect, ready for combat, they are sorry that they have promised not to fight. They do not know who the stranger knight is or what his issues are. They just know that he seems to be a threat, and they are ready to take him on. The youth Segramors is always eager for a fight and cannot resist such a challenge. The other knights often have to tie him hand and foot or he would be in the middle of any fight. They know him to be a reckless warrior.

Segramors remembers that in his oath he has promised to gain King Arthur's permission before fighting, so he hurries to the tent where King Arthur and Queen Guinevere are sleeping. Impulsively, he bursts through the doorway and rudely pulls back the covers from the sleeping king and queen. He appeals to the queen, his aunt, that she ask the king to let him be the first to joust.

Although King Arthur explains why he doesn't want the knights fighting strangers, he gives in to his queen's pleading and allows the youth his wish. Segramors, armed and ready, rides out on his horse to face the strange knight. The contrast is amusing. The reckless youth is ready for a good fight, and Parzival is lost in a trance of love for his wife.

Segramors threatens Parzival, and when there is no response, charges at him. At that moment, Parzival's horse turns. Parzival's eyes are turned away from the three drops of blood, and he comes to his senses. Parzival receives a thrust on his shield, but he returns one so strong that Segramors is thrown off his horse. Parzival rides back to where the drops of blood are on the snow and once again sinks into a trance.

Segramors returns to the encampment with an abusive response to any of the knights who speak to him. He excuses his loss by claiming that anyone can fall in a joust. Segramors boasts that if Parzival had recognized who he was by his shield, he would never have dared to fight against him, but he admits Parzival is worthy of praise for having knocked him off his horse.

When Sir Kei hears how Segramors has been knocked down, he takes it as a personal challenge to engage the Red Knight in battle. He appeals to King Arthur to let him avenge the honor of the Round Table. With Arthur's permission, Sir Kei is armed and rides out to face Parzival, who is still entranced by love.

Kei taunts the stranger knight, accusing him of insulting the king by approaching Arthur's encampment ready for a fight. Sir Kei says that Parzival should let him put a dog's leash around Parzival's neck and lead him to the king. If Parzival will not agree, Kei says that he will take him there by force. Kei gives Parzival such a blow on his head that his helmet sings. Parzival still pays no mind. Kei charges again and this time Parzival's horse turns so he comes back to his senses and is ready for the charge.

Parzival responds to Kei's thrust onto his shield with a return thrust so hard that Kei and his horse fall over a fallen tree. The horse is dead and Kei's right arm and left leg are broken. Kei is carried away and brought into Arthur's tent. Gawain is saddened by Kei's injuries, but Kei is still able to respond angrily to Gawain. "That knight out there can really hit hard. You don't have bravery, that's on your father's side. You are more like your mother and would turn pale at the flash of a sword."

Gawain restrains himself from reacting to Sir Kei's taunts and simply says, "No one has ever seen me turn pale when a sword or lance was thrust at me. You have no reason to be angry with me. I have always been ready to serve you." Gawain leaves the tent and mounts his horse. Without a sword, he quietly rides out to have a look at this bold knight who is still staring at the ground. Gawain tries to engage Parzival in conversation, but Parzival remains with his lance erect and his eyes focused on the drops of blood. Gawain says, "You have insulted King Arthur and his men. If you will come with me to the King, I can influence him to show you mercy and pardon for your offense." But Parsival does not hear.

Gawain reflects on his own life, thinking of times when he has been entranced by love. He follows the direction of Parzival's gaze, takes a silk scarf and drapes it over the drops of blood. With that, Parzival comes to his senses again. In his mind, he speaks to his wife, questioning whether he has really saved her from Clamide, whether he has served her well. As he emerges from the trance, he wonders what has happened to his spear.

Gawain tells him, "It was broken in jousting." Parzival considers it an insult that Gawain comes without weapons. However, Gawain convinces him that he comes in friendship, asking Parzival to come with him to the king under his protection. When Parzival asks the name of the king, Gawain tells him about King Arthur and also identifies himself. This exchange changes the mood between the two knights. Parzival comments that he is aware of Gawain's reputation for kindness. He says that he cannot enter King Arthur's camp until he first avenges the beating of Lady Cunneware by Sir Kei. Gawain lets Parzival know that the beating has already been avenged because Parzival has broken Sir Kei's arm and leg and is responsible for his horse's death. Parzival puts his trust in Gawain and agrees to ride with him to the king.

As Parzival and Gawain ride into the encampment, they are welcomed with great joy. Parzival's radiance shines on all who look at him. King Arthur welcomes him warmly and with much nobility. Lady Guinevere embraces him as a son. The beautiful Lady Cunneware kisses him on both cheeks and Gawain pledges eternal friendship. The knights of the Round Table come one after the other to greet him as one of their own. The members of the Round Table do not want to end the festive meal because everyone is in such high spirits. Parzival is truly happy. He has attained the goal he had set in childhood.

A maiden riding on a mule approaches the Round Table, but she is not a maiden as we would expect. Gawain looks at her with something like inward terror. "Cundrie the sorceress!" he murmurs. "What does she want here?" Silence falls upon the wine-happy knights and the laughing ladies. They all recognize her, but no one knows who she is or where she lives. She always appears when a mysterious crime or an outrage has occurred and mercilessly accuses the criminal.

Cundrie is a learned maiden and speaks all languages well. She knows dialectic, geometry, and astronomy. Her clothes are elegant, a rich blue cape of fine cloth, a silk dress, a hat trimmed with peacock plumes and lined with cloth of gold. But she is frightening to look at. She has a long black braid like the bristles of a pig. Her nose is like a dog's. She has two boar's teeth sticking out from her mouth. Her eyebrows are so long that they are braided together. Her ears are like a bear's, and she has a hairy and rough face. Her hands are like monkey's skin, her fingernails stick out like a lion's claws. She carries a whip in her hands. Poor Parzival, he can barely look at her, yet he cannot stop looking at her.

Cundrie approaches King Arthur, saying, "What you have done here has brought shame to yourself and to many a Briton. The Round Table is ruined; falsity has joined its ranks. Your rising fame is sinking, your honor has been proven false. The fame and power of the Round Table have been weakened because Sir Parzival has joined its company."

She rides over to Parsival who is stunned by this statement. "You are the one to blame. A curse on the beauty of your face and on your manly limbs. Why didn't you ask the question and relieve the wounded king of his sorrow. You should have taken pity on him. You have an empty heart. You are destined for hell. You adder's fang! You saw the Grail pass before you, and the silver knives, and the bloody spear. If you had only asked the question!"

Then Cundrie mentioned something that was new to Parzival. "Your brother is a strange and wondrous man. He is both black and white, the son of the Queen of Zazamanc. He has more virtue than you."

Before Parzival can take in the information that he has a brother, Cundrie continues to blast him. "Your fame has turned into falseness. Your soul is sick in self-love, even if you do good for others you do it only for praise. Your heart is hard and you lack feelings. It would have been so easy for you to ask, but you did not." She weeps and tears at her hands. Her heart is in great distress. Although part of him wants to respond in anger, Parzival is moved by her tears, and something deep down in him tells him that there is truth in what she says.

Gawain jumps up and tells Cundrie to go. He cannot bear the way she speaks to Parzival. Before she leaves, she gives him advice. "Sir Gawain, go and seek Clingsor's Castle of Wonders. Clingsor, with the help of black magic, has stolen your sister Itonje and holds her tight. There are four queens and four hundred maidens locked up there, and that is a great adventure for a noble knight who wishes to win fame."

In great despondency, Cundrie leaves the Round Table with Parzival enveloped in shame. Parzival tells the members of the Round Table that he must leave. "Cundrie is right. There will be no joy for me until I find the Grail castle again. Then I can return to you."

In the midst of all this grief another stranger enters the circle. This joyless knight asks for Arthur and Gawain. He greets the members courteously, except for Gawain, for whom he says he has nothing but hatred. He accuses Gawain, "You killed my lord. If you deny this, you should engage in battle forty days from today. If you have any honor, you should meet me." Other members of the Round Table offer to go in Gawain's place, but Gawain refuses. He says, "I do not know why I am to fight, and fighting for its own sake gives me no pleasure." Yet he cannot bear the shame of refusing to go.

The knight identifies himself as Kingrimursel, nephew of the murdered lord. He promises Gawain safe conduct through all the land except from himself in battle. After he identifies himself and leaves, the members of the Round Table recognize who he is. His reputation is great and he is known as a very brave knight.

This is a day of both joy and sorrow for the Round Table. First there was the cheering as Parzival was welcomed into the Round Table. From Cundrie they learned who Parzival is, his background, his parents. Some even remember the tournament in which his father Gahmuret had won Herzeloyde. Yet these two fair knights, Parzival and Gawain, will leave them in mystery and in shame. Before Parzival goes, however, he is told more about his brother by a lady who identifies herself as the cousin of this mysterious brother. "His power extends far and wide," she says. "Two wealthy lands obey in fear his rule, in water and on land. He is worshiped like a god. His skin is both black and white."

As Parzival reflects on what Cundrie has said to him, he thinks about why he did not ask the question. Gurnemanz had advised him to refrain from impertinent question, so he had remained silent. He feels the grief of his sinful omission, but he still does not understand the reason behind the grief.

Gawain entreats Parzival to spend the night, and the next morning they will ride out together—Parzival to seek the Grail Castle and Gawain to meet Kingrimursel in battle. But Parzival refuses. "You mean well, Gawain, but I must go my path alone. Go well on your journey. I will see you again one day." Gawain pledges that once he finds his sister he will ride to the end of the world to find Parzival and says, "May God protect you."

Parzival responds bitterly, "God? I will tell you something, friend. I have believed in my life to serve God. But it looks as if he mocks me. From this day on, God will have to do without my service and I will live as I please. I advise you to do the same. Ride into the world, meet happy adventures, and gain the love of a beautiful lady. From those you will have more joy than I. Fool that I am, I will pursue the Grail."

Parzival leaves, and the next day many knights of the Round Table leave too, to seek the Castle of Wonders. Gawain also leaves. Deeds of honor have been done by many, the sorrow done to Lady Cunneware and to Lady Jeschute has been avenged, but nonetheless, also shame and remorse lingered in the camp.

Facing the Adolescent with Truth:
Wake up and pay attention

We can find several themes in this chapter of *Parzival* related to our adolescents.

Have you ever had the experience of talking to a teenager, or trying to talk to one, and wondering if anyone was there? At times adolescents seem so preoccupied that it is difficult to get them to focus. Parents say, "Pay attention," "Take out the garbage." "Clean your room." Are teens just ignoring the parent or are they in a dream consciousness? Other times, they respond in monosyllables (OK. Sure. Huh?) and then ignore what we've asked. They don't seem to hear what's being said just as Parzival didn't hear other knights speaking to him.

In the story we see various ways to break through dreaming and try to wake up preoccupied youth. One way is to act aggressively as Segramors and Sir Kei did. When the adult (parent, teacher, or other) behaves in this way, adolescents often respond with hostility as if the adult were an enemy intruding into their world. The other way is represented by Gawain. He observed Parzival. He spoke kindly. He found the source of Parzival's gaze, remembered in his own life when he had been in love, and then he distracted Parzival from the drops of blood. We can distract teenagers from their own soul pain by stimulating their interest in other people, other cultures, in what is going on outside their fragile selves. Such interest often leads to projects such as helping those in need or to travel and study abroad.

There are times, however, when the kind, gentle way is not enough to wake up the teenager. The adult has to penetrate the haze to stimulate a change in behavior. In this chapter Cundrie arrives in the midst of happiness. She destroys the mood and changes the destiny of the Round Table. She speaks the truth to Parzival, and it hurts. Cundrie is a person who understands deep laws of karma. She speaks what is lying unconsciously in Parzival's heart—that he was not pure, that he did not truly deserve to be a knight of the Round Table. Cundrie stings Parzival, and that sting changes his destiny. Just at the moment when he arrived at his heart's desire, he is denied the joy. But Cundrie actually is helping him in the same way Sigune has been helping him.

In a less dramatic way, certain adults play a similar role in teenagers' lives. When a teacher or other adult brings a truth to the teenager, this often is not welcomed. It might be: That paper you wrote is very sloppy and needs to be redone. Bringing such comments to a high school student is one of the most difficult things a teacher faces. Yet it must be done as these situations should not be ignored. Parzival would never have taken the next step in his development without Cundrie's shocking accusations. Parents can be helpful in teenagers' growth by helping them face the consequences of their behavior. Trying to cover up a teenager's mistake or lying to keep the teenager out of trouble only confuses the adolescent with mixed messages about what is ethical behavior.

When the adult confronts the teenager with his or her behavior, the response may be angry and defensive at first. Teenagers do not want to face the discomfort of taking responsibility for their deeds. Who of us does? They do not know how to get out of the situation but will try all kinds of ruses. The teenager may try denial (I wasn't there. I didn't do it. You've got the wrong person.), accusation of others (She asked me for the answers. How could I refuse her?), or making light of the deed (What's the big deal? Everybody cheats.). Deep down in their souls, teenagers know what was done was wrong and feel shame. The way the young person handles the situation will influence the development of his or her character.

One boy said, "I keep wishing I could turn the clock back and never have done such a stupid thing." The adult needs to be objective and not rub the teenager's face in the accusation. It is important to find a way for the youngster to make amends. It is fortunate when the act is not so serious, and the teenager can benefit from taking responsibility, and life goes on. That is not always the case. In the trial of high school student Andy Williams who killed two classmates in San Diego, Williams said he wished he could return to the moment when he pulled the trigger and not have done so. He was sentenced to fifty years in prison.

It helps the adolescent to hear the adult acknowledge that no one likes to face misdeeds, that in the long run the youngster will appreciate having to face the music, but that for now it feels horrible. Separating the deed from the person's character is important.

> "I don't appreciate what you did, but I know you now understand why it's wrong. I respect that in you."

> "I'm really angry about what you did, but I have great affection for you, and when this is over I know we will enjoy each other again."

> "I know you are angry that I caught you. I didn't like being in that position. But you will be a better person for facing it now rather than getting into a bad habit. I'm here to support you and let you know I'll help in whatever way I can."

These kinds of comment can help the adolescent deal with the situation. Of course, there are some teenagers who don't think that they have done anything wrong and do not take responsibility for their actions. At least they do not admit it in the moment.

Responsibility Develops the Higher Self

Each of us in responsible positions with teenagers has to have some of Cundrie in us. It is our responsibility to see the higher Self in each of our teenagers and to raise their consciousness to that level. When teenagers are able to realize the truth of a situation, however unpleasant it is, they grow closer to their higher Self, and this is a significant step in their spiritual development. Because I have been teaching for forty years, I have had the opportunity to meet former students as adults, and they often comment on how much they appreciated a particular high school teacher who told them the truth, even though they didn't like it at the time. They respect that person and are grateful that the teacher had the courage to face them.

This element of character development cannot exist in isolation. It needs the community. It needs relatives, teachers, adult friends, and peers who support the teenager but don't spare him the experience of facing consequences. Even when Gawain offered to ride out with Parzival as they left the Round Table, Parzival refused and said, "I have to go my path alone." This is a major turning point in Parzival's life.

When teenagers arrive at their seventeenth or eighteenth year, they are ready to understand the weight of their deeds. They may lie to themselves, but they know that they are lying. Now the adolescent can begin to measure his or her actions against a sense of who he or she truly is. This is a sign a teenager is entering late adolescence.

When I was giving a workshop in Latvia, a man related the following incident. When he was fourteen he had loved cars. At that time in the Soviet Union, the chance of his actually ever having a car was slight. He had gotten hold of a magazine with wonderful colored illustrations of cars. Although he had a big test the next day, he went into the bedroom and was dreamily savoring the pictures of cars. His mother came into the room, angrily grabbed the magazine, and tore it up because he was supposed to be studying.

The next morning he decided to get even with his mother by joining the students in school who drank heavily. For the next two-and-a-half years, he became a heavy drinker, did very poorly in school, and got into lots of trouble. Then he described how, when he was seventeen, he woke up one morning and said to himself, "This is not really me. I got into this, I can get out of it." From that day on, he worked out a way to extricate himself from the group he was in, stopped drinking, and began to attend to his school work. What he remembered so vividly was the moment in which he realized, "This is not really me."

Each of the three knights described in this chapter represents a part of soul activity—of thinking, feeling, or willing.

Segramors is the impulsive youth just ready for a fight, no matter who is challenging. He lives in his undisciplined will. He doesn't think about what he does; he just does it. It doesn't occur to him how rude it is for him to run into the tent and throw the covers from the sleeping king and queen. He only knows what he wants. He is excited about a fight for its own sake. As he matures, he will need to direct his will in a more helpful way.

Sir Kei has a brooding nature and responds to situations with sarcasm, insults, and taunts. It is difficult for him to accept defeat without justifying it to himself and to others. Sir Kei seems very harsh, but his virtue is his loyalty to King Arthur. He is like the teenager who is very intelligent, who makes scathing comments, and uses his quick wit to cover his sensitivity. Often such a teenager has suffered disappointments and hurts in his earlier years. At this point, he resorts to the negative aspect of his sharp thinking. However, when he transforms this negativity into a positive concern for others, his keen intelligence and wit will serve a good purpose, and he will feel more accepted and appreciated.

Gawain lives in his heart, in his feeling. He comes in friendship and is able to meet Parzival with trust. When Gawain is goaded by Sir Kei, he does not lose his balance, but stands firm in his own position. Gawain neither attacks nor insults. He simply states the case. Gawain is able to accept criticism, deal with unfair accusation, and take responsibility for his actions. In this situation, his feeling life is balanced. Therefore, he is able to shows discernment and to respond to the needs of others.

Waking up and taking responsibility for their deeds helps teenagers mature. If they live by their instincts, their behavior will be antisocial and unproductive for social life. However, as they reflect on their actions and are willing to face their deeds, they use higher thinking skills

Chapter 7

Honor, Jealousy, and Innocence

Book VII. *Gawain's adventure*

*G*awain sets out for Askalon where he will meet Kingrimursel. After a few days, he comes to a broad plain where he meets a large group with fine garments and brightly painted shields. After inquiring, he learns that they are the men of King Meljanz, or of his friends and relations on their way to attack the fortress of Prince Lippaut.

Gawain approaches Prince Lippaut's fortress and sees that attackers surround it, while defenders are ready to repel the attack. Gawain is curious about the situation, but he also has a dilemma. "If I look on at the fighting and don't take part in it, my fame will be extinguished. If I join the battle and it delays me, my fame will also be extinguished." He passes a gate which is walled up, with an archer standing ready to shoot. He continues on up a hillside to the castle. The duchess of the castle, along with her two daughters, looks out the window and notices Gawain. As the duchess wonders who this could be, her oldest daughter, Obie, scornfully replies, "I guess from the look of him, a horse-trader or a shield salesman, perhaps." But the younger daughter, Obilot (still under twelve years of age) sees something special in Gawain and defends him.

The reason for the battle is forsaken love. When Meljanz was a child, his father, the king, lay dying, and asked Prince Lippaut to raise his son as befits a ruler. Prince Lippaut did as asked. When Meljanz came into adulthood, he asked Obie (the older sister) to reward his service with love. She mocked and scorned him in a most embarrassing manner, telling him that he did not have enough experience as a knight to deserve her love.

When the rejected Meljanz reminded Obie of his power over her father, the Prince, she tossed her head and let him know that she didn't want to owe anything to anyone. "My sovereign freedom is great enough for any crown which earthly head has ever borne."

Meljanz blames Obie's father, Prince Lippaut, for putting such ideas into her head and, no matter how the Prince tries to solve the situation, Obie's rejection of Meljanz burns into a dangerous fury in him.

Meljanz's arrogant response is all-out battle against Prince Lippaut. Although Obie feels badly about Meljanz's anger, it is too late. The situation has become very dangerous.

Obie does not only insult Meljanz. She continually insults Gawain, calling him a peddler, until young Obilot comes to his aid and counters her sister's insults with adoration.

Prince Lippaut notices Gawain and, assuming he is there to help defend the castle, has the gate opened and gives him greeting. Prince Lippaut has great hopes that Gawain will aid him in his need. Gawain explains that he has to move on to challenge Kingrimursel in Vergulaht's city.

Young Obilot quickly approaches Gawain and asks him to be her knight and to fight for her love. By chivalric law, Gawain is obliged to accept, except that the law does not relate to a child. Gawain has to choose between disappointing this young girl or being mocked by other adults. Gawain reflects on Parzival's words that it is better to trust a woman than trust God so he gives the little lady his promise that he will bear arms in her honor and that he will carry her in his thoughts during battle. He speaks to her and her playmate with the greatest devotion. "Once you have grown to womanhood, even if the forest grew nothing but spears, as it now grows only wood, the crop would not be enough for you two. If you, so young, have such power over men, how will it be when you are grown? Your love will teach many a knight how spears can shatter shields."

She gives Gawain her silken sleeve, and he sets out in battle with it upon his shield. Many knights are thrown from their horses as Gawain helps bring victory to Prince Lippaut's side. Meljanz fights bravely, and he and Gawain come face to face. Gawain is able to unhorse him and pierce his side, but as he is taking Meljanz prisoner, Gawain's horse escapes. Gawain has the silken sleeve, slashed by blades and spotted with blood, delivered to young Obilot as is the custom.

That evening at the banquet, Prince Lippaut's men and the many opponents who surrendered are feasting. Knights tell of The Red Knight who fought for them so bravely. Parzival, the Red Knight, had sent a knight off to his wife, Condwiramur, with the message for her, "Tell her that he who once fought for her sake with Kingrun and with Clamide now yearns for the Grail and yet also for her love. Both are always in my thoughts. Tell her that I sent you, and may God keep you safe."

After describing the Red Knight's actions, Meljanz scornfully says to Gawain, "If only you had met the Red Knight who fights on my side, you would not have been so victorious in battle." Gawain is surprised to hear that Parzival was nearby, but thankful he has not had to fight against him. During the battle, Parzival's horse was wounded, and he took one that had been captured. This was Ingliart with the short-cropped ears, which had escaped from Gawain.

Gawain orders the captive opponents to do the bidding of young Obilot as he has to move on to meet Kingrimursel. When Meljanz is brought before Prince Lippaut and his council, he says, "Your courtesy was always so complete all the while I lived here among you that your counsel never failed me. If I had followed it better, I would be happy today. . . . I would never have lost his favor if his daughter had not made mock of me and treated me like a fool. That was unwomanly behavior."

Since Obilot had never mocked him, Meljanz is quite happy to give her his pledge which means he will do whatever she asks. Obilot commands him to offer obedience to her sister Obie, and then Obilot commands Obie to accept his offer. It is through Obilot's wisdom, though she is a child, the two are brought together. Obie allows her feelings to show, kisses the wounds Meljanz suffered in battle, weeps tears of sorrow, and she and Meljanz are joined together. Both of them overcome their pride and reconcile.

The foolish arrogance of Obie has cost many men their lives. Obilot's command seems to be just what is needed, and the two reluctant lovers reawaken their love for each other. Gawain treats young Obilot with utmost respect and courtesy. Although Obilot cannot bear for Gawain to leave and weeps bitterly, he makes his way out of the kingdom to a forest and continues on his way to meet Kingrimursel.

Emotional Immaturity: Dealing with rejection

The sarcastic girl and the injured boy
Obie is a haughty, sarcastic girl who uses her words as barbs. She is arrogant and deals out hurtful words. Her over-confidence gives her a feeling of power and protects her sense of freedom. Actually she does not know how to deal with her tender feelings and covers them up with sarcasm.

Meljanz represents the boy who allows his feelings to show, and then is rejected. He expresses his hurt violently, using power to dominate a woman, and in this case, a whole kingdom. Such a boy puts up a macho front, but actually he feels vulnerable. Outwardly, he shows off his power, but inwardly he is threatened by a girl's power to reject him. If she does, his feeling of being emasculated is so strong, he will find a way to make her the enemy and hurt her. He may lash out and insult her, demean her, and humiliate her. The situation can become even more complicated because some girls find super-macho boys very attractive, they are excited by the "bad boy" attitude. He may become possessive, making her obey his every wish. Because she wants his love, she allows herself to become a victim. Trouble is in store for both of them.

How many high school fights have occurred because a boy has wanted to get even with a girl who rejected him, humiliated him, or taunted him, especially if it happened in front of his friends? If a boy feels that he is threatened (whether it is real or not), he often reacts physically. This is especially the case with at-risk youths who are unable to work through a painful situation using words. Instead, they quickly move to using physical force.

In Obie and Meljanz we see adolescents acting out of immature emotions. Emotions of anger, hurt, hate, arrogance, pride, or jealousy are like flashes of lightning aimed at some unfortunate subject. If the teenager does not transform the emotions with thinking, he or she remains stuck in a gut-level response. The irrational emotions create chaos. However, when teenagers (or adults, for that matter) are able to use their thinking to shed light upon these emotions, a heartfelt feeling results. The feeling is deeper and more connected with the teenager's true self. Emotions of joy, excitement, pleasure, delight, or ecstasy tend to brighten up the atmosphere, creating a shared sense of happiness.

For example, Obie insults Meljanz saying that he isn't powerful enough for her. She attacks his self-image and wounds him deeply. He is unable to accept that she would say this on her own, so he claims that her father put her up to it. He wanted to prove his strength to her, but at the same time he wanted to destroy her father and the kingdom in which she lived. He was not going to give her the satisfaction of knowing he cared. The way he shows his power is by hurting her. On her part, she does not take back her words, but arrogantly increases her insults even though she does not really mean them. She is repelling the very person she cares about.

Reactions are quick responses that grow more intense by the moment and can easily leap out of control. Feelings are slower, deeper, more thought-filled. Feelings can help teenagers identify deeper issues that they are dealing with, giving them a chance to look inside themselves. When reactions flare, there is no time for self-reflection, while feelings may take several days to percolate up. If teenagers become aware of their feelings, they may be able to gain control and direct their behavior to effect the changes they really want. Often they cannot do this without help. Having a thoughtful adult to speak with often helps a teenager sort out reactions from feelings.

It is important that adults realize that reactions are not usually about the real issue but are sparks alerting us that there is a feeling underneath that needs attention. We have to sense when to respond and when to let something pass. Sometimes teenagers are letting off steam and do not need to be taken at their word. One day at the end of a particularly difficult eleventh grade class meeting, a colleague and I felt that we had been emotionally drained by the students' immaturity and lack of cooperation. In a moment of frustration, we wondered why we were teaching high school students and subjecting ourselves to this behavior. One of the girls overheard us and cheerfully said, "Don't take it so hard, we're just being teenagers."

Teenagers' emotions change radically from moment to moment, up and down, over the hill, into the valley—a veritable roller coaster. If the adult waits instead of reacting, the emotions often change, and there is peace once again. Of course, there are extremes of emotional expression which cannot be ignored. Adults have to decide when a boundary has been crossed. Enough is enough! Adults should be clear about what they will tolerate— physical abuse or verbal abuse is unacceptable. The adult has to have self-respect, and not allow himself or herself to be violated. In this way, the adult is saying, "I have standards for the way I will be treated. I am worthy of respect from you." Of course, the adult also has to respect the adolescent. Being clear about these boundaries gives the adolescent a framework in which to act. If the adult is inconsistent, tolerates abuse one day, and punishes the teenager another day for the same abuse, the adult's inconsistency confuses the teenager.

In this chapter of *Parzival*, we have a picture of how girls and boys often handle emotional outbursts. The boy reacts with his will—he is going to battle. The girl intensifies her verbal attack. He gets lost in violent behavior. She gets lost in her emotions.

It is Obilot, a child, who is able to move through the emotional wildfire and resolve the situation. Gawain has given her the power to use her wisdom. Even a child can have more clarity than two teenagers locked in an emotional melt-down.

Holding onto grudges and reacting without thinking are typical signs of early adolescence. When teenagers are able to identify their feelings and understand why they are behaving in a certain way, this is a sign they are moving into the maturity of later adolescence. In this stage adolescents are able to take time before reacting (even if it only means counting to ten), and are able to forgive the other person. This is a stage to be celebrated!

Chapter 8

Mixed Messages and Repercussions

Book VIII. *Gawain's other adventure.*

*A*fter many days of riding, Gawain approaches the castle of Schanpfanzun. An army of riders five hundred strong comes toward him led by a well-clad commander, King Vergulaht. Vergulaht's face is shining with beauty, reminding us that he is a cousin of Parzival. The army is on a hunting expedition, and Vergulaht does not interrupt it to host his guest, but instead he says that his sister Antikonie will receive Gawain and entertain him well, so much so that he would be happy his host would be gone for a long time.

Gawain reaches the castle and is, indeed, welcomed warmly by Antikonie who makes herself available to his wishes. She offers him the kiss of welcome. It is much more than a formal welcoming kiss, and so Gawain receives a mixed message. As he continues to press for her favor, she says that they have barely met, and yet, he is already pressing himself on her. Again he asks; she refuses. Gawain lets her know that he comes from as good a family as she does, so that should not keep her from giving in to his requests.

When the ladies who have been with Antikonie take in the scene, they find reasons to leave them alone. He then slips his hand under her cloak and is stroking her thigh; they become passionate and push away all restraints. At this moment, a grey-haired knight sees them and, thinking that he recognizes Gawain as the murderer of his lord, sounds the alarm that this criminal is now about to rape the king's daughter.

Defenders of the city come running into the castle to attack Gawain. Annoyed at the intrusion into their passion, Antikonie tells Gawain that they had better run up to the tower before the attackers kill him. Despite her attempts to get the knights to stop the attack, they do not hold back. Gawain loosens a bolt from the tower door and drives some of the attackers back. Antikonie finds a set of chess pieces and a beautifully inlaid chessboard with an iron ring in its center that she offers as weapons. Gawain uses the chess board as a shield, while Antikonie hurls chess pieces so heavy that they knock down anyone who is hit by them.

As Antikonie is throwing with deadly aim, she is also weeping at the thought of Gawain's being captured and killed. Gawain, fighting beside her, is roused in desire by Antikonie's lovely body, and fights even harder.

King Vergulaht appears and joins the attack against Gawain. He is just unsheathing his sword when Kingrimursel arrives and takes in the scene. Kingrimursel's honor is at stake since he has promised Gawain safe passage until they meet on the battlefield. He joins on the side of Gawain until Vergulaht finally calls a truce and the confused fighters withdraw.

Meanwhile Vergulaht meets with his council to try to sort things out. He, too, believes that Gawain has killed his father, yet he wants to keep the favor of his loyal knight Kingrimursel and his sister Antikonie.

Kingrimursel, embarrassed by the treatment of Gawain, asks Gawain to pledge to meet him in combat in one year. Vergulaht recalls that he was unhorsed in battle recently, and that the victor, the Red Knight, forced him to take an oath to seek the Grail for him. If he does not succeed in a year, he is to go to the Queen of Pelrapeire, Condwiramur, and surrender to her. One of the princes suggests that they send Gawain out of their kingdom to face death elsewhere. In addition to facing Kingrimursel in a year, he should go off to find the Grail. This would not be an easy task since the Grail Castle is well protected. If he is killed, he is killed. Thus Gawain's fate is decided.

In the morning, Gawain takes the oath to find the Grail, reconciliation is concluded, and Gawain reluctantly parts after Antikonie's last kiss and sets off on his way. Weeks later, King Vergulaht learns the true name of his father's murderer, but Gawain is long gone and no one can remember who had originally accused him. So our hero Gawain has set off on a path of great peril.

Learning to Respect Each Other:
Problems of sexual harassment and abuse

Gawain has gotten into another situation. This one is based on all kinds of confusion. In the previous encounter, Gawain was a model of courtesy, but with Antikonie he is impulsive and sexually aggressive. His behavior creates such chaos that knights end up fighting each other without even knowing why.

Vergulaht creates a strange situation at the beginning. "My sister will take care of you so nicely that you won't miss me." Hmm. What does that mean? When Gawain meets Antikonie, she gives him a sensual kiss of welcome, which leads him on, but then she tells him to stop. She is not very clear about her request and, in fact, seems perfectly happy to be involved with him. Later, we see that she has been so moved by him that she weeps at the thought of his being hurt. After the knights meet to decide what to do about all this confusion, Antikonie takes Gawain into her bedroom where he spends the night. The next morning, they bid each other goodbye.

Here we have an image of two young adults who have impulsively chosen to be sexually active. When we look at this from the adolescent viewpoint, a number of questions arise:

What are these two doing? They don't even know each other.
How does the girl feel about this afterward?
Is this behavior a habit?
Is the girl having expectations about the relationship?
What are her options?
Is the boy being rewarded for being so sexually assertive?
What messages is the boy getting from her mixed signals?

Gawain has not yet worked out his relationship to sexuality and intimacy. The motto—From simplicity of sex to complexity of relationships (see Kindlon and Thompson, *Raising Cain: Protecting the Emotional Life of Boys*)—describes the path Gawain is on, as it describes the journey of most boys. This is a very different path from Parzival's. Parzival does not have an issue with sexuality. His struggle is a lonely one—finding the Grail again. He needs to open his heart and activate his feeling life. Gawain's feeling life, however, is an open book. He is friendly, warm, kind, and social, sexually aggressive, and exciting. What does he have to learn? His path has to do with bringing thinking into his feeling life.

In every high school, there are boys who exude self-confidence and who pride themselves on their ability to "make it" with girls. They are usually good-looking, confident with their bodies, and able to project that they are experienced in the ways of sex. They attract girls who are interested in sexual experience and want to have fun. There is a playful quality about their flirtatiousness as each tests the other to see how far he or she will go. Girls often expect that being sexually active is part of a relationship, not a one-night stand. However, if it is only a fling, the girl's reputation suffers, although boys usually get by with such behavior without seriously damaging their reputations.

When a group of high school football players in Southern California boasted about their score with high school girls, many of their fathers excused their behavior, saying, "Boys will be boys." No attention was paid to the girls' experience. Despite, the women's liberation movement, the double-standard of acceptable behavior between boys and girls is still common.

The fighting in this chapter reminds me of a snowball fight or of boys throwing spitwads across a classroom. There is something exciting about the abandon, and one hopes no one will get hurt. It is a good example of boy power that is contagious. Enough danger and risk-taking is present to keep everyone alert and having a good time. That is, until some authority says, STOP! When it is all over, the sides have gotten confused, no one is quite sure who should be punished. They all need to calm down and bring some cool reason into the situation. During the fighting, there was very little conversation, just confused action. It has to be stopped to allow thinking to penetrate.

In many of the scenes in *Parzival*, we see women being attacked and misused, but also dependent upon men's power to give them a legitimate place in society. This was a time in history when women had few outlets for their energy or talent. In the upper class, they learned early how to be attractive, how to speak to men in a courtly way, how to relate to the mating game, and how to behave as women of nobility.

Certainly, girls have more opportunities today than ever before. They are educated, have opportunities in sports, enter professions such as medicine and law in greater numbers. Yet there is a long way to go to change assumptions about women's capacities. A friend was on an airplane, standing in the first class cabin when he overheard the following conversation. A man asked a woman dressed in a business suit, "What do you do?" She replied, "I work for the airline." "Oh, are you a stewardess?" "No, I am a pilot." Old stereotypes take time to disappear.

What messages are given to girls about their position in society? The old ideals of modesty and charity have little power with today's girls. On the contrary, they are encouraged to exhibit their bodies and to use their bodies for power. A thirteen-year-old said, "This is what I've got. I can use it to get what I want." Trying to imitate the omnipresent media images of thinness, girls are constantly forcing their bodies to become something they are not. Not only can this lead to eating disorders or other unhealthy habits, but psychologically these images tell the girl that she is just not acceptable as she is. She's not all right. Girls today are very aware of their vulnerability. They are harassed about their figures, their sex life, their lack of sex life, their hair, their faces, their achievements in school. I have met with girls attending large schools who have described situations where boys they don't even know snap their bras or stroke their thighs as they bend over to get their books out of their lockers. Many girls report that they have experienced unwanted sexual touching in the hallways of their schools. They also report sexual rumors being spread about them. Girls are reluctant to speak up for fear of being further harassed or molested.

Descriptions of date rape, physical abuse in boyfriend-girlfriend relationships, and incest shake a girl's confidence, leaving her feeling suspicious and unprotected. In gangs, a girl acquires social status, which assures her of protection if she is connected with particular boys. However, dependence on this protection leaves the girl wide open to abuse from her protector.

Dating has become a dangerous activity. In many schools, the boy expects that if he pays for the evening, the girl owes him sex. The hassle that erupts in this situation doesn't make dating very attractive. On one hand, the girl has her own curiosity about sex, but she may want to experience it at her own pace. A boy who was pleasant in class when he asked her out can turn into an aggressive lion when they are in an isolated place.

On the other hand, girls in the seventh to tenth grades, have become amazingly assertive. Long before boys figure out what is happening to them, some girls call them and proposition them. Mothers of boys in these grades have reported persistent phone calls from girls, even when the boys have tried to discourage them.

Although they fear AIDS and other sexually transmitted diseases, some girls have the illusion that nothing can happen to them. The combination of the pill and some incorrect information can lead a girl to feel it's fine to explore sex as long as she doesn't get hurt. She doesn't realize until afterward that having a succession of partners may not harm her physically but can be psychologically traumatic. Many girls who become pregnant report that intercourse happened while they were drunk, and they have no memory of it. Teen parties when parents are out of town often lead to girls becoming pregnant. Oral sex and mutual masturbation have become common ways for teens to be sexually active without the dangers of intercourse.

Boys and girls need guidance in developing respect for each other. Because boys mature later intellectually and emotionally, they have more years to deal with their impulses. Girls have become more cautious about going out alone with boys they don't know well. Girls have to be taught how to deal with assertive boys who don't stop when a girl says No!

A dangerous combination is an older boy and a younger girl. The boy's ability to convince her that she really wants sex is stronger the more immature she is. The boy is able to whisper all kinds of loving expressions which are purely manipulative to get the girl to think that he really cares for her.

Despite all the media images to the contrary, I believe that girls still connect sex with love. They still romanticize boys and want to be treated courteously. Girls focus on the relationship rather than solely on sex. In some circles it has become cool to remain a virgin. When enough teens in a group decide that they control their own bodies and have decided that they will not have casual sex, others in the group gain courage to join.

As teenagers enter the world of sex, they are often on their own. The expectations from parents may not be clear, and society sends them mixed messages. When parents give their teenagers guidance, they have a standard to consider, even if they choose to disregard it. Parents have more power than they may think on this subject. By discussing sex with teenagers, parents are offering them something to think about, and that is helpful.

It is not surprising that teenagers are so focused on sex. Developmentally, they have awakened to their own sexual desires and are curious to explore them. However, the flooding in of sexual imagery and the encouragement to be sexually active accelerates adolescents' sexual experimentation before they may actually be ready for it.

Chapter 9

The Adolescent's Spiritual Life

Book IX. *Parzival and Trevrizent*

*P*arzival and Gawain have ridden out into the world of the unknown to seek the Grail. Parzival goes out of his own free decision, but with sadness and bitterness in his heart. Gawain goes under the oath he has taken to save his life.

On his journey to find the Grail Castle once again, Parzival traveled through many lands, on horseback and on ships at sea, winning every encounter. He has relied on the sword that Anfortas gave him when he first visited the Grail Castle. During one battle, Parzival brings the blade down on his opponent's collarbone and the sword shattered in many pieces. Nevertheless, he won the battle, and then went off, as Sigune once instructed him, to the spring at Lac. He placed the pieces under the flowing stream and pulled the sword out completely whole and ready to use again.

As Parzival rides through the forest, he spots a hermit's cell and knocks on the window to ask directions. An emaciated woman dressed in a gray robe has a garnet ring upon her finger and a band in her long, gray hair that symbolizes widowhood. She offers him a bench outside the window, and she sits down inside, talking to him through the window.

He asks her how she can live in so isolated a place and where she gets her food. "My food comes to me directly from the Grail. Cundrie the sorceress brings it to me once every week," she replies. Parzival asks whether she lives alone, and the woman explains that her beloved is always with her. Parzival makes out the form of a coffin, and as he looks more closely, he realizes that she is Sigune, and it is her dead lover Schianatulander in the coffin. In this, his third meeting with Sigune, he recognizes the deep grief that she carries.

Parzival takes off his mail, and she recognizes him as well. She is the one who told him his name and later cursed him when he came from the Grail castle without having asked the healing question. Now she asks him how his journey to find the Grail has been. He tells her how miserable he is, how he misses his wife, and how, more than anything, he wants

to reach the Grail castle and behold the Grail once more. Sigune sees that
he has suffered. In his eyes she sees sorrow and pain, and she is moved to
help him.

She tells him that, if he hurries he may be able to catch up with
Cundrie, who has only just left her. He will find Cundrie by following the
tracks left by the mule she is riding. Parzival quickly follows the hoof-
prints along a winding path, but soon he loses the trail. Then he meets a
rider on a black horse with trappings and weapons bearing the symbol of
a turtledove. The knight does not let Parzival pass, because this is the
forest of the Grail castle and those who trespass into it face death.

The two attack each other with great strength. Parzival knocks the
other knight from his horse and into a chasm. Parzival's horse is going
so fast that he too goes right over the edge and is dashed to pieces.
Parzival survives by grasping onto branches and gaining a footing
among rocks. The Grail Knight escapes up the opposite slope, but his
black horse is nearby. Parzival climbs back up the slope, swings himself
onto the back of the Grail horse, and rides away. He now has a Grail
sword and a Grail horse, but alas, he has again lost the trail to the Grail
castle.

He wanders for weeks, when one morning he enters a forest where a
light snow has fallen. Here, Parzival meets a group of pilgrims including
an old knight, his wife, and their two daughters. They present a stark
contrast to Parzival, who is dressed in rich garments and armor. He
pulls his horse off the path to let them pass, and politely inquires the purpose of their journey. The old knight comments that it is Good Friday, a
holy day, not one to be riding a horse or to be dressed in armor. Parzival
responds that he has no idea what day or year it is, and that he has no
confidence in God who has never helped him.

The old knight tells Parzival not to be so negative but to think
about the sacrifice that God made by sending his son to Earth to die for
the purpose of helping human beings. He counsels Parzival to follow the
path to the home of a holy man who will help him and absolve him from
his sin.

The young maidens ask Parzival to join them, and he is tempted to
stay with them even though he hates God and they love Him. But he bids
them farewell and rides away. As he rides, his mind goes to the deeds of
God and, for the first time, he reflects on how God had created the world,
and how powerful He is. Parzival decides to test God and give Him a
chance to guide him on his journey. He lets the reins fall loosely over the
horse's ears and urges it on. The horse leads him on the path to the cell
of the hermit Trevrizent.

Trevrizent welcomes him and invites him to warm himself by the fire. Parzival complies and with great courtesy tells of the people who have led him to Trevrizent for good advice. Parzival asks Trevrizent for counsel. "I am a man who has sinned," says Parzival. When Parzival asks Trevrizent if he is afraid of him, Trevrizent explains that he himself was once a knight and that he is not afraid of any human being.

After they take care of Parzival's horse, they go into a warm cave where Parzival accepts Trevrizent's hospitality, takes off his cold armor, and puts on a warm cloak. He is led into another cave with an altar stone and a casket of holy relics. Parzival recognizes that this is the same casket on which he had sworn the oath that Lady Jeschute was innocent. He also recognizes that here he had found the spear with which he has won many battles. But he recalls to Trevrizent that when he left the cave, he had been lost in such deep thoughts of his wife, that he did not even know what he was doing. Trevrizent tells him those events occurred four and a half years ago. Parzival admits it has also been that long since he praised God, that in all this time he focused only on fighting. However, he is so filled with grief that he is ready to give God another chance to help him.

Trevrizent then describes to Parzival the history of man's relationship with God, the power of God, and His Love. He comments that anger will not be the way to reach God; Parzival has to atone for his sins. Parzival replies that in his youth he had been open to God, but had received only sorrow. Trevrizent asks Parzival to tell him about his sorrow and his sin so he can give him advice. Parzival says that his greatest sorrow is that he longs for the Grail and for his wife. Trevrizent praises Parzival for his faithfulness in marriage, but tells him that no man can win the Grail unless he is known in Heaven and can be called by name to the Grail.

Parzival indicates that he wants to learn more about the Grail. Trevrizent tells him that a well-known medieval master, Kyot, had first heard of the Grail in Toledo, Spain, from Flegetanis, a scholar descended from Solomon. Flegetanis was an astronomer who was able to understand the constellations and their connections with human destiny. There he had read the mystery of the Grail, which had been brought to the earth by a host of angels. Since then, a special group of noble baptized men have guarded it. Kyot traced this story further, through many lands, until he learned of the Grail family down to Titurel and his son Frimurtel who bequeathed the Grail to Anfortas, whose sister Herzeloyde married Gahmuret and gave birth to Parzival.

Trevrizent explains that many brave knights live in the Grail Castle, often riding out to seek adventure. He also tells about the power of the Grail. Knights who are ill or becoming old are renewed by being in the presence of the Grail. On Good Friday, a dove wings down from Heaven, brings a small white wafer, and leaves it on the Grail. The dove soars up to Heaven again. From that Grail can come the most perfect earthly drinks and foods, whatever one wants and needs. People learn that they are called to the Grail when their names appear on it. They come as children, rich or poor, from many lands. Once the name is revealed, it fades away. The Grail servants live a pure life and are rewarded in heaven.

Parzival responds that he has been a brave knight and has won fame and honor. If God is a good judge of fighting, He should summon him to the Grail. Trevrizent, however, cautions Parzival not to be proud, saying that he should live in moderation. He should learn from Anfortas's mistake which was to seek love through power and excess. Humility is the quality of the Grail brotherhood. The Grail knights have kept secret the knowledge of the Grail except to those who have been called to it. Only one person came to the Grail whose name had not been revealed. That man sinned because he failed to ask about the suffering he saw in Anfortas. This mistake has caused him grief and he will have to atone for it.

Then Trevrizent, noticing the resemblance between Parzival and other members of the Grail family, asks him for his background. Parzival reveals his lineage, his father Gahmuret, his mother Herzeloyde, who he learns is the sister of Trevrizent. He admits that he killed Ither, the Red Knight, which brings great sadness to Trevrizent, because Ither was not only a noble knight but was related to him. It will be up to God to punish Parzival for this. Then Trevrizent reveals that Parzival was also responsible for killing his mother, who died the moment he left her. Trevrizent has two other sisters, Schoysiane, the mother of Sigune, and Repanse de Schoye, who tends the Grail. Their brother Anfortas was supposed to be Lord of the Grail.

Trevrizent goes on to relate how Anfortas became wounded. When Anfortas and Trevrizent were children, Anfortas was chosen to become the Lord of the Grail. If any Lord of the Grail craves a love other than she whom the writing on the Grail allows him, his life will be filled with misery. Anfortas disobeyed this and chose his own love and fought for her with an exuberance of pride, not out of humility. One day, he went out in search of adventure and love and was wounded in jousting by a poisoned spear thrust through his testicles. The person who wounded him wanted to win the Grail by force, but he was killed by Anfortas in the battle. Anfortas rode away with the poisoned spear in his body. A physician removed the spear but could not get all of it out.

Trevrizent recalls how at that moment he had prayed and vowed he would give up knighthood and become an ascetic if God would help his brother. The knights carried King Anfortas to the Grail hoping for healing. However, the power of the Grail kept ill or wounded persons alive, therefore he could not die but received only further suffering. The Grail knights and maidens applied all kinds of medicaments and herbs, but nothing helped. One time when the moon was just beginning to wane and the wound hurt the most, the Grail knights fell on their knees and saw it written that a knight should come and, if he asked the healing question without any prompting, Anfortas would be healed. If he asks the question, he shall be king of the Grail. Then Trevrizent left to become a hermit. He recalls to Parzival that a young knight did come, but failed to ask why the king suffered so much.

After Trevrizent finished telling Parzival the history of the Grail, they went out to search for roots and herbs and to feed Parzival's horse. Then Parzival speaks the important words, "Sir, and dear uncle of mine . . . by your kindness I beg you, forgive me. He who rode to Munsalvesche, he who saw the true sorrow there and who put no question—that was I, misfortune's child." After Trevrizent recovers from his shock, he says, "I will do my best to give you counsel. And you must not grieve too much. You should in right measure grieve and abstain from grief."

Trevrizent describes his own history and how he met Parzival's father. Any man who has pledged himself to serve the Grail must renounce the love of women. Only the King of the Grail can have a wife. However, as a Grail knight, Trevrizent had fallen in love with a woman and had gone to battle in Europe, in Asia, and in far off Africa, in order to earn her love. During one of these battles, he met Parzival's father, Gahmuret. Trevrizent relates how Gahmuret had recognized the family resemblance between Trevrizent and his wife, Herzeloyde. Gahmuret had given Trevrizent a gift—the stone of which the casket is made. He also gave Trevrizent his kinsman Ither as a squire. Trevrizent reminds Parzival, "God has not forgotten that you killed Ither, and He may still call you to account for that as well as for your mother's death."

Trevrizent now gives Parzival counsel. "Do penance for your sins, and one day your soul may find peace." Parzival stays with Trevrizent for fifteen days, eating herbs and roots, and learning how to live a spiritual life.

On the day Parzival takes his leave, Trevrizent tells him, "Give your sins to me. In the sight of God, I am the guaranty for your atonement." Parzival, having gained knowledge of his family history, his mother's death, and of his relationship to Ither, leaves Trevrizent and goes on his way.

The Spiritual Life of the Adolescent

Parzival has had three main teachers in his life. His first teacher was his mother, Herzeloyde, who taught him that God was light and the Master of Hell was darkness. She told him to follow the light, to honor God's wisdom, and to pray to him when he was in trouble. His second teacher was Gurnemanz, who told him how to behave as a knight and taught him the skills he needed to make his way in the world. His third teacher was Trevrizent, his spiritual teacher, who taught him the destiny of his family, the role of God in human history, and why and how Parzival should develop a relationship with God. Each teacher helped him on his spiritual path.

We can see a parallel in the lives of many children. The development of spirituality in the teen years has a foundation in the early years. When children are young, they look to their parents to explain the world, to tell them about good and bad, to give them a feeling of being protected and loved. Many children feel a connection to the invisible world. They speak about their time before birth or of a guardian being who walks beside them. The young child has a naturally religious attitude toward the world, a devotion to the small as well as the large things. Young children are open to the mysteries of the world. However, if they speak of such things, and they are told that they are just imagining them, this rejection may close the door on their connection with the spiritual world.

When children come into their elementary school years, they begin to hear other ideas and become aware that their parents' answers are not the only ones, but they still look to their parents as well as to their teachers for answers and for guidance.

During the years from eight to ten, children often go through a period when they feel alone, insecure, and unsure of themselves. They ask questions about illness and death, they wonder if their parents are their true parents, they may feel vulnerable to other people's power over them. They mainly look to their parents and other adults in authority for guidance in their spiritual life.

During the years of ten, eleven, and twelve, they begin to form their own beliefs as to what is good and true. They watch what adults do and enjoy being around adults who are active and who make things happen. They learn by example.

In the early adolescent years, idealism fills their hearts, and they look around to see how ideals are realized in society. They notice hypocrisy and contradictions and may raise doubts and questions about religion. They want to make a difference by helping those in need, by raising money to build orphanages or playgrounds for children in need or to send to victims of tragedies such as earthquakes or hurricanes. In order to do this, they raise money through carwashes, bake sales, and garage sales. By participating in these specific projects, children feel the satisfaction that they are serving others.

Teenagers in middle and later adolescence are interested in service also, but they want to establish a larger context for their activities. It is not enough to do something "good," but they need to figure out whether this will make a difference. They may contemplate deep questions whether or not they voice them, such as: If I am a good person but I haven't faced temptation, am I truly moral? What is the role of virtue? Is there a God or do we only imagine God exists? If there is no God, does that mean people can do anything and there is no punishment? "

Teenagers enjoy discussions about these topics so they can hear what other people think. They are coming to their own answers, and they can begin to hold their own, even in the midst of very different opinions. When they realize there are no simple answers, they are maturing. While teenagers are thinking about such deep matters, they often feel lonely and confused. When teenagers meet adults who are strong, loving, honest, and down-to-earth, this makes a great impression on them. The strength may be deep faith or it may be honest questioning. On the other hand, teens can be very cynical about people who use spiritual words but who do not live their meaning in daily life. It is very helpful during these adolescent years that a teenager has an adult mentor with whom he or she can have real conversations, an adult who listens carefully and values the thoughts and feelings of the teenager.

Teenagers are looking for answers to three main questions in spiritual life.

1. *What is the meaning of life?* On what can I build my life? Is there some kind of plan that organizes everything?

2. *What is the purpose of life?* Is my life important? In what way? Do some things matter more than others? What do I do when I am lonely and feel as if I cannot go on?

3. *Is there hope?* Can I hope that life will seem more meaningful? Can I hope to feel more positive in the future?

In an article entitled "Searching for a Holy Spirit" (*Newsweek*, May 8, 2000), the authors stated from the results of a poll that "78 percent of adolescents said their religion was important to them, but only half said they attended services regularly, a figure that has declined since the 1970s" (p. 62). The authors comment that youth are interested in spiritual things, but "rather than seek absolute truths in doctrine, they cross denominational boundaries. . . . In place of strict adherence to doctrine, many teens embrace a spirit of eclecticism and a suspicion of absolute truths" (p. 62).

It is important that parents share their beliefs with their teenagers, but it is also important that parents leave the teens room to have their own beliefs. If they feel smothered, adolescents may reject any form of belief and become cynical. If parents are honest about their beliefs, whether those are strong and clear or whether the parents aren't sure what they believe, teenagers will respect them. What teenagers respect most about adults is their integrity,

The teen years are often a time of learning about different religious beliefs, and trying to see if any fit their own sense of what is true. Gaining respect for people of many beliefs is essential to fostering an atmosphere of mutual understanding.

An important source of spiritual exploration may come through literature. Through reading about and experiencing the moral dilemmas of characters, the adolescent can examine points of view and may identify with particular ones. There are many short stories and novels that deal with these questions. One of my favorites is *Franny and Zooey* by J.D. Salinger, because his characters struggle with the search for spirit, with the nature of love, and with what it means to be authentic. Another is *Grapes of Wrath* by John Steinbeck, in which the Oakies are struggling to find a new life in California. The most noble deeds are done by common people, especially Jim Casey and Ma Joad, who aren't able to articulate them philosophically, but who live them in daily life.

I have taught *The Brothers Karamazov* by Fyodor Dostoyevsky to twelfth graders for over twenty-five years, because he brings spiritual dilemmas in such a vivid way. The characters approach life's situations very differently. Through turmoil and struggle, they undergo transformation and become conscious and responsible for their actions. Of course, *Parzival* is another such book that can be very helpful for adolescents because it presents a path of development with all of its pitfalls and strengths.

As part of developing a spiritual life, teenagers struggle with questions of moral action. What is good? Is there evil? Do good and evil live only outside us? What is the source of moral behavior? What is the relationship of moral behavior and society's laws? In the Greek drama *Antigone* by Sophocles, Antigone must decide which is higher—the law of the government or the law of the gods. The law of the gods states that a corpse must be buried with particular rites to ensure that the being does not go to the Land of the Shades. The law of the king states that her brother, a rebel, should be denied proper burial. Antigone decides that spiritual law is higher and she defies the laws of the land, even though she knows she will be put to death.

Another example of a moral dilemma is Henry David Thoreau's *Civil Disobedience*. Thoreau decided to go to jail rather than pay taxes to a government that supports slavery. *Letter from Birmingham Jail* by Martin Luther King, Jr. is a moving piece of writing in which King explains to white ministers why the civil rights struggle is a moral struggle.

In addition to examples from literature, teenagers can think about moral or spiritual questions in contemporary life such as the preservation or destruction of the environment, exploitation of people in developing countries, cloning, and genetic engineering.

Spiritual development is an on-going process of relationship between a person and a higher being or a higher source. Expressions such as conscience, inner guidance, higher truth, inner light, inner self, or nature may be used to describe the source as well as angel, God, Lord, Christ, Jehovah, or Allah. This relationship is the source of moral action. However, a person can also lead a moral life by following guidelines of "right" behavior without struggling to find a connection to a spiritual source.

Aspects of Spiritual Development

Parzival offers many images of how teenagers develop their spiritual life. Five examples follow. These are: facing oneself, transforming one's feeling life, transforming one's will life, developing resilience, and transforming one's thinking life.

Facing oneself

Parzival says to Trevrizent, "I am a man who has sinned. Give me counsel." An important step in moral development is being able to face oneself and admit one's guilt. This is the first step in accepting responsibility. Being able to say, "I was that person" or "I am truly sorry about what I did" opens the soul to a process of self-awareness. Once these statements are made, the teenager can find ways to make amends. One reason that it is so hard for teenagers to admit guilt is that it is painful for them to accept the negative behavior as part of themselves. Yet, they cannot transform their behavior until they can clearly take responsibility for their actions. A parent or teacher who is able to support a teenager's process in accepting responsibility is acting as a guide for the youngster's spiritual development.

Transforming one's feeling life

Trevrizent teaches Parzival lessons about his feeling life. He praises Parzival for his faithfulness in marriage, a positive accomplishment, but he also tells Parzival no man can win the Grail unless he is known in Heaven and can be called by name to the Grail. Parzival is still impulsive, however. He says, "If God is a good judge of fighting, He should summon me to the Grail." Parzival doesn't yet understand that gaining the Grail has nothing to do with fighting. However, he realizes he had no sense of what he had done to Ither at the time of the fatal battle. But now, he does realize it and feels sadness. He also confesses that he was the knight who had not asked the healing question. Although Parzival still has a long way to go, his feeling life is changing, and the experience with Trevrizent has awakened his heart.

Likewise, when teenagers are able to awaken their feelings and acknowledge them, this is the beginning of transformation. As they mature and reflect on their feelings, they may gain perspective and transform them. For example, over time, anger can give way to forgiveness, and distrust can give way to trust.

Once Parzival realizes what he has done, he is distraught. Yet Trevrizent cautions Parzival not to go to extremes in his feeling, but instead, he should live in moderation. Trevrizent models self-control and equanimity. Even after Parzival admits that he was the youth who did not ask the question, Trevrizent tells him, "You must not grieve too much. You should in right measure grieve and abstain from grief." In other words, find a balance. This attitude is a guide to a teenager's maturing—don't get too angry, don't become too passive, but learn to stand up and deal with situations that meet you without going to extremes.

Whereas Gurnemanz gave Parzival advice for social interaction as well as the basis for spiritual development, Trevrizent gives him advice to consciously develop his spiritual life, such as, foregoing anger, being grateful to God, turning his heart to God and accepting His love, and atoning for his sins. Gurnemanz' advice helps Parzival know how to behave in his chosen role. It serves as preparation for going out into the world and doing good deeds. However, Trevrizent's advice goes deeper because Parzival is at a different stage of maturity. He is awake to the results of his actions and is feeling pain for what he has done to others. Therefore, he is open to hearing what Trevrizent has to say, and he wants to enter into a new relationship with Trevrizent as a teacher. One can feel real engagement between Parzival and Trevrizent.

Transforming one's will life
In addition to transforming their feeling life, adolescents need to transform their will life. How do they do this? One way is by setting meaningful goals and figuring out a strategy for attaining them. Youths who are not able to delay gratification and must have what they want when they want it are stuck in an earlier stage of childhood. Their will is held hostage to their desires and impulses.

Only as they bring thought to bear on their actions can they begin to transform their will.

In order to transform their will, teenagers need to get out of old habits and find new ways of behaving. They need new perspectives. However, this is not easily done if they are locked into destructive ways of behaving. Destructive behavior may be all they know, and it is a pattern they are familiar with. They may lack basic social skills in getting along with people they disagree with. They may not know how to communicate feelings, but only how to react physically. Because of their insecurity and lack of skills, they need skills to help them deal with crisis.

Developing resilience
Adolescents who are resilient are most able to change their behavior when the situation warrants it. What do teenagers need to be resilient?

They need a stable, positive emotional relationship with at least one person who understands and commits him- or herself to the adolescent—someone the adolescent trusts. This person may be a close friend, a teacher, a parent, a neighbor, a coach, or any other person in the environment who is willing to give time and attention to the teenager.

Adolescents need to be able to cope with stress, rather than just reacting to it or seeing themselves as victims. Such stresses such as deadlines, changes in relationships, normal responsibilities in school and at home, and time management are *appropriate stresses*. Teenagers learn that these stresses are a normal part of life that they will need to address from time to time. They have to learn to take personal responsibility for their decisions. However, teenagers who see these stresses as too much of a burden, or see themselves as victims in these situations, have difficulty responding to them effectively, and become overwhelmed and unable to function well. They are not resilient.

Other stresses that are beyond the normal ones and evoke tremendous anxiety are inappropriate stresses. They are sometimes more than the teenager can bear alone. Some examples are accidents, serious illness, family dysfunction or breakdowns that the teenager has no power to change, inordinate pressure, unexpected pregnancy, teasing based on sexual orientation, and addiction. Teenagers have difficulty taking responsibility for these situations by themselves, and they need help from adults.

Learning to manage appropriate stress helps teenagers develop resiliency, and prepares them for future challenging situations. However, *inappropriate stress* can drive a teenager into depression, extreme anxiety, violence, destruction or self-destruction. Supportive adults are essential to intervene and help teenagers deal with these situations.

In order to be resilient, a teenager needs enough intelligence to be able to think about complex situations and to be able to understand the world. Youngsters who have low intelligence or who are immature for their age have difficulty understanding causes and consequences. They are unable to think clearly and may react to words and situations they don't really understand. For example, if they are sexually active, the girl may not understand the relationship between menstruating and getting pregnant, or they may not understand how protection works during sexual activity. They may be manipulated by older teenagers into criminal behavior because they want to be liked, and they don't understanding the consequences. Such youngsters especially need to be guided by a caring, ethical person who looks out for them.

Authentic self-esteem in which the teenager feels worthy helps develop resiliency. Boys and girls often act tough when underneath they feel they are losers. Having opportunities in which to excel and shine helps a teenager feel valued. They do not need a course in self-esteem as much as they need opportunities to feel the joy of accomplishment.

Social support from persons or institutions outside the family helps the teenager feel connected to others outside the immediate environment who model appropriate behavior; this helps develop resiliency. Teachers who teach juvenile offenders, for instance, are very conscious that they are modeling how people relate positively to one another, how to express disappointment or joy, how to work out frustrations and hurt. Over and over, they have to show these young people that there are ways of behaving that do not involve violence. They also bring tremendous love and commitment to these adolescents. The teenagers in their care are accustomed to adults who leave when things get tough. These teachers tell their students that they are there for the long haul.

An ability to incorporate in oneself both feminine and masculine characteristics also helps develop resiliency. In many cases, adolescents depend on their friends or the media to provide them with images of appropriate behavior. These images may distort healthy behavior by encouraging adolescents to be precocious, provocative, or even degenerate. They need the presence of caring adults who are comfortable with their identity to be models for them.

Transforming one's thought life
There are stages in the development of one's thought life such as the following:

1. The adolescent's thinking can stay at the level where it is dominated by satisfying desires (I want this. I will take it now. Don't get in my way.), or it can begin to take in spiritual values such as truth.

2. The next step toward conscious thinking is: I want this but I haven't earned it. I will work toward gaining it. Help me.

3. There are positive and negative reasons why I want that.

4. I understand your perspective, although I don't agree with you. I really want that, but I can see reasons why it might not be good for me to have it.

5. People have different motives. It is important to hear each other. I respect each person's goals. I have my own idea, but I know not everyone agrees with it. I may or may not pursue my desires.

6. What is the ethical way to behave in this situation?

7. What is truth?

We can look at the image of the Grail sword and the Grail horse as aspects of the thinking life. In mythology, the horse is often a symbol of thinking at different levels from instinct to spiritualized thought. Controlling the horse is a symbol of the power of thinking controlling unbridled will. In Greek portrayals of the half-horse/half-man, we have the image of wildness or sensuality that has not yet been transformed. In the figure of Pegasus, the flying horse, we have the image of ideas that are flying to the world of spirit.

Parzival has the Grail horse that leads him along the path to the Grail Castle. Here we have the image of clear thinking that is moving from the physical world to the spiritual world. The horse knows where it is going.

The Grail sword is the image of the will that serves the spirit— it will cut through the chaos so the bearer will be able to move in an upright and honorable way. If broken, the sword can be renewed in the spring, just as a person can renew his or her intentions by returning to a spiritual source, to one's conscience. What is Parzival missing? He still does not have his feeling life completely in order. His spiritual development is only in the early stages.

A teenager moving into maturity needs to find a source of renewal within the heart. No matter what challenges will come, a sense of stability, clarity, and love will give a foundation of strength. Parzival becomes depressed because he feels his journey is one of loneliness. He trusts no one, not even God. He longs for his wife, but he knows he can't return to her until he finds his higher self, the Grail. He separates himself from humanity. This is always dangerous. One can only imagine that had Parzival not met Trevrizent, he could have become isolated and might even have taken his life. It is in the joining of his heart with Trevrizent's that he becomes fully human. To find such warmth, love, and forgiveness is the birthright of adolescents, but they don't all have that in their lives. When a teenager has such a lifeline, it is amazing what difficulties can be overcome.

Developing a relationship to a higher being
Parzival is changing his relationship to God. In this chapter Parzival reflects on how God had created the world, and how powerful He was. Parzival moves through doubt to blessing God. It is after he does this that his eyes are opened and he notices how inwardly beautiful the maidens are. When the adolescent is able to open up his heart to the experience of gratitude, beauty, truth, and goodness, his or her attitude toward everything around changes. Wonder and mystery are the portals to this higher development.

The strength of a spiritual community

The spiritual community of the adolescent is made up of all those who love him or her. They offer the most powerful gift to help a young person develop a strong and positive sense of self. This may come from a religious community or from a group of concerned and loving individuals who have a more informal relationship to the youth. An adolescent can expand his or her spiritual community to include those who are willing to speak the truth in order to awaken the adolescent to his or her deeds. They are connecting with the higher nature of the young person and want to help anchor him or her in positive behavior and hopefulness. The spiritual community can also include those who have died and can help from the other side.

Adolescents are awakened to their special place in life when they realize how many people are there to help them. When teenagers can experience gratitude, their heart is full. If they recognize and appreciate the role of parents, teachers, and mentors, adolescents are able to feel they are part of a spiritual community in which they are growing stronger. Their conscience is awakened and their gratitude gives them strength. This may exist within or without a specifically religious community.

The power of poetry in adolescent searching

Many young people struggle with these questions in poetry. They explore the darkness as well as the lightness of life. They confront their fears and their hopes.

When my friend Linda Bergh's seventeen-year-old daughter Kirsten was killed in an automobile crash, her mother collected her poetry to share her journey through the travails of the soul. Readers of her book, *She Would Draw Flowers*, have the opportunity to take the journey with her as she comes of age and develops insight and respect for the mysteries of life. I am grateful to Linda Bergh for allowing me to use some of Kirsten's poetry to illustrate how resilience can help a youngster transform difficulties and come to a new appreciation of life.

As a ninth grader, she was realizing what a protected and loving life she had.

Purple Violets

My path has never been strewn
With broken glass
And cutting words.
No,
I have walked my life
With feet pale and tender
On pillows of purple violets,
Embraced by yellow voices
That enfold me.
Leading me, with trusting eyes closed,
Away from the sharp, slippery rocks,
Away from the sucking pool
Which threatens to pull me under,
Shielding me with gentle blue-sky wings
From the screaming, tearing, empty wind
Which tries to blow me away.

I did not ask for this path,
For the loving smiles
And guiding hands,
But they are mine.
This is how I am.
This is my path.
It is mine to walk,
To change as I please,
To take care of
Forever.
I must cherish my violets,
Or they will die.
So I will,
Forever.

Kirsten explores nature and finds strength in her connection to it.

Ode to My Tree

Even now, as I sit, cradled
In your leafy embrace,
Gazing through your speckled leaves
I feel no difference between
Today and yesterday.
Your strong branches have always
Supported me,
Held me,
Caught me when I slipped.
Your dancing leaves have always
Created a canopied chamber
Where I can hide.
When the wind swayed your branches,
I clung to you, feeling your breath.
When I come home,
Your feathered arms greet me,
Beckoning,
And I answer your call.
No one else responds.
Only I have explored your kingdom,
Stood balancing on one bare foot,
Trying to move with your rhythm.
Although others have climbed
The flimsy ladder into your arms,
They grew tired of your silence,
Of your stillness.
But we are alike, you and I.
We have changed together,
Adapted to each other.
Now, as your newborn leaves
Flicker and flash in the sun,
I can see your smile.
We share a secret,
You and I.

Here is an excerpt from the poem "Open Your Eyes" in which Kirsten challenges the reader to wake up to the joys of life. She ends with the following lines:

The air is filled with song:
The wind whispers in the trees,
Blackbirds warble out their melodies,
The water chuckles happily to itself,
Distant thunder grumbles harmlessly.
Will you shut your ears to their gentle voices?
Will you shut your eyes to their compassionate smiles?
Do not close your heart to the joy and beauty around you,
Rather embrace it.
For if you cannot love the world, you cannot love yourself.
And without love,
There is nothing.

When Kirsten was 16, her father Paul died of cardiac arrest. Her way of dealing with it was through her writing. "My life is a confused heap of memories and dreams. Sometimes I wish I could've remained back there—back then. But I have to move on. I will be happy no matter what happens. My tears of grief will mix with those of joy."

Her writing is an example of an adolescent with tremendous resilience. She does not hide her feelings but honors them. Yet she finds a way to bring perspective to her sorrow. She captured the intimacy and the loss she felt with her father's death in the poem "Just Paul and Me."

And then it's just
Me and Paul
And the night
Him just crooning
About playgrounds
And women
And nonsense
With a scratchy
Old record sound.
And me just
Twirling
With my reflection
Like some
Fancy-dancy
Make-believe queen
Dancing the polka

And the night
Just sitting there,
Staring at us
As if we were
Crazy,
Or something.
I guess we are,
Because I'm all alone,
Just me
And my reflection.
Put that in one of
Your songs, Paul:
A crazy girl
Dancing with her
Shadow
Because there's
No one else left
For her
To dance with.

As Kirsten processes her feeling about her father's loss, she thinks about the past and the future, and she reflects on her mother.

Mother

The sun filters through the ripples of white swirly lace.
Dapples, yellow, a paper valentine heart
Of shadows and sunlight on the countertop.
A soft image, of sunlight, of yellow warmth, of lace hearts.
Contentment, peace.
Your arms surround me,
Enfold me in yellow warmth,
Shining loving light into my heart from yours:
A lacy heart, beating with your strength and love.
In your softness I find my contentment and peace
You rock me, cradle me with your assurance,
Your knowing of me, your selflessness.
Hold me in your soft embrace a while longer,
I will spread my wings and take flight soon enough.
And when I do, my heart will always cherish
The comfort and love that I find only in you.

The resolution of her father's death comes in the beautiful poem "For You, Papa."

I thought I heard your footsteps
running toward me,
disturbing the stones.
But when I opened my eyes,
I saw it was only the waves,
Pulling and swirling like hands.

I thought I felt your smile,
Warm and loving upon my face,
But when I opened my eyes,
I saw it was only the sun,
Beaming at me from across the water.

I thought I heard you
Whisper my name.
But when I opened my eyes,
I realized it was only the wind
Playing in my hair.

I thought I felt you
softly kiss my cheek.
But when I opened my eyes,
I saw it was only a leaf
Caressing me with gentle strokes.

And then I felt your love
In and all around me.
Powerful yet gentle like the waves,
Warm and shining like the sun,
Soft yet strong like the winds,
Tender and alive like the leaves.
And I didn't even have
To open my eyes.
I knew you were there.

One of Kirsten's great strengths was her love of life and her reaching out in friendship. This last poem was dedicated to her deep friendship with Nina. They were both killed in the accident.

To Nina and Me

When we're grandmas together
Maybe we'll be soft and beautiful like clouds
And sweet and rosy with laughter like apples
And we'll be free and graceful
Like the summer grasses
Of our barefoot youth.
Maybe you'll still have dimples, Curled up like two fetuses in
your cheeks
Creased with countless births and smiles.
And maybe there will still be
Freckles scattered across my nose
Like the huts of an African village in the heat
Hiding in the wrinkles that gather at my eyes
Like animals 'round the water hole.

And we'll tell our wide-eyed grandbabies
About iced-grapefruit chapstick.

It is often through poetry that teenagers will share their soul and ask the existential questions of life. How fortunate are those of us who are privy to such gold.

Chapter 10

Eroticism Rules, Confusion Reigns

Book X. *Gawain chooses to serve Orgeluse*

*W*e rejoin Gawain who has spent a year riding in search of the Grail. He returns to the kingdom of Kingrimursel to fight him as he vowed he would. However, now that the real murderer of his lord had been identified, Kingrimursel has forgiven Gawain. That puts an end to the dispute, and both Vergulaht and Gawain ride off in search of the Grail.

One morning, as Gawain rides out onto a meadow, he sees a woman sitting in sorrow with a mortally wounded knight on her lap. Having a good idea about healing, Gawain takes a tube of bark and inserts it into the knight's body through the wound. Then he has the woman suck on it until the blood flows toward her instead of inward. The knight regains his strength and tells Gawain that he was on his way to the kingdom of Logrois for adventure when he was attacked by a knight named Lischois Gwelljus. Gawain wants to find Lischois Gwelljus and avenge the wounded knight, despite pleas from the knight that this is too dangerous.

Gawain follows the path until he sees the Kingdom of Logrois. The winding road that circles a mountain leading to a fortress gives it the appearance of a spinning top. The fortress is surrounded by trees and vines making it very difficult to attack. Gawain makes his way along the path, and beside a spring he sees a most beautiful woman, the Duchess Orgeluse of Logrois.

Gawain is fascinated by her beauty and offers her his company. She chastises him for commenting on her beauty and urges him to move on. She lets him know very clearly that she has no interest in him whatsoever. That doesn't dissuade Gawain who tells her that she has captured his heart. She promises him nothing but trouble if he persists in giving her his attention. This only makes him the more interested in her; he continues to promise her his love and says he is ready to do anything she asks.

She takes him at his word and gives him the task of looking after her horse. To get to it, however, he must go down a path, over a high bridge into an orchard. However, there is a crowd of people dancing and singing, playing tambourines and flutes. He is to ignore them and walk directly to her horse, untie it, and it will follow him. In order to do this, Gawain has to dismount from his own horse, and since there is no place to tie it, Orgeluse tells him to leave it with her. She continues to taunt him, and he is made to look like a fool.

He follows her directions and makes his way through the celebrating crowd. To his surprise, they start wailing because they know that Orgeluse is going to make his life miserable. He continues until he comes to her horse, standing by an olive tree. A knight with full beard weeps when he sees Gawain come to the horse. He warns Gawain to leave the horse alone and to be careful of Orgeluse. Gawain bids goodbye to the people and makes his way with the horse back to her.

Instead of being grateful to him, she yells, "Welcome, you goose!" calls him stupid, and lets him know that she has no appreciation for him whatsoever. He responds by letting her know that he will continue doing her service despite her abuse.

They ride out onto a heath where Gawain notices an herb growing which he could use to help the wounded man. After he digs up the root, he remounts his horse despite her jeers. A strange-looking man comes up from behind them with a message. He is Malcreature, brother of Cundrie. Malcreature and Cundrie had been sent to Anfortas as a gift from Queen Secundille. Anfortas had given Malcreature to Orgeluse to serve as her squire. This is the first time the reader learns of a link between Orgeluse, Duchess of Logrois, and Anfortas.

Malcreature does his best to anger Gawain, calling him a coward and a fool. When Gawain grabs Malcreature, his prickly skin cuts Gawain's hands which became covered with blood. This makes Lady Orgeluse chide Gawain even more.

When they return to the wounded knight, Gawain presses the root upon the cut. The wounded knight keeps warning him about Orgeluse. Disgusted by Gawain's attempt to help him, he asks Gawain to take him to a nearby hospital. He orders Gawain to use Orgeluse's horse, lifting Orgeluse onto it and the knight behind her. As Gawain swings her onto her horse, the wounded knight tricks him by jumping onto Gawain's horse and riding away. Orgeluse laughs at Gawain and asks him if he still wants her love. He responds, "If I can't win that, then a bitter death must soon be mine." It doesn't matter what she calls him, he still intends to serve her in love.

At that point, the wounded knight comes riding back. Gawain now recognizes him as Urians, the knight who raped a maiden and whom Gawain had captured and brought to Arthur. After being sentenced to death by hanging, Urians reminded Gawain that he had given Gawain an oath of surrender in order to save his life. Gawain stood by his word and begged for clemency for Urians, that his life should be spared and that he be pardoned as well. Instead of being executed, he was made to eat with the dogs for four weeks. Because of this humiliation, Urians declared Gawain an enemy and rode off again, taking Gawain's horse Gringuljete with him.

Orgeluse still has no pity for Gawain but lets him know that, since this is her land, she has jurisdiction, and Urians will be punished for his offenses. Having lost his horse, Gawain accepts Malcreature's sad-looking nag, but realizes that it is too feeble for combat, so all he can do is walk beside it, carrying his shield and spear. Orgeluse continues to taunt him. He responds to her nasty remarks with love.

Gawain and Orgeluse emerge from the woods, and Gawain looks up at a castle such as he has never before seen. Its towers and halls are impressive. At its windows he sees four hundred or more ladies. They continue on until they come to a meadow where jousts are held. A knight comes up from behind, ready for battle. Orgeluse reminds him that she had promised him trouble and that he must take up battle with this man who will surely knock him off his horse. At the edge of the meadow is a river, and a ferryman offers Orgeluse a place on his ferry. Orgeluse gets into the ferry and travels to the opposite shore. As she leaves the ferry, she calls out to Gawain in a mocking voice.

Next, Lischois Gwelljus comes riding right toward Gawain who quickly decides that he will be better off fighting on foot. They clash and both break their spears and are thrown to the ground. They jump up and resume fighting, now with swords and shields. After fighting each other bravely, Gawain pins Lischois down under him and tells him to give his oath of surrender, but Lischois refuses, as he has never been in this position before. Instead of surrendering, he offers his life—better to die than to live defeated.

Gawain decides to let him go, but he still needs a decent horse. Why not take Lischois' horse, all armored for battle? What a happy situation to find that this is actually his horse Gringuljete whom Urians had stolen from him. Gawain notices on the horse's hock a turtledove brand, the insignia of the Grail.

Gawain, however, is not paying much attention as he is still infatuated with Orgeluse. Lischois grabs his sword from the ground and attacks Gawain. A second time they fight till both shields are filled with holes. They then fight hand-to-hand.

They are not alone as they fight, for ladies are watching them from the castle windows. The two knights deal each other swift blows, until Gawain grabs Lischois, throws him down violently, and again demands that he surrender. Again Lischois refuses, but offers to let Gawain kill him. He speaks of how for love of Orgeluse he has driven back many worthy knights. Gawain realizes that he cannot kill Lischois, and that both of them are being driven on by love of Orgeluse.

The ferryman, who had taken Orgeluse across the river, comes, carrying a sparrow hawk on his wrist as he walks. He has the right to claim the horse of any man who loses in a joust on that field. Gawain tells him that he must take the nag because at first Lischois defeated him, and only then had he defeated Lischois. Gawain has no intention of giving up his own horse, which he had lost and now gotten back. There, instead of a horse, Gawain offers the ferryman the knight Lischois, a good prize. After he delivers Lischois to him, Gawain accepts the ferryman's offer of a night's rest.

The ferryman explains to Gawain that this is all Klingsor's territory, a place of fantastic adventure, and that the castle he had seen, with four hundred ladies at the windows, is the Castle of Wonders. Then, Gawain leads Lischois onto the ferry and across to the ferryman's house, where Gawain is offered both the house and the ferryman's daughter, Bene, for his needs. She helps take off his armor and Gawain asks her to join him as he eats the evening meal.

The finest fowl is served to Gawain. As Bene cuts up the morsels of meat and puts them on a slab of bread, she mentions that he should send one of the fowl over to her mother, who seldom enjoys such a feast. He gladly does this. After the meal, cushions are brought in for Gawain to sleep on. Gawain remains there alone with the ferryman's daughter, but he does not require anything of her, and he sleeps peacefully through the night.

Developing equanimity:
Becoming the ruler of oneself

Gawain's task is to fight his way through dangerous territory to the Grail, but on the way Gawain passes through this realm of the Castle of Wonders where he is tested through sensuality, trickery, insult, and combat. This chapter on the Castle of Wonders is a contrast to the one on the Grail Castle. It was difficult to find the Grail

Castle. In fact, one had to stumble on it by chance. The opposite was true of the Castle of Wonders. One could even see it from a distance. When Parzival experienced wonders in the Grail Castle, he did not ask any questions, but when Gawain experiences confusion in the Castle of Wonders, he asks right away, "What is going on there?" Everything connected with the Castle of Wonders has to do with magic, enchantment, illusion, and mystery.

Parzival had been called a goose by the squires of the Grail Castle, because he had not asked the healing question, Gawain is called a goose by the Duchess Orgeluse as she taunts him over his lovesick adoration of her. Gawain has given away his heart on first sight. As we saw in his escapades with Antikonie, he struggles with his emotions in connection with women. This time, however, he is not interested in some quick sexual encounter. He sees something deeper behind her beauty and attractiveness.

She is giving him the test of his life, and yet he cannot get near her. He has to endure her mockery as he pledges to love her no matter what she does to him. Parzival was a fool as a young man; Gawain now is a fool even though he is a noble knight. However, through his devotion, he will turn out to be a wise fool. He senses that he has a powerful connection with Orgeluse, and he ignores all the warnings about her.

Gawain is known as a just knight, fair in all matters of knighthood. He had already had to face Kingrimursel because of unjust accusation. Now Urians wants revenge against Gawain even though Gawain actually saved Urians' life after Urians had raped a woman. Over and over, Gawain proves his courage against knights who challenge him. This he must do because responding to challenge is a rule of knighthood. However, when he responds to Orgeluse, he is acting out of freedom. At any point he can walk away, yet he chooses to continue the relationship with her, showing kindness, restraint, and courtesy.

In a mature relationship, each partner acts out of freedom. Loyalty and devotion spring up to replace the initial sexual attraction. As mentioned earlier, one of the key steps in the maturing of the adolescent male is the step from the simplicity of sex to the complexity of the heart. As Gawain continues to be true to his feelings for Orgeluse, he enters late adolescence.

Gawain is a representative of the feeling life. He shows kindness, virtue, and honor in relation to his peers, knights of chivalry.

He doesn't have any problems in the world of combat. His challenge is in the realm of sensuality and women. He shows courtesy to Obilot, but succumbs to Antikonie who invited his advances. That relationship was healed, and now he is challenged to demonstrate loyalty in the throes of insult and abuse and calmness in the midst of accusation.

This is a picture of the adolescent's having to bring equanimity into his feeling life. Gawain has different tests to master with males and with females. Honor and virtue in relationship to male challenges is one thing, but honor and loyalty in relationship to the females in his life is much more difficult. His feeling life must go to a much deeper level. This is what he has to develop with Orgeluse. He has to tame his sensuality, learn clear thinking, and bring them together. Once he makes his choice, he stays loyal to it. In that he will be free.

What is the test for Orgeluse? What does she learn? We have to wait a few more chapters before we understand her situation.

In late adolescence, boys confront the world of feelings. As they move beyond crushes they search for the truth in relationships. They are willing to go through the difficulties of sharing intimacies, supporting a partner's needs, and being loyal to the relationship. They discover that a girl will open her heart to a boy who is loyal. This is particularly true when she has been hurt by other boys.

We also find that boys and girls in late adolescence develop the ability to form deep friendships. The relationship may never become sexual, and each one learns so much from the other about communication, sharing, and supporting each other. In the maturing relationship, the boy relates to the girl in a more comprehensive way. He comes to know her as a person first, and then perhaps in an intimate way. Other deep friendships occur between boys and girls that never become intimate. They share many interests, feel comfortable with each other, and give each other strength and support.

There are also very shy boys who reach out of their shell only as they approach eighteen or nineteen. The idea of having a relationship is threatening, and they cannot even imagine it. These boys are so tender and so vulnerable. Yet if a relationship blossoms during this later adolescent time, it is most wonderful to behold. The boy's heart opens wide; his sense of joy is unending. He cannot believe his good fortune, and he treasures the trust and love that he and the girl share. The relationship becomes a key that opens him to new kinds of friendships, to relationships with adults, and, most of all, to himself. He discovers talents he hardly knew existed. He is exhilarated. Old friends hardly recognize him. As long as the girl is sincere in the relationship, he will find a new footing in life. Even if the relationship ends and he grieves, he will value the experience and know that it is possible again. If he is very fragile, he may close himself off for a long time, angry that he has been hurt. Then his friends need to surround him with support and warmth so that he feels trust in life again.

Relationships during the adolescent years test the teenager's capacity to gain self-control. Am I in control of myself, or am I at the mercy of my sexual desires? How do I behave with someone I am attracted to? How do I handle the confusion of these situations? Relationships are as mysterious to the teenager as the Castle of Wonders—with its illusions and confusions—is to Gawain.

Chapter 11

The Adolescent Gains Self-control

Book XI. *Gawain in the Castle of Wonders*

*W*hen Gawain awakes in the morning in the ferryman's house, he rises, breathes in some fresh air, listens to the birds, and looks out the window. To his surprise he sees the castle he had seen the night before, and the four hundred ladies are still looking out the windows. Exhausted, he returns to sleep, but when he wakes up, he finds the ferryman's daughter Bene seated by his side. She pledges the service of the entire household and herself for whatever he needs. Gawain wants to know who those ladies are, looking out the window. At this question, however, Bene reacts with fear and refuses to tell him anything. She is willing to answer any other question but not that one.

Gawain persists with his question, but all he gets from Bene is tears and deep pain. When her father comes into the room, he misunderstands Bene's tears and thinks they come from their having been in bed together. But Gawain explains that nothing happened between them, except that he has a question which Bene is not willing to answer. Could the ferryman answer it?

When Gawain repeats the question about the ladies in the castle, he receives a similar reaction. "For God's sake! Do not ask! Sir, there is misery beyond all misery." Gawain's heart is moved, and he wants to know why the question distresses the ferryman so much. The ferryman tries to deter Gawain from this line of questioning but realizes that Gawain is not going to stop with the first question. This will result in sorrow and pain to the ferryman and his family.

Nonetheless, Gawain persists until finally the ferryman relents and unhappily explains that Gawain is in the Land of Wonders, with the Castle of Wonders and the Wonder Bed. If he goes any further, this will be the greatest and most difficult challenge he could possibly have. He needs to be ready for battle, and the ferryman will lend him a stone shield to take with him.

Gawain remembers that he had heard about the ladies from Cundrie, and he is determined to do something to help them. He asks the

ferryman's advice for the battle to come. Amidst sorrowing and lamen-
tation, the ferryman tells Gawain that if he survives this test, he will
become lord of this land and everything in it. All the ladies were brought
to the castle by enchantment, and many noble knights have tried and
failed to free them. If Gawain takes up the challenge, he will face death
in the Wonder Bed. If Gawain succeeds, however, God will honor him.

Gawain learns that Parzival has passed this way the day before on
his search for the Grail, but he did not know anything about the Castle
of Wonders and had not asked any questions. The ferryman gives
Gawain some intriguing information. If Gawain is able to free the ladies,
he will not only help them, he will also do good for the ferryman, bringing him great riches. Thus, if Gawain doesn't die in the battle, many people will benefit from his triumph.

Bene helps Gawain put on his armor, and the ferryman brings his
shield and Gawain's horse. He gives Gawain very specific advice: carry
the ferryman's shield, buy something from a rich trader sitting outside
the castle, and leave his horse with the man and it will be safe. "When
you enter the castle, you will see no one. It will seem deserted. When you
go into the room with the Wonder Bed, be prepared for a fight. Never let
go of the shield, no matter what. You may think the struggle is over, but
it is just beginning."

Gawain leaves the ferryman's household amidst much weeping and
grieving and goes to the castle gate, where he finds the trader selling precious goods that could not be equaled anywhere. When Gawain asks to
look at the goods, the trader responds, "I have been sitting here for many
a year and no one—except noble ladies—has dared look over what is in
my booth." If Gawain succeeds with the Castle of Wonders, he will become
master of everything there and all these precious things will belong to
him. The trader invites Gawain to trust him and leave his horse. As the
ferryman had said, the trader also says, "If you succeed, I will belong to
you."

Gawain is ready now. He enters the castle on foot. The castle is very
well fortified. In the middle is a great open field. The roof of the great
hall is like peacock's plumes, bright-hued and brilliant. Inside the great
hall the woodwork and the arches are beautifully decorated. A large
number of beds lie side by side, each covered with a rich coverlet. The
ladies are not permitted to meet Gawain, so the room is empty. Gawain
walks around the hall and comes to an open door. This is the room with
the Wonder Bed.

The floor is shiny and smooth as glass, made of magnificent precious stones. The bed sits on four round wheels made of rubies. The floor

is so slippery that Gawain has difficulty walking on it. Every time he takes a step, the bed moves away from him. The shield feels heavy in his hands, and he longs to put it down, but he remembers the ferryman's words. Gawain leaps into the middle of the bed, and now the battle is on. The bed swerves back and forth, hitting all four walls with such force that the whole castle resounds. A bed is usually a place for sleep, but Gawain has to stay awake every moment to keep from being thrown off.

Gawain puts the shield up over him, and he prays to God. Suddenly, the bed stops moving and the room is still. What will happen next? Five hundred slings let loose with hard stones aimed directly at him, but luckily his shield protects him, even though some stones pass right through it.

The battle isn't over. Five hundred crossbows are aimed right at him and arrows whiz by him. Although his armor has been dented and slashed and he is exhausted, he has survived the onslaught. But no, it isn't over. The door opens and in comes a figure frightful to behold, a stocky peasant clothed in fish skin. He lurches at Gawain with a threatening, fat club. Gawain is puzzled by him since he has on no armor and his weapon is crude. The angry peasant tells him that what's coming is much worse than what he has had so far.

The sound of rumbling fills the castle, and in through the door rushes a lion as tall as a horse. Gawain springs up and defends himself against the ravenous beast. Again, the ferryman's shield protects Gawain, but it receives mighty blows and is ripped through in parts. Gawain slices off a leg of the lion and the leg is caught on the shield. The floor now is even more slippery, thanks to the lion's blood. The lion lunges toward him on his three legs and tries to grasp Gawain in his claws, but Gawain thrusts his sword into the lion's breast, and the lion falls dead.

Gawain has not come through this battle unscathed. His wounds are deep, and he is beginning to lose consciousness. His head is resting on the lion, his shield underneath him. He looks as if he, too, is dead. A maiden peers in and sees the brave knight apparently slain and she wails. But she keeps her wits about her and tends brave Gawain. All the maidens pray for Gawain's life. One of them unties his helmet. Another checks to see if he is breathing. They bring clean water and pour it into his mouth. Gawain opens his eyes and thanks them.

Ever the courteous knight, Gawain apologizes for the condition he is in, but the maidens rejoice and tell him that he has won the battle. The victory is his. Now the most important thing is for him to recover from his wounds. But Gawain isn't sure that it's really over and asks for help in treating his wounds. The wise Arnive directs the maidens to make up a bed and to prepare salves for his wounds. They gently take off his armor and bring him to the bed. Although he has over fifty wounds, the shield has done its work and no arrowhead has punctured his body. There are swollen places on his head where his helmet was dented, but wise Arnive cares for those. She has medicines from Cundrie. In fact, she is using the same salve that Anfortas used for his pain. It is from the Grail Castle, she tells Gawain.

When Gawain hears the words "Grail Castle," he is overjoyed, thinking that it is close by. Now, however, the most important thing is for him to heal. He is given an herb to sleep, and rest comes to him. The ladies check on him throughout the day as he sleeps and heals. When he wakes, his appetite is back and is taken care of lavishly. As he glances at the lovely maidens caring for him, his heart is aroused and he thinks once again of Orgeluse. But Gawain's healing is not yet complete. After eating, Gawain again falls into a deep sleep.

Gaining Control of Speech and Instincts

Gawain does not take advantage of Bene even though she is willing. Instead, he is faithful to Orgeluse. Unlike Parzival, whose feelings of empathy for others were not so developed, Gawain does not fail to ask why people are suffering. Gawain's heart forces are too strong for him to just ride away from other people's pain.

My colleague Brian Gray describes Gawain's experiences in the room with the bed as a metaphor for gaining control of one's speech. The bed knocking back and forth against the walls is the tongue, says Gray. Gawain, who is glib and smooth of speech, has to learn to hold his tongue. The stones and arrows are the barbs and insults that attack him. I find this metaphor convincing and very applicable to the challenges teenagers face when confronted by taunts and insults.

The lion, says Gray, represents Gawain's feeling life. He has to tame his feelings, his passions. The lion specifically represents eroticism which Gawain needs to transform into love. Gawain only partially passes the test, and he becomes unconscious. If the test is to show mastery rather than killing, Gawain is only partially successful. Gawain is almost killed in this encounter, but he survives and thus frees the ladies. He is then reunited with his family—his sisters, his mother, and his grandmother (Arnive)—three generations of women.

Gawain's strength and his weakness are related. Both have to do with an active feeling life. On the strength side, he is a noble knight, gregarious, interested in bringing people together, a mediator, someone who is comfortable in the social sphere. His weakness is that he is a captive of love; he has not yet figured out how to control his sexual desires, how to have an appropriate relationship with women.

The women have been captured by Clingsor, and in their enchantment, they are not able to speak to each other. He frees three aspects of the feminine—the maid, the mother, and the crone. It is Gawain's ability to relate that allows him to free them and makes it possible for them to resume their lives. A true relationship frees women to become themselves. Allowing women the freedom to speak their mind has been a challenge over millennia It is interesting that Gawain does not recognize his mother and sister because he has not seen them for many years. In his struggle in the Castle of Wonders, Gawain has now developed qualities of humility, equanimity, perseverance, and inner courage.

Teenagers need to control their instincts

Teenagers are beset with desires which they do not know how to handle. After the seventeen-year divide, a transition period that lasts about two years, adolescents start to take hold of these powerful feelings and direct them. What is going on in them? It is not only their sexual drives that are pushing and pulling them. Aggression, manipulation, power, seduction are other powerful drives.

The trader who sits at the entrance to the castle is master of the precious objects in his booth. If he succeeds in the castle, Gawain will become master of everything and all these things will belong to him. As long as Clingsor is master, however, no one except for the noble ladies, is interested in them. The trader sits at the entrance to the castle. The ferryman tells Gawain, "Buy something from the rich trader and leave your horse with him."

Let's look at this in terms of adolescent development. The castle is enchanted, danger lurks inside, people are frozen in time; the wild bed, the barbs and arrows, the churl with a club, the vicious lion are all there. If Gawain masters them, he will possess the precious objects. When the adolescent masters his or her instincts, a reward is in store—the precious objects. His Higher Self has transformed desires into ideals such as compassion, purity, truth, or service. As described in an earlier chapter, the adolescent's spiritual life is enhanced by such an experience. His ideals are no longer abstractions, but they are becoming part of his soul life. Now, he can identify ways to serve humanity. Of course, this transformation is not completed in adolescence, but continues throughout our lives.

As long as the adolescent is at the mercy of his or her instincts, these precious aspects of the adolescent journey are ignored. Adolescents need to leave their instinctive will behind when they enter the bewitched castle. Thus, they are beginning the journey to a balanced soul life.

Here is another way to look at this. The floor is magnificent, made of precious stones. Each step is dangerous. Gawain could fall and get hurt. The bed is enticing, it is shining and dazzling. If the teenager jumps onto the wild, banging bed, he or she is at the mercy of sexual instincts. The adolescent is going to get into trouble. He or she needs to calm down the emotions. Only a shield will help. The adolescent needs to be steady, hold the protective shield, no matter what comes. Don't put the shield down. How often do we use the image, don't let your guard down? You will be tempted by alcohol, drugs, and sex. Keep your guard up. Don't give in to temptations. You may not come through it unwounded, but you'll make it, and there will be people to help you.

After adolescents come through this period, their life of will is changed. Rather than being swayed by temptations, they are better able to discriminate and choose their responses. It is not a matter of running away and hiding from temptations, but it is a matter of being clear and making conscious choices. This conscious activity forms their character. Temptations will present themselves over and over, and each time the adolescent has an opportunity to meet them with firmness and clarity.

Chapter 12

Awakening the Thinking

Book XII. *Gawain captures the wreath*

Gawain is restless in his sleep, filled with intense longing for Orgeluse. The tossing and turning loosens some of the bandages. When he wakes up, he notices that fresh clean clothes have been put near his bed to replace the bloodstained ones. He dresses and walks into the castle hall. At one end of the hall rises a narrow tower, high above the castle roof with a winding staircase inside it. In the middle of the jewel-encrusted tower stands a shining circular pillar which Clingsor brought from the lands in the East. A person can look at the pillar and see all the lands for six miles round. Gawain is fascinated with the pillar and is looking at it when the wise Arnive enters with her daughter Sangive and Sangive's two daughters Itonje and Cundrie (not the sorceress Cundrie.) They scold him for being out of bed when he needs rest to recover from his wounds, but he feels that through Arnive's help his strength is being restored. She asks him to kiss all three ladies—Sangive, Itonje, and Cundrie—but even though they are beautiful, all he can think of is Orgeluse. Gawain does not reveal his identity to them.

Gawain asks Arnive to tell him about the crystal pillar. As she does so, Gawain sees a fully armed knight and a lady coming toward the castle. The lady is Orgeluse. Gawain sees that the knight is looking for battle and he prepares for combat. Despite the ladies' protests that he is in danger of re-opening his wounds and bleeding to death, Gawain reminds them that he is now master of the land and needs to defend it against anyone who comes in search of combat. The women are terribly worried about him, but they quietly help him prepare to go out.

Gawain mounts his horse, Gringuljete, receives a spear from the ferryman, and crosses the river. Gawain learns that the knight, the Turkoite, has vowed to fight with only a spear. Anyone who knocks him from his horse is the victor. The joust is on. Gawain catches the Turkoite's helmet and knocks him off his horse.

Even though Orgeluse is aware of his victory over the Wonder Bed and the lion, she continues to taunt him, saying, "You would not dare seek the combat which I would have to demand if your heart desired to serve me for love." Gawain calmly replies that just being with her has made him stronger, and he pledges to serve her in whatever way she wants. She allows the joyous Gawain to ride off with her while the four hundred ladies mourn for him. Orgeluse challenges him to fetch a wreath from a branch of a tree in a nearby ravine. She tells him the tree is guarded by a man who robbed her of her joy. If Gawain is successful, she will give him her love.

After agreeing to the challenge, Gawain rides with Orgeluse through a forest to a ravine and looks at the tree from which the wreath must be plucked. Orgeluse tells Gawain to make his horse leap across the waterfall that formed the ravine, and she will watch him. Her tone is different now. "May God watch over your fortunes!" she calls.

Gawain rides on past the waterfall. He digs in his spurs, and his horse makes a mighty leap but reaches the far side with only his two front feet and then falls into the rushing water below. Gawain, however, saves himself by grabbing a hanging branch. Orgeluse weeps, but Gawain manages to pull himself onto land.

Gringuljete is in danger of being swept down the river, but Gawain leans over, holds out the spear, and catches the bridle in his hand. Thus he pulls Gringuljete out of the water. He climbs back onto his horse, arrives at the tree, plucks the wreath from the branch, and puts it on his helmet.

Just then, the bold and proud knight Gramoflanz arrives. Neither Gawain nor Gramoflanz recognizes the other. Gramoflanz arrogantly calls to Gawain that he will only fight with two people, because one man could never defeat him. Despite the fact that Gawain has plucked the wreath, Gramoflanz refuses to acknowledge it has happened. Gramoflanz is an impressive figure, with a hat of peacock plumes, a cloak of green silk trimmed in white ermine, a beautiful horse, and a falcon on his hand, but he has no weapons.

Gramoflanz looks at Gawain's damaged shield and figures out that Gawain must have been fighting in the Wonder Bed. He tells Gawain that he killed Orgeluse's husband, Cidegast, and his three companions. Then he took Orgeluse captive and offered her his crown and all his lands. But she responded only with hatred toward him. Gramoflanz went as far as holding her prisoner for a year, but she never changed her mind, so he is at war with her.

Now, however, Gramoflanz desires another woman, Itonje, the daughter of King Lot, even though he has never seen her. Since this knight who has mastered the Castle of Wonders is lord of the land, it is in his power to help Gramoflanz gain her love. He asks Gawain to bring a ring as a token of his love to Itonje as he has been carrying out deeds of courage in her name.

Gawain realizes that he would gain no fame defeating an unarmed Gramoflanz, and he agrees to carry the ring to Gramoflanz's love. He also asks Gramoflanz to identify himself. Gramoflanz says that he is the son of King Irot who was killed by King Lot, and that the only knight he will fight alone is Gawain. He looks forward to meeting Gawain in battle and gaining vengeance for the death of his father. Gawain reveals that he is Gawain, son of King Lot, and brother of Itonje. He is willing to fight Gramoflanz to defend the honor of his father.

Hearing all this, Gramoflanz still challenges Gawain to a battle, but not here away from admiring eyes. It will be a huge public event with each side bringing about fifteen hundred guests, including King Arthur and the Round Table. The date is set sixteen days hence on the Plain of Joflanze. Each pledges to be there.

Gawain rides with the wreath on his helmet, jumps across the ravine, and heads toward the proud duchess who now proclaims her anguish over his risky jump and admits that he is her beloved. He presents the wreath to her but chides her for using her beauty to dishonor a knight. Now, Gawain responds differently, and he tells her that he will not love her if she continues to scorn him, that he doesn't need to accept this behavior anymore.

She is now ready to open her heart and share her suffering with him. She asks his forgiveness and explains that she loved her husband so greatly that when he was killed by King Gramoflanz, the light of life went out of her. She tells Gawain that she has been testing him to see if he were worthy of her love. She realizes how good a person he is and how his courageous deeds have impressed her.

Gawain vows to conquer Gramoflanz and knock the arrogance out of him. Orgeluse, weeping, agrees to accompany him to the Castle of Wonders and to care for him until he is healed. When he asks her why she is weeping so much, she tells the rest of her story. She has been trying to take revenge on Gramoflanz by sending strong knights against him. One of those who agreed to kill him was Anfortas who pledged his love to her. He had given her the booth of precious wares in front of the castle gate as a token of his love. Clingsor used black magic to wound Anfortas who was in service of her love. Anfortas now lies helpless, suffering greatly. Clingsor is such an evil man, she said, that he can't bear to leave good people unharmed. "I did not want him to hurt the noble Anfortas. Because he desired the booth with the precious wares, I gave it to him on the condition that if anyone should withstand the test in the Castle of Wonders and win the prize, then I was to seek his love. If I did not please him, the treasure would be mine once more." She had hoped to lure Gramoflanz with the treasure, but it did not work.

Orgeluse tells Gawain that every day she sent knights against Gramoflanz, but he was never defeated. Some knights did it for pay, others for her love. Only one knight refused her love, she said, and his name was Parzival. He defeated five of her knights, but when she had offered herself to him, he refused, saying that he already had a beautiful wife whom he loved. He also said that he had enough sorrow with the Grail.

Gawain asks Orgeluse to keep his identity a secret from the people in the castle. Gawain and Orgeluse ride back to the castle where the knights plan to celebrate the great hero who has defeated the lion and the Turkoite. They come galloping so quickly with banners flying that Gawain thinks they are planning to attack him. But no, they are Clingsor's army, come to honor him as the new lord of the castle. The ferryman and his daughter also come. Gawain and his lady love Orgeluse sit side-by-side and feast. In her company, all his pain disappears. The ladies of the castle greet him with pleasure and gratitude. Then Arnive leads him to his room to receive more treatment for his wounds.

Gawain sends a messenger to King Arthur and Queen Guinevere, requesting them and their whole court to attend the joust when he will defend his honor. He pledges his loyalty and service to the court. He tells the messenger to speak to the queen early in the morning and to do as she advises. "Do not reveal that I am lord of the land here," he instructs.

The messenger leaves on his errand. Arnive tries to get the information from him as to where he is going and what his instructions are, but he is true to Gawain and reveals nothing.

Gaining Control of Thinking

Gawain has succeeded in partially transforming his will and feelings. Because he was obsessed with thoughts of Orgeluse, he still needs to transform his thinking. After a restless night, he explores the castle, climbing up a winding staircase to a tower with a shining circular pillar. From here he could see six miles round. I suggest this is a metaphor for Gawain entering into his head, being able to see things from different perspectives.

Gawain's major task in this chapter is to pluck the wreath from the tree. If he succeeds, Orgeluse will give him her love. When he leaps across the ravine and plucks the wreath from the branch, he puts it on his helmet. Continuing with metaphors, I suggest this is a picture of Gawain's new thinking being placed on top of his old warrior-like thinking.

It isn't easy to develop thinking that is reflective and comprehensive. Gawain almost loses himself and his horse in the process. Once he gains the wreath, he is able to jump over the ravine with ease and grace. As Gawain matures, he comes into himself. He faces Gramoflanz and says, "I am Gawain." He tells Orgeluse not to use her beauty to dishonor a knight. If she continues to mock him, he would rather be without her love. Gawain is no longer a man helpless in love. He is upright and clear about where he stands. When he shows his strength, he frees Orgeluse to be vulnerable and sincere, and she asks his forgiveness. The two, who are now truer human beings, commit themselves to each other.

Gaining control over their lives

In the adolescent, clarity of thought is often seen at about seventeen when the teen is able to stand upright and listen to conscience. The inner intelligence shines forth.

Adolescent boys love physical challenges which include danger and risk-taking. Often, reckless behavior has serious consequences such as a close call with death or with the law. Girls also act out risk-taking behavior, although it is not usually a physical challenge. It may be sneaking out, drinking, joining a gang, or being sexually promiscuous. Being caught or being hurt often shocks teenagers into realizing they need to do things differently, and they especially need to weigh the consequences of their actions beforehand.

When they succeed at re-gaining control over their lives, they gain a sense of accomplishment and satisfaction. When they look back over their previous behavior, they often wonder how they could have been so stupid.

Gawain gains confidence when he stands up to such a strong man as Gramoflanz. Boys need to find their own boundaries in relation to a man. Gramoflanz switches from his arrogant and aggressive attitude to a more gentle attitude when he speaks about Itonje, and Gawain is affected by this. Gawain's tone changes, he softens, and he is able to identify himself with Gramoflanz.

Let's remember that Gawain was not reared by his father, but by Arthur, his uncle. He also has not seen his mother since he was little. Arthur has been a significant mentor for Gawain, and it is to Arthur that he turns when he is in trouble. However, Gawain is the darling of the Round Table. He has learned to do well by being sociable and charming. However, Gawain has to learn to be strong in his heart and steadfast in his will, different from being strong on the battlefield or a charmer in social situations.

I find it interesting that Parzival, Gawain, and Feirefiz all lacked fathers during their childhood. They seek father figures who will help them understand what it is to be a man. Steve Biddulph, in his book *Manhood*, says that most boys in our society are under-fathered and not given the processes or the mentor figures to help their growth into mature men. Boys need to interact over and over again with men. When they don't, they become emotional children in men's bodies who spend their lives pretending. They are uncomfortable with their feelings and lack the know-how of intimacy. They need men to encourage them but also to point out mistakes and hold them to a high standard of behavior.

Much greater familiarity is needed with men so that boys can make connections with various expressions of manhood. When they lack such positive contact, boys suffer from isolation and loneliness, compulsive competition, and lifelong emotional timidity. Boys need men to set them rites of passage, and when the boys meet the expectations, they need the men to acknowledge their accomplishments publicly. We will see how Gawain experiences this in the next chapter.

Chapter 13

Having a Good Time

Book XII. *Unveiling the secrets*

*A*rnive is offended that the squire will not reveal the message to her, nor will Orgeluse reveal the name of her knight-love. When Gawain wakes up from a sound sleep, he asks that the ferryman send his daughter and Lischois Gwelljus to the castle; also the Turkoite is invited. Attired in beautiful clothes, Gawain, Lischois Gwelljus, and the Turkoite, walk into the great hall. Gawain, lord of the lands, sets free the Turkoite and Lischois at the request of Orgeluse.

When everyone is seated, Gawain asks Bene, who has been acting as a secret messenger between Itonje and Gramoflanz, which of the maidens is Itonje. Bene tells him, and Gawain sits next to Itonje, but she does not know she is speaking with her brother. He tries to find out if she loves Gramoflanz. Only after he shows Itonje the ring sent secretly by Gramoflanz does she confess her love for him. This ring becomes the symbol of their mutual affection and is sent back and forth as a confirmation that the message accompanying it is real. She asks him to keep her secret and asks for his help and counsel. He does not tell her that he and she have the same mother, or that their father killed the father of her beloved.

The great feast is about to begin. Knights and ladies sit at separate sides of the hall. The mood is festive as Gawain exhibits his hospitality. This is a significant occasion since they who were enchanted by Clingsor never knew each other's identity and had been unable to speak to one another for many years. Now they can meet and rejoice. Music and dancing follow. What a jovial atmosphere it is!

Gawain and Sangive, his mother, with Queen Arnive, his grandmother, watch the gaity, while Orgeluse comes and sits hand-in-hand with her love. Orgeluse will spend the night taking care of him as he is still quite weak. The evening comes to a close. All the guests leave, and Gawain and Orgeluse at last can share their love

The squire arrives at the place where King Arthur has set up his tents and delivers the message to Guinevere of Gawain's perilous situation and his hope that Guinevere and Arthur will attend the joust. Guinevere is elated that Gawain is alive and well, and she recalls that terrible day when the members of the Court of King Arthur were separated after the harsh words of Cundrie. Guinevere instructs the squire on the way that he should deliver the message to Arthur. When Arthur receives the message, he agrees to bring the entire court with him to the Plain of Logrois, but he is furious that Gawain's father is being accused of killing Gramoflanz's father. When Gawain receives this good news, he is relieved and overjoyed to know that King Arthur and his army will attend the great event when he will battle King Gramoflanz.

One morning, Gawain has occasion to sit next to Arnive and thank her for saving his life with herbs and tender care. He asks her about Clingsor's magic. She tells him that Clingsor had been famous all over Italy, but that he lacked judgment in sexual matters. When he was found in bed with the wife of the king of Sicily, the king had had Clingsor castrated. Clingsor learned magic and now takes out his bitterness and humiliation on anyone who is respected and honored. One particular king who feared Clingsor offered him this castle and the kingdom with thirty years of food supplies if he would leave him alone. Although Clingsor uses black magic to hurt people, he is still a man of his word. He promised that any knight who could withstand the challenges of the Castle of Wonders would win the castle, all its surrounding land, and all the people who had been locked up in the castle. Now that Gawain has accomplished this, Clingsor's power is broken and all the inhabitants are free.

When Arthur and his army arrive, Gawain is so deeply touched by his loyalty that he cannot keep from weeping. He loves Arthur who reared him from childhood and with whom he has shared mutual service and loyalty. Arnive notices that Gawain has been crying, and, thinking that it is from fear of such a threatening army, she tries to comfort him by telling him it is the army of Orgeluse. Of course, Gawain knows it is Arthur's army. Gawain is keeping many secrets at this point, and he is carefully developing his plan that will climax on the day of the great confrontation with Gramoflanz.

Then, Arnive recognizes the coat of arms of the Round Table, but she does not know that her husband has passed away. The army settles on the plain, with properly chosen campsites for the ladies as well as a circle of tents for Arthur and his knights.

Gawain tells the ferryman to tie the boats and the barges on the other side of the river so that none of Arthur's people can use them to cross over. Gawain tests the loyalty of his newly acquired knights of the Castle of Wonders by telling them the great army camped outside the gate is a threat. When young and old alike swear loyalty to him and pledge to defend the castle, he is satisfied. Orgeluse realizes that this is not her army. In fact, her army has suffered terrible consequences from meeting up with Arthur's knights. Because Orgeluse did not know Arthur's army was coming for the joust, her army treated his army as enemies and attacked them. Both armies are exhausted, having lost many men. Had Gawain shared his secret with Orgeluse, much blood would have been spared. But he keeps his secret.

Gawain showers gifts upon his knights, foot soldiers, and ladies, displaying his wealth and generosity. The next day, Gawain leads his army in all its regalia to the Plain of Joflanze. This is a day of great busyness. Tents are set up, and there is a great procession composed of Gawain, Orgeluse, the queens, and all the knights and ladies of the castle around King Arthur's encampment.

Arthur asks Gawain, "Who are these ladies?" Gawain introduces five ladies to him amid much weeping and happiness. Their relationships are now revealed. Arnive is the wife of Utepandragun and the mother of Arthur. Sangive is Gawain's mother. Itonje and Cundrie are his sisters. They all kiss one another and feel overwhelming joy at their reunion. The fifth lady is Orgeluse, Gawain's love.

Even though Arthur's and Orgeluse's armies have fought each other and experienced much suffering, Arthur invites Orgeluse's army to join his own as part of this splendid reunion. Arthur's army is delighted to see Gawain whom they had missed for almost five years. Only Sir Kei is less than gracious. Remembering that day when Gawain had not avenged Kei's broken arm and leg when Parzival knocked him off his horse, he sarcastically asks, "Where did Gawain get that swarm of women?"

Arthur sends a message to Gramoflanz, informing him that they are ready for the joust if that is what Gramoflanz still wants. Meanwhile, Gawain decides to test himself and see if his wounds have healed enough so that he can go into battle without concern. He gives his horse Gringuljete free rein out on the open plain, far from his army. As he practices, in the distance a knight approaches, lance erect, ready for battle.

Issues Challenging the Adolescent Boy

This chapter deals with three issues that challenge the adolescent—appropriate use of sexual energy, appearances and reality, and finding a new relationship with the mother and father figure.

We learn that Clingsor could not contain his sexual energy and was caught in bed with the Sicilian king's wife. His way of dealing with this humiliation was to hurt others through black magic.

One of the adolescent boy's great challenges is to find an appropriate way to deal with his sexual desires. If he cannot handle these urges, he is probably going to get himself in trouble. He may be mocked by his enemies, beaten up, or even killed. His behavior brings consequences that are no longer under his control. Boys today are rarely at risk of castration, but may well contract AIDS or some other sexually transmitted diseases. In addition to endangering his health, a boy who uses girls as tokens of his macho powers, endangers both his character and his reputation. Such a boy is, in a word, a creep, and soon will be known as one.

Clingsor is a creep—big time. His behavior is a great contrast to the courtesy Gawain shows toward Orgeluse. Boys need to be taught the difference between liking, loving, and lusting. In addition to being a creep, Clingsor represents the schoolyard bullies. He covers up his humiliation by hurting others.

This is a chapter about appearances—reality and fantasy. What is real? What is illusion? The adolescent is struggling with this question. When am I really myself? When do I feel that I am in enchantment? Do I have a true relationship with others? Is it all a sham? When I look into my world, do I see what I want to see or do I see what is truly there?

This also is a chapter about splendid reunion and rejoicing. The secrets are beginning to be revealed. Mothers are reunited with sons and grandsons.

Earlier in the book, Parzival had left his bride Condwiramur to find his mother. This had to be done before he could begin his quest for the Grail. Now, Gawain cannot become the true king of the Castle of Wonders until his mother is freed from her enchantment. What does that tell us about the journey of the male? Although he needs time away from his mother, at a certain point there must be a reconciliation, whether it is in this world or the next. Such a reconciliation seems necessary for him to have a healthy relationship later on with a wife.

Gawain now feels complete. His uncle and father figure, King Arthur, supports him in the moment of his greatest need. His mother and great-aunt (Arthur's mother) are present also. He is standing tall. With this support he can publicly introduce his love Orgeluse and hold a large public display of his power and wealth. This reminds me of a line from a Southern hillbilly song, "That's what all the young folks are doing all the while, Puttin' on the agony, puttin' on the style." Gawain is definitely putting on the style. He is also showing us how much he is able to control his life by keeping things secret. He is truly coming into his manhood and wants to be recognized in front of the community he loves. For Gawain, this event is a rite of passage. It includes all the elements of a rite of passage: risk, high stakes, identity, recognition, and reward.

How often do boys crave for their fathers or uncles to come watch them pitch a game or play basketball, so they can feel the attention and support of the important people in their lives. One thirty-year-old man sulked because his parents never had managed to come and see him play an entire hockey game during his high school years. Even though they gave him many other things, he blamed them for not having taken the time to give him the kind of attention he really wanted.

Arthur is an example of a man who gives attention and love to an unfathered or under-fathered boy. Such boys often don't know how to ask for help. Steve and Shaaron Biddulph write, "Under-fathered boys unconsciously want men to be involved and address the problems of their lives, but don't know how to ask. Girls ask for help, but boys often just act for help." (*Raising Boys*, p. 152)

They list four main clues to spotting an under-fathered boy: an aggressive style of relating; hyper-masculine behavior and interests (guns, muscles, trucks, death); an extremely limited repertoire of behavior (standing around grunting and being "cool") and a derogatory attitude toward women, gays, and minorities. (*Raising Boys*, p. 165).

Had Arthur not responded to his request, Gawain would have been devastated and perhaps would not have turned to him again. Guinevere also showed an understanding of a man's need to control his life. She told the messenger to take the message to King Arthur so he could show his court his decisiveness in supporting his nephew in need. Had she not understood this, she could have accepted the message herself and asked Arthur to go help Gawain.

The great feast is also a common fantasy for boys (and girls) who have been adopted, imagining what it would be like to reconnect with their birth mothers or birth fathers. I have known a number of boys and girls in this situation. Even when the adoptive parents are loving and supportive, the questions remain: Who am I? What would I have been like if my real parents had reared me? They fantasize about what it would be like if they were to find their birth mothers or fathers. Everyone would celebrate and rejoice. All the extended family would come, and there would be a great reconciliation. The reality is often much different. In some cases, the birth parent, after an awkward time, does reach out and accept the young person. However, it is rarely a fairy-tale ending. In some cases, the birth parent rejects the child again, which is devastating. Adults who experienced this as children or teenagers carry feelings of rejection and anger into their adult relationships and often have great struggles in social interaction.

Gawain does not know how the great festival is going to turn out. He hoped that Arthur would come. At first, he did not know that he had freed his true mother, grandmother, and sisters. He has his friends and the woman he loves as part of the great entourage. However, it is a great risk because Gramoflanz could kill him—yet Gawain has to risk it. He cannot feel like a whole person unless he brings his family together around him on the day that he fights his greatest battle, publicly assumes his role as King of the Land of Wonders, and marries Orgeluse.

Chapter 14

Integrating Feeling and Thinking: The Adolescent in the Community

Book XIV. *Reconciliation*

*I*t is early morning. Far from the camps, Gawain has been practicing for the great joust with Gramoflanz. A knight in shining red approaches, ready for battle. He, too, had plucked a wreath from Gramoflanz's tree and Gawain assumes that the knight approaching is Gramoflanz. For honor's sake, he must accept the challenge and fight, even though no ladies are there to witness it. The two knights, both riding Grail horses, charge each other, slashing and hacking with great fury.

The story is interrupted here as we follow the squires who bring King Arthur's message to King Gramoflanz, saying that if he still wanted to joust, he should appear, but he should know that Gawain will always be protected by the brotherhood of the Round Table. Proud Gramoflanz is not one to be cowed by this message. He respects Gawain's brave reputation as evidenced by his agreeing to fight Gawain alone. He considers Gawain a worthy opponent and hopes that Itonje, the object of his love, will witness the battle. His grand army, over one thousand knights and ladies representing many countries, is already preparing to move to the Plain of Joflanze to witness the great event. Bene has brought the love-token ring back from Itonje to Gramoflanz. Bene does not yet know that Gawain is Itonje's brother. Bene brings the message that Itonje and the other ladies have ridden from the Castle of Wonders to be present for the joust.

Elegantly attired and shaded under a silk canopy carried by twelve maidens riding horses, Gramoflanz rides toward Arthur's camp; two little maids ride beside King Gramoflanz and support his arms as they ride.

As Arthur's messengers ride back to Joflanze to prepare for the big battle, they pass the area where Gawain is fighting the stranger. Gawain is doing poorly and the battle is nearly lost. They recognize Gawain and shout his name. Upon hearing the name Gawain, his foe throws down his sword and states, "It is myself I have vanquished, and misfortune met me here." Gawain is surprised by this behavior and asks the foe to identify himself. His foe reveals that he is Parzival.

Gawain is so weak from his wounds old and new that he can barely stand. His head swirling, he falls to the grass. One of Arthur's squires runs over, holds up his head, undoes his helmet, and fans the air before his face. Thank goodness! Gawain recovers. At this moment, the armies of Arthur and Gramoflanz line up on opposite sides of the field, ready for the proclaimed joust.

Men from both armies have been watching this combat between Gawain and the stranger knight. When Gramoflanz arrives, his men tell him about the brave battle that had taken place. He and Bene both move closer to see who is fighting. When she sees Gawain in such poor condition, Bene does everything she can to relieve him of his pain and exhaustion, and Gramoflanz offers to postpone the match for a day, to give Gawain a chance to recover.

Parzival offers to fight in Gawain's stead, but Gramoflanz says, "You may well be a hero, but this battle is not destined for you." Bene becomes furious that Gramoflanz would fight Gawain in his present condition, and when Gramoflanz lets out the truth that Gawain is Itonje's brother, Bene is even more angry.

Gawain escorts Parzival to his camp, orders fresh garments for both of them, and introduces him to the four ladies. Parzival is concerned that they may have heard about how he was shamed by Cundrie and resists meeting them. However, the warmth of their meeting allows him to feel joy. Orgeluse still resents Parzival since he had rejected her. However, she obeys Gawain's request that she tend to Parzival.

Bene understands the gravity of the situation with Gawain. If Gramoflanz kills Gawain, Itonje will lose a brother. If Gawain wins, Itonje will lose her love. Gawain insists that Bene not reveal his relationship to Itonje. Bene is alarmed, devastated, angry, and passionate that he must not continue the fight against Gramoflanz. She shouts at him, "It is against her heart you intend to fight." Meanwhile, Itonje notices Bene's tear-stained eyes and senses that something is wrong. Itonje has sent Bene with the love-token ring for Gramoflanz. Now she wonders if Gramoflanz has changed his mind and rejected her love.

With their lords and ladies, Arthur and Guinevere approach Parzival and acknowledge his fame and purity. The crowd grows and the different armies, once foes, gather and proclaim Parzival's honor and nobility. Parzival asks Arthur that he be reinstated in the Round Table and that is graciously done.

Parzival also requests that he be allowed to take Gawain's place against Gramoflanz. Since he has come to this land to fight against Gramoflanz, and has plucked the other wreath, he had approached the meadow with his spear erect, expecting to fight Gramoflanz, not Gawain. Never could he imagine that the person whom he thought was Gramoflanz would turn out to be his dearest kinsman, Gawain. Now that Parzival's shame is gone and he is part of the brotherhood again, he really wants to take on this battle. Courteously but adamantly, Gawain refuses.

Before turning in for the night, Parzival makes sure that all his equipment is in perfect condition and ready for use. Gramoflanz also prepares his equipment and is ready. At dawn, he rides onto the field in elegant attire, hoping to impress Itonje. Impatiently, he waits for Gawain. Early in the morning, Parzival secretly makes his way out onto the field, sees a king waiting there, and the battle begins. Parzival and Gramoflanz clash, splinters flying, each putting all his energy into the attack.

Meanwhile Gawain also prepares himself. As daylight comes, rumors are flying around that Parzival is missing. A special Mass is sung for Gawain and his knights who join him. King Arthur also attends. When it is over, Gawain completely outfits himself for battle. As the army moves over to where the battle is going to take place, however, they can already hear sounds of weapons striking each other. The battle is moving along as Gramoflanz fights for his love and Parzival fights for his friend. Gramoflanz will never again boast that he will only fight two men at a time. Just at the moment when Parzival is on the verge of victory, Gawain and Arthur and several knights of Gramoflanz ride onto the field and all agree to stop the fighting and proclaim Parzival the victor. Although Gawain is still planning to fight Gramoflanz, he can see that Gramoflanz is exhausted from fighting Parzival. Gawain offers Gramoflanz a night's rest just as Gramoflanz had done for him.

Arthur confronts Parzival with the fact that he has entered to fight with Gramflanz despite Gawain's refusal of permission to do so. "You crept away from us like a thief, else we would have restrained your hand from this combat," says Arthur, sternly. At the same time, Arthur tells Gawain not to be angry that Parzival is being praised for his brave fighting. The day is filled with messengers going between Gramoflanz's camp and Arthur's. Gramoflanz gives his messenger the love token ring and a letter to give to Bene. In Gawain's camp, Itonje has overheard that Gawain is her brother and that he is going to fight her sweetheart, and she is devastated. When Queen Arnive grasps the complexity of the situation, she summons King Arthur, hoping that he will call off the combat. Itonje is convinced that Orgeluse has put Gawain up to slaying Gramoflanz in revenge for what he did to her love Cidegast. Itonje also begs King Arthur to stop the battle. He agrees, after it is proven to him that Gramoflanz and Itonje love each other even though they have never met. Gramoflanz agrees to come to King Arthur's camp under safe escort.

Arthur is successful in obtaining a truce from the duchess Orgeluse, and he places all the ladies including Itonje in a nearby tent. When Gramoflanz with his retinue enters the tent, his uncle Brandelidelin enters and is greeted by Queen Guinevere and King Arthur. Arthur tells Gramoflanz to look around and see whether the lady he loves is present, find her, and kiss her. Remembering the appearance of her brother Beacurs, whom he had previously met, Gramoflanz picks out Itonje and kisses her. They courteously exchange greetings.

While the knights and ladies socialize, Arthur takes aside Gramoflanz's uncle Brandelidelin, and they agree that the only thing that can come out of the present situation is sorrow and hatred and that the battle must be prevented. Each takes the responsibility for making peace on his side.

It is done! Orgeluse agrees to a reconciliation with Gramoflanz, but only if Gawain renounces the battle for her sake, and if Gramoflanz stops accusing Gawain's father of killing his father. Gramoflanz, on his side, agrees to renounce his hatred for King Lot of Norway. Arnive, Sangive, and Cundrie also come to the reconciliation. Brandelidelin kisses Orgeluse, and she kisses Gramoflanz although it is difficult for her to do so. Gawain and Gramoflanz give each other a kiss of reconciliation.

With that, a great wedding feast is planned, with many couples to be wed. Arthur gives Itonje to Gramoflanz; Cundrie, Gawain's sister, is married to the Turkoite; Orgeluse announces to all that Gawain is lord over her and her land. The army of Gramoflanz joins the festivities with a great display of splendor and wealth. This is a time of great celebration, happiness, and joy, except for Parzival who still longs for his wife Condwiramur and who still strives for the Grail. He puts on his armor, saddles his horse, and departs from the merriment at dawn.

The Role of the Community

Gawain asks Arthur and the whole court to come as witnesses. All the entanglements get sorted out. However, this is not Parzival's community. He still needs to find the Grail, so he must leave the happy gathering and travel on.

Parzival's search for community

Although Parzival wants to be a knight of King Arthur, it is possible only if he is invited. The first time he enters King Arthur's court, he is a simple fool who knows nothing of knighthood, so he is not invited to become a member of this noble community. Parzival was invited by Gurnemanz to join his community, wed Liaze, and be a son to Gurnemanz, but he left. He knew that this was not the community for him at that time of his life.

Parzival wanted to stay with Condwiramur. He knew that she was his true love and that they belonged together. However, he was not ready to settle down in the community. First, he had to take care of past situations, such as finding his mother. He searches for the community of his childhood where he first experienced love and nurturing. He cannot be a full member of Condwiramur's community until this has been accomplished.

Parzival arrived at the Grail Castle through the working of fate, not through his conscious efforts. He was not yet mature enough to become a member of the Company of the Grail. He didn't have the capacity to take his place there. He was over his head. Yet he had a sense that something important had taken place there, even though he didn't understand it.

He was brought into King Arthur's Court and welcomed as a member, but he had not sought the court consciously. He had been in a dreamlike state when he first ventured into the territory of Arthur's knights. He was overjoyed to be part of the court and experiencing the fulfillment of his childhood dream. The story could have stopped there as Parzival found the community he thought was his goal. However, Cundrie knew from a higher level of understanding that this community was not his destiny. She shamed him into leaving.

During the Easter Holy Week, he met the family of pilgrims. The daughters invited him to join them; although it would have been very pleasant to join them, he knew that this was not his community and he declined.

On his journey to find the Grail Castle, Parzival passed by many castles and kingdoms including the Castle of Wonders, but he was always on the outskirts, never entering into the center of activity. These were not his communities either.

All the court of King Arthur joyfully celebrated Gawain's victory. Many weddings took place, but Parzival knew that he didn't belong in the merrymaking. This was not his community. Although he was welcomed to stay, his goal was elsewhere.

Parzival betrayed the trust of Arthur by sneaking out and fighting Gramoflanz when he had given his word not to. Although he is not yet ready to become a true member of a community, Arthur's forgiveness helps him stay on his path.

When Parzival finally reaches the Grail Castle, everything will fall into its rightful place. He will be reunited with his wife and children, and become King of the Grail. At last he will find his true home, his community for life.

Parzival's search for community reflects the search of all of us, either consciously or unconsciously. The formative years of a child's life in a community lay the foundation for intimate relationships, a sense of belonging and feeling comfortable. Searching and seeking adventure may take us all over the world, but there is a golden thread leading us back to the community of our childhood and youth. We need to revisit this community and heal relationships before we are free to find the community of our adult years—a community of souls based on neither blood ties (family) nor tradition, although both family and tradition may play a role in the community that we freely choose to connect with later.

In the ancient world, place was very important. A person was connected with the land, with the rhythms of the seasons. This is the old way. The new community is a very different experience. Because people often live far away from family members, they form new communities based on friendship, common values, or common life-style. In the new communities, members support each other and come together to celebrate, just as old communities did. However, they are chosen communities rather than arising out of family ties. Finding a new community to belong to can be time consuming and frustrating.

Adolescents need a solid and wholesome community life before venturing out on a lonely path. Youngsters who don't have such a foundation often long for this missing piece of their life and search for people who can offer them the stability and support they missed in their childhood. There are three major communities that influence the life of the child—the extended family, the school, and the neighborhood. town, or city. Earlier in the book, I discussed the role of the family. Now I would like to focus on the school community.

The School Community

The healthy school community has many significant features. It is made up of people of various ages—young children, adolescents, and adults who spend their days together over several years. The variety of adults offers different opportunities of mentorship: opportunities for growth, for learning, and for changing behavior. Adults who are willing to stand up for values of integrity, honesty, and forgiveness become models of virtue for young people. Adults who are able to hold a mirror up to the adolescent's face to awaken self-knowledge and reflection, even when it is not welcomed are respected for their devotion to truth. The nurturing school community is a village in the sense that there is stability, a size in which everybody can get to know each other, a sense of belonging rather than of anonymity, rituals marking life changes, and opportunities for public acknowledgement of new capacities and shared memories.

In considering the adolescent, let us look at five levels of a high school community.

1. Relationship to adults

Adolescents need to have meaningful relationships with adults in school. They will be drawn to some more easily than others. Yet, over time, adolescents also come to value qualities in adults that they did not appreciate or acknowledge earlier. A particular student was explaining to a new ninth grader, "That teacher gets better as you get older." The student's parents chuckled, "She doesn't seem to realize that she is the one who is changing."

It is not the task of the adults to do things to be liked. In fact, this is often troublesome. If the adult cultivates a relationship with a teenager to feel liked or appreciated, this will eventually backfire. Either the teenager will reveal a confidence, causing great embarrassment to the adult, or the teenager will change his or her mind and turn on the adult. It is not the teachers' task to become friends with the students while they are in high school. They need to be free to establish as much of a relationship as they choose, without any expectations beyond what is required in the classroom. Our task as teachers is to do our job, set clear boundaries in our work, serve the unfolding capacities in the student, and be objective, fair, and supportive. If we focus on being their friends, they will expect friendship, which crosses professional boundaries.

It is often the case that young teachers especially want to be liked. They may ask to be called by their first names in a school where that is not usually the case, or socialize with students outside of school. This is always risky. As one student said to a young, vulnerable teacher, "Come on, you're our friend. Come drinking with us." Or "How can you give me that grade? I thought we were friends."

We are called upon to be midwives of our students' learning, serving their developing minds and hearts. They are always in a process of becoming.

I was especially struck by how much growth and development take place in young people when I attended a funeral of a thirty-seven-year-old former student. If we had had to make a judgment at the end of twelfth grade, we might have said about this boy: He has many strengths and some weaknesses. He brings joy and love to all his classmates and friends. Yet he has a weak will. He has difficulty finishing what he starts. He struggles with concentration.

However, twenty years later, when people who had known him as an adult spoke about his accomplishments, it became clear that the delightful capacities he had shown earlier had only grown stronger and more powerful. The weaknesses had been tempered by life experiences and maturity. He had developed strength of will and had become very capable in a number of areas. What was in seed form at eighteen had truly flowered in his thirties. It was a great pleasure to hear of the many accomplishments he had achieved in his twenties and thirties. They hadn't come easily, but with maturity and a passionate love of life, they had come.

Ten years after they graduate, our students will not remember whether they liked us on a particular day, but they will remember whether we held a standard and inspired them to become more than they realized they could be. They will remember how they grew when we were truthful with them about their work rather than rewarding them with empty praise. They will remember our own passions in life and how we modeled life's joys and showed that we, too, were part of life, not isolated in an ivory tower.

To be a high school teacher or the parent of an adolescent is to be on one day a Gurnemanz setting down the rules, on another day a Sigune telling them their name and origin and reminding them where they have gone astray, on another day a Trevrizent revealing to them aspects of their destiny. Sometimes we even have to be a Cundrie, letting them experience shame.

The community of adults in a high school environment is a community of trust in which we need to foster hope, belief in positive change, and commitment to serve the highest good. This is our charge and we must never forget it. We have the responsibility to believe in the capacity for change, for maturing, for transformation in every young person we serve. When these qualities live in the souls of the adults in a high school community, adolescents can thrive, can meet their own dark night of the soul and come through it into the light.

2. The community of peers

Whether or not one is accepted by at least some portion of one's fellow students is one of the greatest anxieties in the adolescent's experience. Groups in a high school have implied or direct membership issues. Which group should the student join? What are the requirements? What are the intentions of the group? How does one join? There are the in-groups, popular students who are looked up to and admired by those outside the group. What is the price of membership? How high school groups form has always been a mystery for me, despite decades of teaching high school students. There is an unspoken, unclear aspect of why one person is welcomed and another isn't.

Those outside the in-group may feel inferior, lonely, and unworthy. If they are satisfied with their own group, they may feel quite secure and uninterested in whether they are accepted by the in-group. However, if they yearn to be in but are either excluded or simply ignored, their high school years may be miserable. These feelings are not logical, and despite many conversations about finding other friends, realizing that their own small group of friends is just as good, the feelings of rejection don't go away.

In large high schools, students are often grouped by club membership (newspaper staff, drama club, football team, etc.), racial or ethnic groups, or by life-style preferences (the techno-geeks, the preppies, the stoners, etc.). Students often connect with a particular group early in their high school years, and even when they try to change, they find it difficult to do so. Fixed on early impressions, classmates find it hard to recognize new or different qualities in the teenager. Schools where students have many opportunities to be seen in different ways, rather than becoming stuck in old perceptions, help students develop individual identities. Yet, even in such schools, the situation of rejection or stereotyping still may exist, and many hurt feelings, tears shed, and frustrations abound.

For a student who cannot find strong friendships in a class, at least he or she may feel satisfaction as a member of the larger community of the school, in relationships with teachers or staff members, or students in other classes or groups. Having many friends throughout the school is a compensation, but the longing for a best friend or a solid group identity usually remains.

3. The social life of the community

Over three decades I have been connected with high school life, I found that many of the most cherished memories among former students were of the customs and traditions. Our society is weak in ritual, rites of passage, and other markers that designate a particular achievement or privilege. A school community can offer these to students. One has to be careful to make the customs and traditions meaningful, for there are also trivial ones that may satisfy in the moment but in the long run appear hollow.

What is important in a custom or tradition? There needs to be truthfulness. Tradition for its own sake can be fun, but it lacks weight. In the school I was connected to, the faculty gave serious attention to the question of rituals, customs, and traditions. We understood that such acts should be spiritual deeds supporting the inner development of the adolescent. What are some of the events to mark in a high school community?

The beginning of the school year. Each new year is a beginning, a marking of a stream of experiences, a gathering of events, learning moments, accomplishments, times of growth, friendships made and friendships lost. It is as important to focus on beginnings as it is to acknowledge endings. There are many ways to celebrate the beginning of the school year. In some schools teachers present twelfth graders with a flower and a wish for a productive senior year; in other schools, the twelfth graders may welcome the ninth graders with a flower as a token of welcome, or they may welcome the first graders by planting a tree together so the young children can watch the tree grow as they advance grade by grade. There is no prescribed ritual; each school will choose its particular way of welcoming the students to a new school year. What is important is that the ritual be taken seriously, that it be an expression of human relationship, that it show respect, and that it have an aesthetic quality.

Birthdays. With younger children, celebrating birthdays is a very significant time in a community life. With high school students, it is often more a private affair with special friends. Even in a high school, however, it is special to acknowledge students' birthdays. Although some adolescents may posture that it is just another day, they look forward to that special attention. In some way a birthday is much more an individual experience than a community holiday. It is the only time that person is singled out just for being born. In countries where name days are also celebrated, there are two occasions for this special recognition. Teenage birthday bashes may be exciting in the moment, but they actually have very little to do with honoring the birth of the person. In our materialistic society, birthday celebrations are getting out of hand. Bigger and bigger extravaganzas are encouraged where parents put out thousands of dollars. This is especially true for the birthday that marks the coming out of the child into adulthood—the bar or bat mitzvah, the quinceañera celebrating a hispanic girl's fifteenth birthday, the sweet sixteen party. Commercial establishments enter the family's planning and these events can become competitions of opulence.

The ending of a school year. In many schools, this occasion is marked with parties, exchange of gifts, and thoughts about the coming summer. The sports banquet is another form of ending. But there is more that needs to be acknowledged. It is a time of looking back as well as forward. What was learned? What relationships were special? What accomplishments need to be public? In some schools, students do a review of the courses they had over the year, together remembering the highlights of each course. It is amazing how much is forgotten, and it is special to share the highlights with each other. The same can be done reviewing the year as a high school community. What events stand out? What serious events? What humorous ones?

One of our most touching experiences was one that took place in Latvia and which I shared with my faculty at home. Our school was so impressed by it that we adapted it as an end-of-year ritual. I will describe the way the Sacramento Waldorf School created its version of Final Bell. On the last day, when the lower and high school students are together, the twelfth graders visit each class in the school. The first graders line up in two single lines facing each other. The first graders hold flowers. The twelfth graders stand in front of the two lines while the first graders recite a poem or sing a song to the graduating seniors. Then the seniors walk in single file between the two lines, the first graders giving flowers to whichever seniors they wish. This then is repeated in each grade.

The seniors experience the grades they themselves had gone through in their earlier years as the children shower them with poems and songs. At the same time the seniors' bouquets of flowers grow larger and larger. When they complete the eighth grade lines, they meet the rest of the high school which serenades them with song and then forms into lines as well. The procession ends with the seniors walking between the two lines of their teachers and being given flowers. With the school bell tolling for the last time, the twelfth grade speaks the verse which they have said at the opening of school every day for many years. There is hardly a dry eye left in the group. Parents have also been invited to observe this ritual and the seniors' parents say that being present at this ritual also acts as a closure for their own years in the school. Involving the parents extends the boundaries of the community and honors their efforts and responsibility.

Festivals. Each school has its own range of festivals. It is important that there be meaning, that the students have a role in the celebration by which they learn skills and ways of celebrating. Through this they may learn about holidays in various cultures. They may celebrate seasonal holidays repeated yearly or have assemblies in which they share aspects of their schoolwork and learn how important it is to share these moments together.

It is especially beautiful to see the high school students involved with the younger children in a K–12 school. Here the students begin to assume responsibility in guiding young children. One year, the twelfth grade was invited to the first grade classroom to help the younger children carve pumpkins. Each first grader sat at a newspaper-covered desk with a pumpkin ready to be carved. Each twelfth grader went to a desk and worked with a younger child, carving, scraping, laughing, sharing. The mood was intimate, almost somber, as the seniors took their responsibility very seriously. However, when lunch bell sounded, the seniors were ready to rush out of the classroom to join their high school friends for lunch, but they didn't. They waited until the desks were cleaned, the knives washed and put away, and the newly carved pumpkins lined up in a row. From that day forward, the first graders looked up to the seniors with awe, and the seniors looked at the first graders with warmth and affection.

These kinds of event awaken a sense of belonging, broadening the sense of identity, and stimulating interest in others. Other such events include tutoring younger children, doing building or gardening projects for the school, cleaning the school together, and making toys for the kindergarten.

I recall one year when high school students built the fence around the kindergarten play yard. Weeks later, the kindergarten students came to the high school meeting bringing applesauce they had made and pictures they had drawn for the high school students. It was a sweet moment.

Even when schools are separated into elementary, middle, and high schools, it is possible to connect high school students with children in the larger community or to form a relationship between a high school and a particular elementary school.

4. Relationship to the past, present, and future
Adolescents gain a sense of time through their relationship to a community. In a time when there is so much mobility, being able to stay in one place for a number of years offers teenagers a sense of their own history. Moving from community to community or school to school puts tremendous pressure on adolescents to create an identity, to make quick decisions about whom to befriend, and to make relationships with teachers.

Of course, there are times when a change is healthy. By and large, it is valuable for children and adolescents to make lasting relationships that see them through their changes, lows and highs, success and failure—all within a context of support and familiarity.

While it may seem easier to leave a class or school when there are difficulties, a better lesson may be learned by the students' or teachers' making a new start together. Finding the strength to heal broken relationships, finding ways to improve misunderstandings, and gaining perspective on other people's ideas and actions develop important capacities that will serve youngsters well in life. It has become common in our society to follow the slogan, "Ending is better than mending" from *Brave New World* (by Aldous Huxley). However, students who have the opportunity to mend rather than end are learning important social skills.

5.The individual in the community

High school students have individual destinies just as Gawain and Parzival did. Gawain's destiny was to restore integrity in society, to behold beauty in another person, and to heal relationships between people. He lives in the social realm, learning lessons in love. What are Gawain's obstacles? He is impetuous. What are his trials? He is mocked by Obie, tempted by Antikonie, and scorned by Orgeluse.

When we meet teenagers in high school, we must always keep in mind that they are at a particular stage of their journey. Just as Gawain should not be judged by his behavior with Antikonie, high school teachers and parents need to leave space in judging teenagers. The facts of what they do stand as facts, and often come with consequences, but they should not be final judgments on their character. Each student is going through his or her version of temptations, trials, and overcoming of obstacles. Our task is to keep an image of the youngster's higher self, keeping faith in who he or she will become and offering a helping hand along the way.

We have all known high school students with a Gawain-like capacity for warmth and friendship, sociability and charm. They seem to know how to behave in a group, are sought after for advice, and admired for their fun-loving quality. They seem to have everything they could want. Yet they, too, make big mistakes and have to recognize this and overcome them. Behavior that one can forgive in a fifteen-year-old should not be as easily forgiven in an eighteen-year-old. When high school students make the same mistakes over and over again, a habit is developing that hinders healthy development. One hopes that adults will step in, form a relationship with the youth—reflecting the problem behavior—and help him or her to make changes. When that doesn't happen, the youngster will have many hard knocks ahead to awaken him to the results of poor judgment and anti-social behavior.

While Gawain's journey is horizontal, in which he has adventures and opportunities to grow, it is different from Parzival's vertical path in which he is single-mindedly focused on pursuing the Grail and then returning to Condwiramur. We meet high school students who continue on their path through school with a particular goal in mind. They may or may not have friends, but, as wonderful as friends are, these students do not have the same need for them as others do. This student has a clear goal, may have mentors either in or outside of school, and is focused on the future. This doesn't mean there aren't lonely times, but an inner steadiness acts as a guide. The task for students on this vertical path is to reconcile head, heart, and limbs. Left to themselves, they may become one-sided, focused on one idea, swayed by emotions, or propelled by action. They also may be given to depression. They need to bring all aspects together in harmony. This can be helped by a single close friend, a loved mentor or teacher, or any other adult who shares common interests. The journey can be difficult and lonely, but when the youth awakens to compassion and empathy, this is a big step toward inner balance.

Parzival needs shocks to wake from his dream. Sigune provides them. Gradually, he takes responsibility for his behavior. That is our hope for high school students. Will they wake up, experience the needs of others, look outside themselves, and begin to gain perspective? Cundrie shocks Parzival further. Who is the Cundrie in the youth's life? Who tells him or her the truth?

We can also look at the community experience of the women in the story. They also have varied paths. Their challenge in so many ways has to do with relationships, with the life of the psyche. Whether it is Herzeloyde and Sigune struggling with loyalty and protective issues, Jeschute and Cunneware being abused by aggressive out-of-control males, Obi and Obilot caught up in pride and jealousy, Antikonie in impetuousness, or Orgeluse in anger and vengeance, they are one-sided and need balance their lives. Condwiramur, Bene, and Repanse de Schoye seem to have a spiritual anchor that guides them. Perhaps their path is more like Parzival's.

Important to the adolescent journey is the cultivation of idealism over self-indulgent sensuality. The teenager who is focused only on him- or herself doesn't leave room to appreciate others. Instead there is an emptiness in the heart that gets filled only by self-indulgence or by criticizing others. This is a sad state of affairs and such immature students lose the respect of their classmates. This situation calls for a respected adult to step in and speak directly to the teenager, appealing to her or his conscience to take responsibility for his or her behavior, and to realize that what may be a temporary satisfaction doesn't satisfy in the long run. This Cundrie-like encounter can make all the difference in a teenager's life.

Although the story of Parzival takes place centuries ago, many aspects of the relationships described are current today. It is necessary for the girls (and women in the story) to find resolution in their personal relationships before they can feel a part of a community. If they feel that their relationship is secure, they can give a great deal to the community. The men have many trials to face as well. They usually identify a goal and focus on attaining it before being acknowledged by the community. In both cases, the community is a healing agent for inner growth.

Chapter 15

Integrating the Will:
Boys without Fathers, Girls without Fathers

Book XV. *Feirefiz appears on the scene*

*P*arzival rides out toward a great forest when he sees a heathen stranger, rich in adornment and precious jewels, approaching. Heathen was the term used for a non-Christian during the Middle Ages. Who was this stranger? One who traveled the world, bravely defending women, receiving their precious gifts, and gaining fame. He wears on his helmet an ecidemon, a little beast that kills poisonous snakes. His horse is draped with rarest silks. He is the commander of twenty-five armies, each speaking a different language. Countries look to him as lord and master. His armies were left on ships in the harbor while their commander rode off alone in search of adventure.

The two men spot each other and attack. Neither one can unseat the other, so even is their match. They close in on each other with swords. The heathen's helmet is dented. The horses are sweating. The two leap off their horses and continue their encounter on foot, sword against sword.

This is a battle of sorrow. These two are sons of the same man, each is part of the other. The heathen charges into battle, yelling "Tabronit" (the land of Queen Secundille near the Caucasus mountains). Through this shout, the heathen gains new strength. Parzival is exhausted and needs something to spur him on. However, he is weakened under the blows of the heathen's sword and sinks to his knees. Each is loyal to a woman—the heathen to Queen Secundille who has given him the richly ornamented helmet, and Parzival to Condwiramur the beautiful and pure.

At last Parzival thinks of his wife, and it is as if her strength pours into him, as he shouts "Pelrapeire!" This is just in time. Parzival regains his power, breaks his sword over the heathen's helmet, and the heathen falls to his knees. When he raises himself up, he realizes the other no longer has a sword. The heathen acknowledges that it would be cowardly to fight his opponent who has lost his weapon. He declares they call a truce until they have rested. Acknowledging the greatness of the other's capacity in battle, the heathen asks Parzival to identify himself. Parzival refuses because it would mean that he had lost the battle and was forced to reveal himself. Since there is no clear loser, the stranger agrees to go first. "I am Feirefiz the Angevin."

Parzival is confused. "How do you come to be an Angevin? Anjou is mine by right of inheritance. The castles, land, and towns of Anjou are mine." Parzival acknowledges there is only one knight who can claim this land besides him, and that is the brother he has never met but whose exploits and fame have reached his ears. If he could see the stranger's face, he could see if he were the one. Parzival pledges he will not attack the stranger if he takes off his helmet. The stranger is not concerned, because he still has a sword and Parzival has none. But to make things even, he hurls his sword into the woods.

The heathen asks Parzival to describe his brother. Parzival tells him that his brother has been described to him as black and white all mixed up. Feirefiz says, "I am the one."

Each removes his mail and helmet, kisses the other, and recognizes the joy of the moment. Feirefiz gives honor to his gods and goddesses for this event, attributes to Parzival the honor of the elder son, and offers him two rich countries. He tells Parzival that he has undertaken this journey to find his father. Parzival responds, "I never saw him either." They speak of their father's reputation, his fame, his nobility, his steadfastness, faithfulness, and praiseworthiness. Parzival tells his brother that their father died in a joust in Baghdad.

Feirefiz is in deep sorrow. "In this hour I have both lost and found my joy. If I am to grasp the truth, my father and you and I, we were all one, but this one appeared in three parts. . . . You have fought here against yourself; against myself I rode into combat here and would gladly have killed my very self."

Feirefiz wants Parzival to come down to the harbor and see his great army. Parzival is surprised that an army would sit and wait for its commander. Since there is no hurry, Parzival invites Feirefiz to Arthur's camp to meet all the ladies there. This gets Feirefiz's attention; he is interested in following up on this, as well as in meeting relatives.

Parzival picks up Feirefiz's sword and gives it to him. Then they ride off to Arthur's camp, where the knights and ladies have been saddened by Parzival's early morning departure. Someone had come from the Castle of Wonders to tell of a raging battle that was seen in the crystal pillar. Arthur is sure one of the knights is Parzival. At that point Parzival and Feirefiz come riding into the camp. Everyone is very much impressed by the jeweled garments Feirefiz wears. Parzival introduces Feirefiz—the king of Zazamanc and his brother—to Gawain who kisses him and orders that richly textured garments be brought for both of them. The ladies also give him a kiss. Gawain invites them for a meal and asks King Arthur and Queen Guinevere to join them.

The whole company of the Round Table joins them and all receive Feirefiz warmly. Arthur and Feirefiz exchange greetings and knowledge of their fame. Arthur is particularly interested in how Feirefiz had come to this land and how his wife would let him travel so far away. Feirefiz describe his queen whose desires he serves, her love being his reward for knightly victories. Whenever he faces danger, he thinks of her and this gives him strength.

Arthur says, "From your father Gahmuret, my kinsman, you fully inherit the habit of long journeys in the service of ladies." He tells Feirefiz that Parzival is searching for the Grail. He asks both men to name all the people and countries they have known in battle. The list is long from both men's encounters. Feirefiz's list includes his desire for knightly deeds; Parzival's for encounters that happened as he was striving for the Grail.

Gawain has Feirfiz's battle equipment brought out, and it is much admired. While Feirefiz is being admired by the ladies, Arthur proposes a festival to be held the next morning as a reception for his relative Feirefiz and his induction as a knight the Round Table.

The day shines sweet and clear. Knights and ladies gather in their best finery around the Round Table circle. Arthur grants membership also to Gramoflanz and two other worthy knights. Feirefiz and Parzival enjoy the company of many beautiful ladies.

Into the festivities rides a maiden wearing sumptuous garments bearing the emblem of the Grail. Her face is covered by a thick veil. She is immediately brought into the circle of the Round Table. She bids greeting to King Arthur in French. She asks the King and Queen to listen carefully to her words. Then she dismounts and goes directly to Parzival, falls at his feet, begs him for a greeting. Parzival, reluctantly forgives her, but does not give her a kiss. At the urging of Arthur and Feirefiz, he gives up his grudge toward her. She springs to her feet, bows to them, undoes her headdress, and reveals she is Cundrie the sorceress. She still looks the same way she did when she appeared at the Round Table to curse Parzival.

This time her message is quite different. "Blessed are you, son of Gahmuret. You shall be Lord of the Grail. Condwiramur, your wife, and your son, Lohengrin have been named along with you." Cundrie then tells Parzival that he has two sons born soon after he left Pelrapeire. She instructs Parzival that he will now ask the question of King Anfortas and help his suffering. Parzival has now achieved peace of heart and is worthy of the Grail.

Parzival weeps with joy at the news. He thanks God for showing him favor to serve the Grail. He recognizes and states that if he had not done wrong, she would not have been furious with him. However, in his youth, it was not the time for his salvation. Orgeluse weeps for joy that Anfortas's suffering will come to an end; she had been the cause of his pain. Parzival asks Cundrie what he should do next. She tells him he cannot go alone. He must choose a companion. She will lead the way.

At Arthur's invitation, Cundrie goes to rest and visit with Arnive. Parzival asks his brother to go with him, and Feirefiz agrees to go with him to the Grail Castle. Before they leave, Feirefiz wants to distribute gifts to all present. Everyone agrees they will not leave the field for the four days it will take Feirefiz to go to his ships and return. Arthur gives him messengers to help him. Then Parzival tells the group what Trevrizent had told him—that no one ever fights his way to the Grail. He will not reach it "unless he has been summoned to it by God."

The two brothers bid farewell and set out for the ships. When they return, they give each person gifts of great wealth before riding off with Cundrie to the Grail Castle.

The Adolescent's Soul Experience

In this story we are dealing with three castles—the Grail castle, Arthur's castle, and the Castle of Wonders. Each represents a level of the adolescent's soul experience.

The Grail castle is the aim of Parzival's journey. He cannot achieve his goal until he understands the purpose of the Grail and transforms himself to be worthy of achieving it. Parzival's approach to life is through his thinking. Only by bringing light into his thinking is he able to fulfill his life destiny. The Grail castle represents the *spirit*. When he grasps his spiritual destiny, he awakens to his Higher Self. This path is the path of One. He can integrate other soul forces into himself, but in essence it is an individual journey. Anfortas is the ruler of the Grail castle who misused his power and now must be healed by the true magician, the one who transforms himself spiritually from dullness to compassion.

The Grail Castle is the place in the soul where the adolescent is striving to reach ideals, to find a relationship to God, to find that there is meaning in life beyond the senses. The awakening of empathy, developing an awareness of spiritual life, sensing moments of destiny, relating his or her behavior to an inner truth are all aspects of the experience of the Grail Castle in the soul. Rules are different here. They are not the rules of convention, but the unfolding of destiny, of higher laws. Usually adolescents have mentors or guides to help them in the Grail Castle of their soul.

Arthur's castle has to do with earthly deeds of protection and knightly valor. Parzival and Gawain are members of Arthur's castle and court. At times they are members in good standing, and at other times they are shamed and have to leave. This castle is a place of hearty feelings, nobility, and honor, of comraderie and fellowship. King Arthur's court and castle represent the *soul* expressed through the feeling life. Arthur bestows earthly wisdom on the members of his court. Through meeting the challenges brought to them, the knights elevate their souls and purify their feelings.

The Castle of King Arthur is the place in the adolescents' soul where they learn how to have healthy peer relationships, value friendship, act with loyalty, honor, and virtue. Teenagers spend much time in the soul realm of King Arthur's castle as they learn how to become social beings. They need to learn to respect their elders, treat their peers with courtesy and care, appreciate what is given to them, and be patient. The knights of Arthur's Court go off into the world, defending the right and protecting the weak. This is a good example of how a high school student would work within this castle in the soul life. When the student is being overly competitive, jealous, or self-serving, he or she is having problems remaining at the Round Table. In this realm there are rules of behavior and they must be obeyed.

The Castle of Wonders. This castle has to do with power connected to the body through the *will*. Misuse of sex, personal power, vengeance, drug-induced illusions, hypnotic trances, misuse of speech, and lack of control are all aspects in which the person dishonors the body rather than respecting its qualities. Gawain has to

197

gain control over his body and use his sensual experiences appropriately. Clingsor is the magician who controls the Castle of Wonders, using power to seek revenge.

The Castle of Wonders is the place in adolescents' soul life where they become whipped about by their sensuality and lower nature. When their lower nature—their instincts and drives—overpower their consciousness and sense of responsibility, they are stuck in the Castle of Wonders. How do they get out? In the same way Gawain mastered the challenges. They have to learn to control their behavior, master their mouth so that they are responsible for what they speak. They need to overcome anger, not lose their temper when insulted or treated unfairly, not insult others, avoid seeking revenge, find ways to solve problems peacefully.

The three castles represent the paths by which we transform ourselves and purify our bodies, our soul, and our spirit. Adolescents are just beginning this journey. They experience each of the three castles at different times of their youth.

Boys without Fathers

Feirefiz and Parzival meet in this chapter. They discover they are both sons of the same father. They have grown up without ever having met their father, without the benefit of having a father to guide them. Both suffer from father loss because of their father's restlessness. Gahmuret abandoned Feirefiz's mother Belakane because she wasn't baptized and because he was restless and wanted to go seek adventure. He married Parzival's mother, excusing the fact that he was still married to Belakane by the statement that she wasn't a Christian. Then he went off to seek adventure and was killed in battle. Both women suffered from Gahmuret's behavior. Belakane was heartbroken. She would have been baptized if he had asked her. Herzeloyde overprotected her son to keep him from becoming a knight and dying in battle. When young Parzival leaves her, she dies of heartbreak. However, both boys know their father was a brave knight, and this sustains them and gives them a model to imitate.

Both sons carry the double loss—lack of a father and a mother who is incapacitated through the loss of her husband. Because of his mother's fear that she would lose her son if he learned about knighthood, Parzival is held back in a state of innocence of the young child. He is naïve about the ways of the world. Feirefiz is searching the world for the father he never knew. He is like an early adolescent, naïve, captivated by beauty and romance, and generous.

As was typical of the knightly class in the Middle Ages, Gawain had been sent to be a page in another castle when he was a young child. His father, King Lot of Norway, was a brave warrior who died on the battlefield. He was accused of killing King Irot, father of King Gramoflanz, and thus Gawain has to meet the revenge Gramoflanz now carries for the son of King Lot. Although it is not clear that the accusation is just, it does not matter. There is something unreal about the scene. Yet, Gawain has to meet the challenge and defend his father's reputation. Gawain's relationship with his mother also seems unreal. As a child he did not spend time with his mother and sisters. As an adult, when Gawain enters the Castle of Wonders, he does not recognize his grandmother, mother, or sisters. Yet through his courage and bravery, he is able to liberate them from their enchantment. This is indeed a land of unreality.

In Gawain's case, the society structured the education of the male by providing stages of development—page, squire, knight—under the guidance of a male mentor. Our modern society has the ideal of the nuclear family with the father as an integral member of the household. However, for those boys whose fathers are absent, the society provides no structure. Organizations such as Big Brothers try to provide older male models to befriend boys and guide them. This is very helpful in many cases. However, the reality is that many boys whose fathers are absent are bereft of a significant male in their lives.

I have worked for almost a decade training staff who work with juvenile offenders. As I have become familiar with many of the boys' biographies, two patterns emerged. One was that there was no father present; the other was that the father was a negative role model. In the first case, the boys were at a loss, not able to find a relationship to authority, and therefore they were defiant, confused, and lacked direction. These boys struggled to find an identity. They carried a sense of rejection and felt resentful. In the case where the father was a negative role-model, the boys at least had someone to look up to as they adopted their fathers' attitudes towards society.

They saw nothing wrong with criminal behavior, because it was what they knew and saw around them. Although they were adopting a lifestyle that was anti-social, they felt they belonged to someone.

Boys who grow up in a more positive social environment also feel the rejection and resentment, but they are fortunate enough to have mothers, grandparents, and family friends who provide them with nurturing surroundings. Yet, they carry the loss within their psyche and feel something is missing. Some boys search for their fathers and idealize them. If they do find them, they take the chance that they will be rejected again.

One man described how, when he was in high school, he asked his mother for his father's telephone number. He had not known his father since he was three years old. He traveled to the state where his father lived, called him and asked to come over to the house. The father had never told his wife about this child and didn't want to do it at this point. The father and son met at a restaurant, spoke, and that was the end of it. In the past ten years, they have not contacted each other again. However, the young man said, "At least I could see where I get some of my physical features."

Boys need fathers to do things with, to find out what the life of a man is, to test themselves against. Fathers represent the outside world, the society, the rules, and the expectations. They teach the boy not to give in to his wants, but to overcome his instincts, take himself in hand, and take responsibility for himself. Often fathers teach sons to overcome their fears and dependencies. While this can sometimes be harsh, boys long for the authority of a caring father. When it is not there, they have to father themselves. The problem emerges when they become fathers and have not worked through their feelings towards their own fathers. The father has a strong influence on the boy's sense of self. He defines himself as like his father or unlike his father, but his father is his point of reference. When that is not there, he is unsure of who he is.

Boys without a positive relationship to their fathers grow into men who have something in their soul life that does not feel complete. Peace has to be made eventually, preferably before the father passes on. The death of a father has a significant impact, even on the adult male. The need for a father-son relationship is not only important for the son; it is also important for the father.

Girls without Fathers

In the Medieval setting of the story, it was typical that girls would not have a close relationship with their fathers who were knights. However, in modern society this relationship is an important one. Girls need their fathers as a model of a man in their lives.

Over and over again I worked with adolescent girls who experienced pain that their fathers had disappeared from their lives. The girls fantasized who their fathers were and wanted to reconnect so that they could have a "Daddy." Many times when the situation was arranged so they could live with the father they had not really known, the results were very disappointing. In many cases, they moved out-of-state to try this new living situation, and often it meant giving up their school and friends. But the need was so great that they chose to do it. A few months later, they returned to school disillusioned with their fathers but determined to make their lives meaningful without them. If they had never left to try to renew the relationship, they would have lived in illusion from then on. The experience, although unpleasant, broke the illusion and allowed the girls to move on with their lives.

Girls have expectations that their fathers will support them, look after them, protect them, and help them make their way in the world. When their fathers disappear, they are left feeling abandoned and vulnerable. When they have a strong mother who models for them independence and inner power, the girls are able to develop their own independence. But the feeling of being left never quite goes away.

Elyce Wakerman, in her book *Fatherloss*, traces the effect on girls based on the reasons their fathers left and their attitude toward men. I have lent this book to girls without fathers many times in hopes it would help them become aware of their unconscious needs. There are various reasons why a girl doesn't have a father; divorce, death through illness or accident, abandonment, suicide are the most common. In addition, there are girls who never knew their fathers. Either their mother never told them who he was or she didn't know.

It is generally accepted that a father is particularly important for a girl's sex-role development. Wakerman quotes psychotherapist Marjorie Leonard:

It is not enough that the mother is available for identification. The girl also needs reassurance from her father that he sees her as a budding female, so that she can have confidence that males her own age will also accept it. . . . Crucial to the girl's development is whether or not her father was available to her as a love-object and whether or not he was capable of offering her affection. (p. 19)

Some of the issues that arise are:

- The discomfort of a girl when people ask her who her father is, what he does, and where he lives.
- The feeling that something is wrong with her. A cloud hovers over her house.
- A feeling that she and her father would have been very close.
- Proving she can do things on her own without a man.
- Wanting a man who could take care of her.
- Feeling rejected because he had left her.
- Feeling he must not have loved her enough.

These feelings are transferred to boyfriends and husbands. A man is the most important figure in a family. He is almost godlike. She looks for an older man she can count on. She expects the man to disappear. She is afraid of commitment. She is ambivalent. She longs for a man, wants to hold on to him at all costs; at the same time, she doesn't trust him.

Wakerman explores the relationship of a father's disappearance to the daughter's stage of development when he leaves. She also comments on the influence of other men in a girl's life.

Though it is widely believed that a father substitute can go a long way toward alleviating the absence of the biological father in a girl's life, the women in our study were surprisingly indifferent toward and unaffected by, men who acted as surrogates—except in the case of grandfathers! Alone among surrogate fathers, these men were able to make a positive contribution to their father-absent granddaughters' lives, helping them to feel more confident and assertive than fatherless women whose grandfathers did not participate in their upbringing. (p. 53)

Girls who grow up without fathers are less traumatized when they have a brother. Perhaps it is because they have the experience of interacting with a male, feeling his protectiveness and observing his way of being. They also get to meet his male friends, so their experience of growing up is not only with women.

Some of the qualities girls who grow up without fathers may have are insecurity, hostility toward life, anxiety, caution, and a need to prove herself.

As adults working with teenagers or parenting them, it is important for us to realize the impact on boys and girls when they are fatherless. This has become a common factor in modern American society, affecting the choice of partners as well as parenting attitudes.

Relationship between Muslim and Christian

The interconnection between Muslim and Christian knights was already referred to when Gahmuret chose to serve the strongest leader in the world, the Baruch of Baghdad. Although Wolfram describes anyone who is not Christian as heathen, he respects Muslims' courtly behavior, their courage, and their wealth. There seems to be little difference between Christian and Muslim knights. Knights of either religion share traits of knightly manner and courtly love. This unites them and creates a brotherhood between them. "Heathen" also refers to those who believe in gods and goddesses. Feirefiz is a heathen in this sense.

This is particularly interesting because the story is set in the 9th century. For hundreds of years, Spain had been the cultural center of Europe, where Christians, Muslims, and Jews lived and interacted with each other. From the universities and scholarly tradition in Spain, much knowledge especially in science and mathematics came into Europe and influenced European culture. However, the Muslim influence weakened through religious schisms and infighting. The Reconquest of Spain by the Christians ended this period and both Jews and Muslims suffered through the Inquisition.

However, Trevrizent tells Parzival that the knowledge of the Grail comes from Flegetanis, a learned Muslim scholar from whose book Kyot first learned about the Grail. Regardless of whether Flegetanis actually existed, Wolfram's mention of him is an acknowledgement of the great debt that medieval Christendom owes to Islamic learning .

During the Middle Ages, Africa and Asia were both referred to as the East. Feirefiz and Parzival as half-brothers of East and West, North and South, unite these two traditions of knowledge and custom. Gawain, carrying more of the European flavor, adds a third element, heralding a future time when races and religions will be integrated as parts of one whole.

Placing the legend of Parzival in its historic context highlights the importance of adolescents' developing an understanding of history. The task of each generation is to make decisions concerning the future. Without a good sense of historical perspective, it is difficult to have a breadth of vision. Questions that can be addressed are: What are the patterns of behavior? What is the relationship between nations? What is the history of a people? What are the differing values?

Only by studying history can a teenager place himself or herself in the stream of time. As Thoreau said, "Time is the stream I go a-drinking in." In other words, we are influenced by the time in which we live, we participate in its past as well as its present. Just as each of us carries our biographical experiences hidden within our judgments, decisions, and attitudes, so do people in a region or country. It makes a big difference in understanding a political decision when we understand the spiritual life of the people, their religion, their customs, their tastes, their fears, and their dreams.

Teenagers can deepen their understanding of history by taking courses in school, by participating in extra-curricular activities such as the Model United Nations, Junior State, or Amnesty International. They can become interns in their local government, participate in living history projects such as Foxfire, or oral history projects in their local retirement center. Reading newspapers, magazines, using the Internet, and seeing films are all important ways to stay in touch with history and the present. Some of the most exciting ways to bring history alive is through travel. Whether it is a summer exploration, a service project abroad or within one's own country, a student-exchange term, travel gives the student a direct experience of history, geography, anthropology, and art. What is most important is the need to avoid knowledge by sound-byte, but to penetrate deeper to gain understanding. The appearance of Feirefiz in the legend awakens us to the themes of the relationship between adolescent and father and of historical perspective.

Chapter 16

Each Person Has Masculine and Feminine Qualities

Book XVI. *Parzival becomes Lord of the Grail*

The planets have returned to the conjunction during which Anfortas experiences the greatest pain. His agony seems relentless, and he begs to be relieved of the pain by death. Only because his attendants place him before the Grail, does he continue to survive. Deeply angry that they will not let him die, Anfortas says he has atoned for his sins, and they will be sorry that they don't have enough pity on him to let him die.

The Grail knights are holding out for the second coming of the knight who has not asked the question on his previous visit. It is only because Trevrizent has read this on the Grail that they keep Anfortas alive. They do whatever they can to make him comfortable and sweeten the air to ventilate the stench of the wound,

Parzival, Feirefiz, and Cundrie faced danger and attack along the way, but now they approach the Grail castle. Templars ride out to defend the Grail Castle against strangers, but when they see the turtledoves on Cundrie's cloak, they remove their helmets and honor Parzival and his brother Feirefiz. They accompany them into the great hall where they are received with complete courtesy, given rich garments, and brought refreshing drinks.

Then they go over to Anfortas. He is resting on his ornately decorated couch in both anguish and joy. Anfortas begs Parzival to encourage his attendants to let him die, or if he is Parzival, keep him from the sight of the Grail for seven nights and eight days, at which time he would die. Parzival, sobbing at the suffering Anfortas is experiencing, asks, "Tell me where the Grail is kept here." Then he bows three times in the direction of the Grail, stands up, and asks Anfortas, "Uncle, what is it that troubles you?"

Anfortas is healed and made well again. As Anfortas regains his life forces, he becomes more beautiful than any of the other knights. Parzival is proclaimed King and Lord of the Grail.

Condwiramur received the message that her time of waiting was over. She is guided to the forest on her way to the Grail Castle.

Meanwhile, Parzival takes some of the Grail knights and rides to see Trevrizent who is relieved and happy that Anfortas is now healed. Trevrizent says, "A greater miracle has seldom come to pass, for you have forced God by defiance to make His infinite Trinity grant your will. I told you a lie to keep you from the Grail. I grieved for your trials, for it had never happened that anyone could ever fight his way to the Grail."

Parzival asks Trevrizent for his advice and permission to depart to meet Condwiramur. Trevrizent blesses him and sends him on his way. The next morning he comes to an area where many tents are set up with identification that reveals they are Parzival's countrymen. Duke Kyot of Catalonia recognizes the turtledoves and welcomes Parzival and his men with courtesy. After making sure the knights would all be well cared for, he takes Parzival and guides him to the queen's chambers. Parzival removes his armor and enters the chamber. There he finds his twin sons lying in bed with their mother. She awakens and sees her husband, jumps up and they embrace. Parzival lovingly kisses his boys who also woke up. Kyot has the boys taken away, bids all the ladies to leave, and leaves Parzival and his wife to themselves for a while.

Then they arise and a priest sings Mass. The grand army that had once fought against Clamide welcomes Parzival. He announces that his young son Kardeiz will become the ruler of all of his lands. He asks them for their support until the boy comes into adulthood, and the boy is crowned.

After a fine meal, the army sets out with the young king to return to their homeland. After farewells are exchanged, the Templars, who are the knights of the Grail, accompany Parzival, Condwiramur, and Lohengrin to the Grail Castle.

Parzival asks the Templars whether they know where a hermitage is with a brook running through it. They do know and they agree to lead him there. When they arrive at the hermitage, they find Sigune still in a posture of prayer, dead. They raise the stone from the coffin and place her beside Schianatulander and close the grave. This is especially painful for Condwiramur because Sigune is her cousin and childhood companion.

When they arrive at the Grail Castle, there is Feirefiz waiting for them. He leads Condwiramur into the great hall with three large fires burning and takes Lohengrin into his arms, but the child is unsure of him due to his black and white color and does not kiss him. Feirefiz laughs at this. There are many maidens standing nearby, but Feirefiz walks up to the Queen Condwiramur. She kisses him and also kisses Anfortas. There is much rejoicing.

On this special occasion, the hall is glowing from all the lit candles. The Grail procession will precede the dinner. Parzival and Feirefiz sit together with Anfortas. Twenty-five maidens walk in front of Parzival. Feirefiz is most interested in the beautiful maidens, and especially in Repanse de Schoye who is the only one allowed to carry the Grail. It becomes clear that Feirefiz cannot see the Grail so he cannot figure out what keeps filling the dishes and goblets. However, he is most moved by Repanse de Schoye who has captured his heart.

The old man with white hair in the inner castle supposes the reason Feirefiz cannot see the Grail is that he is not baptized. What he can see is the beauty of Repanse de Schoye. Under the spell of her beauty, his love for his wife dies away. He is totally captivated by Repanse. He expects his god Jupiter to help him gain her love.

In the morning Parzival and Anfortas walk with Feirefiz into the temple of the Grail to the baptismal font. Parzival tells him he will have to give up the gods and goddesses he believes in, and also his wife Secundille because she is not baptized either. The only reason Feirefiz agrees to be baptized is that he thinks Repanse de Schoye will be more responsive to him then. Feirefiz will do anything to be rewarded with her love, and so he is baptized.

Now he can see the Grail. Written upon it is that any Templar whom God appoints as ruler in a foreign land can help the people gain their rights, but they cannot ask him any questions. If they do, he must depart and that is the end of the help he can give them. Eschenbach tells us that the Templars don't like questions because Anfortas had to wait so long for the question to be asked of him.

Feirefiz invites Anfortas to go with him on adventures, but Anfortas explains he has left that life behind him. "Wealth and love of women are now receding from my mind." He tells Feirefiz that he will go out to battle in the service of the Grail, but not for women. Then Feirefiz wants to take Lohengrin with him, but Condwiramur does not allow that.

For eleven days festivities continue until on the twelfth day Feirefiz, along with his new wife Repanse de Schoye, leaves to join his armies at the harbor. Parzival has sent Anfortas and soldiers to clear the way for them, and Cundrie the sorceress also went in front to make sure they were well treated and arrived at the harbor safely. Many tears are shed as they disappear from view. When they arrive at the harbor, they receive the news that Queen Secundille has died. Although Feirefiz is saddened by this, Repanse de Schoye can be relieved about the journey to the East now.

The happy couple travel to the East. In India Repanse gives birth to a son named John. People called him Prester John. From that time on, all kings have been called Prester John. Feirefiz orders writings about Christianity to be sent throughout the East, and he continues to send messages back through Cundrie to let Parzival know how he is.

Lohengrin grows up to be brave and a true servant of the Grail. He is chosen to marry a pure and noble woman, the princess of Brabant. He is brought to the shore of a lake by a swan. He becomes her husband on the condition that she will never ask who he is or she will lose his love. Later on, she does ask him, and the swan returns to bring him a boat by which he will return to the Grail Castle. He left as remembrances a sword, a horn, and a ring. Here was a case where a maiden was forbidden to question.

Out of Many One

All the characters in the story of Parzival can be seen as aspects of one human being. Some aspects are more identified with the masculine side and others with the feminine, but we all have all of them in our soul life. Some are overt and others hide in the shadows ready to emerge in particular situations.

Masculine Qualities

Feeling restless, longing for adventure—Gahmuret, with his choice of an anchor as his shield, is a good example of the adolescent's desire for excitement and willingness to break new ground, go to new places, try new experiences, and even participate in risk-taking behavior. The key word here is excitement. A twelfth grader expressed his feelings in this way:

> What is it about man's being that causes him to strive for greatness, for knowledge, insight, understanding, and freedom? Why does man strive to find meaning in life? Why is he not just content to carry out life meeting the basic needs of survival? Why is it that man strives to express himself? Why is there music or art? Why is there such a need for self-expression? What is there that is

working in the universe that is working in man, some-where deep in man, which compels him to strive at all? What is at the root of man's spirit? . . . I want to carry out my life to the fullest, ready to experience as much as possible. I see my role on earth as a man of men—to live life to the fullest.

Lusting—Clingsor. This occurs at least in the imagination, in fantasy, in many teenagers. There are others who go beyond imagination and are driven by desires to use another youngster solely for his or her pleasure. One body will do as well as another. The lusting part can also be the older boy looking at the younger girl, or the older girl using power over a younger boy. The key word here is power. The lusting part of the human soul today is encouraged by song lyrics, television, movies, and video images that connect sex with violence. It is expressed in the increasing rate of date rape on our campuses.

Thinking—Parzival shows us the aspect of the soul that tries to understand the world. He is not interested in the activity in the castles along the way. He has a clear goal—to find the Grail again. The goal itself is not the important thing; what is important is that he gains understanding through Trevrizent's teachings. He still has the warrior in him and wants to fight his way to the Grail, but it is in his understanding that he realizes his destiny, his family lineage, and his future. As a twelfth grade boy put it, "It is my feeling that ultimate truth lies within the individual. . . . The future will teach us many things, maybe even the meaning of life."

Suffering—the wounded King Anfortas. This part of the teenager is the aspect in which he or she feels wounded. This can be a physical hurt, but more usually it is a soul hurt. This can range from rejection by a parent to rejection by another teenager. The youngster often cannot heal this by him or herself. Help from a wise adult or a professional is needed to help the teenager understand the cause of the hurt and what can be done about it. Someone important to the youngster needs to ask, "What ails thee?"

Contemplation—Trevrizent. Teenagers have the need to go inward, to find times of solitude to keep their own counsel. This spiritual task helps the youngster sort out priorities and make inner commitments. This quality acts as a balance to being active so much of the time.

Innocence—young Parzival in the forest of Soltane. This is the part of the adolescent that still carries the child within. Unwilling or unready to face growing up, he or she wants to hold back and stay young and innocent. This quality is seen in the naïveté of Parzival's orientation in life, in the way he went off in fool's clothing, and in the way he spoke to people "the way my mother told me."

Friendliness—Gawain is the aspect of the adolescent that reaches out to bring harmony and reconciliation. He represents the part of the teenager that listens to friend's problems, supports them in their struggles and perceives their needs. At times the friendly aspect has to recede as the teenager needs to find time for him- or herself. But in general, this quality radiates love.

Charm—Feirefiz is a delightful character. He represents the part of the teenager that is direct, honorable, and spirited. His buoyancy brings a lightness to the scenes he is in. There is a generosity and joy to his actions. The part of the teenager that makes a room vibrate with excitement and joy reflects this quality. Friends gather round this person and enjoy this quality. It enhances their own sense of life.

Fatherly protection—Arthur is the lawgiver, the overseer, the father quality in the teenager. This quality comes out when the teenager is with younger children, protecting and guiding them. It is also an inner quality in which the teenager begins to direct his or her own actions in a lawful manner.

Feminine Qualities

Grieving—Sigune represents the part of the teenager that feels the losses in life. Adolescents take the loss of a parent, a grandparent, an early love, or a family pet very deeply. When parents divorce, teenagers grieve and hold on to images from the past when the family unit was intact, as well as considering themselves causes of the divorce. Sigune is an example of one who grieves in an exaggerated manner until she herself dies. The adolescent whose grief is exaggerated cannot move ahead in his or her life, just as Sigune could take no further step beyond being loyal to the dead Schianatulander. One of the hardest situations in this regard is the loss of a parent through suicide. The teenager has a hard time letting go of the thought: He or she didn't love me enough to stay alive.

Protection—Herzeloyde. What part of the teenager is this protective gesture? When an adolescent has been hurt through abuse or loss, he or she may put up defenses to keep from being hurt again. She may protect herself by being aggressive toward others before they can hurt her, become ill to keep from having to venture out and leave home, or create a wall around herself as a fortress of protection. She cannot bear it when she is unable to protect herself any longer and may become self-destructive or, as Herzeloyde did, die of a broken heart. It may be that eating disorders are connected with this Herzeloyde gesture.

Ideal love—Condwiramur represents that part of the adolescent that longs for ideal love. Condwiramur's relationship with Parzival was a spiritual one. For three nights they did not touch each other. Then he remembered his mother's advice to take a woman in his arms, and he did. Condwiramur lives in Parzival's soul as an anchor as he makes his journey. She is the image of the perfect feminine which, united with his masculinity, creates a unity. At the end of his journey she is there to join with him in fulfilling his destiny. She may be the symbol of the crush which the adolescent has and who is placed on a pedestal.

Messenger between our inner world and the outer world—Cundrie represents that part of adolescents that lives in the darkness of their soul, confronting them with the things they don't like about themselves. She is the teacher within who wakens them to their shadow. She stings them to get them moving to go beyond the obvious and take on the task of their hidden destiny.

Temptress—Antikonie is the part of the adolescent's soul that flirts, lures on the other, and seduces. She is openly suggestive, unafraid of who is watching or telling. She is reckless, and exciting. She allows the adolescent to be daring, sexual, and risqué. This is all in a wholesome open way. She does not lurk in shadows but acts in the light of day. Yet she is ready to take risks, defy authority, and do what she wants with her head held high.

Loyalty—Bene is the part of the adolescent that is devoted to others, willing to sacrifice herself for the joy of others, the needs of others, and the well-being of others. She feels deeply. She is that part of the teenager that goes between boys and girls, finding out who likes whom, delivering messages from one to another, yet she does not give much attention to her own feelings.

Shrewishness and testing—Orgeluse is that part of the teenager that tests others to see if they are worthy of attention. At times haughty, at times sorrowful, she is prepared to go a long way to find out if a fellow teenager is worthy or not. She may scheme and manipulate, but underneath there is a soft heart that has been hurt. When she is convinced she is valued, her strength and grace prevail and she takes on some of the Arthur role as a lawmaker.

The Journey through the Sacred Passage

In the journey through adolescence the teenager passes from an old place to a new place and to a new position in the community. These changes can be assisted by trials and rites of passage that mark a new status and a new awareness. In traditional societies in the past elders knew what they had to teach their young. Today there are differences that affect the teenager's pathway—elders are going through their own transition, adolescents are more individual than they were in the past, and few cultures are homogenous so a sense of continuity and sameness is difficult to sustain. While this makes life exciting, it is also destabilizing. There is little one can count on, especially during adolescence when everything is internally chaotic. Girls need older girls and female elders to guide them, with male elders in the background as support. Boys need to separate from their mothers and find a relationship with an all-male group. Their mothers, as female elders, need to continue to support them but at the same time to let them find their relationship to men.

Rites of passage help this transition because they include a connection between the generations. A significant rite of passage recognizes those in the community who have supported the child up to this time, and it creates a new role for the adults as well as for the youngster who takes on a new status in the community. As the teenager takes up responsibility and is able to be given more freedom, he or she begins the exploration, the adventure, out into the world. This is the winding path of life through which he or she will discover the connection between love and wisdom.

When the teenager hears the call to begin the journey of separating from the family (early adolescence) through the peers (middle adolescence) into the Self (late adolescence), everything depends on what he or she will meet along the way. What will be the trial of water, the trial of fire, the trial of earth, the trial of air? When the youngster returns to the family at whatever time that is, he or she will be a different person. What kind of different person will depend on the nature of the experiences, the lessons learned, and the consciousness gained about life. In this journey toward wholeness, the soul and spiritual "I" or Self of the adolescent meets the Self of the world. This meeting may be traumatic, even life-threatening, or it may be a smooth passage. On the nature of this passage depends the quality of the decades to come.

The Boy's Development through the Sacred Passage

Internalizing the Gawain character. Gawain represents the feeling part of the boy's development. He has to learn to balance his feelings, tame his desires, urges, and impulses, and find an appropriate relationship to the women in his life and to the feminine in himself. He becomes the true lover. The Castle of Wonders is Gawain's rite of passage. The tasks along his journey are:

1. To find a balanced respectful relationship to a woman in which he is upright and clear.
2. To find balance in his wish to compete and best his challenger.
3. To control his tongue.
4. To control his desire.
5. To distinguish between fantasy (illusion) and reality.

6. To find a new relationship to his family—saving the honor of his father's reputation, freeing his mother, sisters, and grandmother from their frozen state so they could become part of his life again.
7. Gaining the support of his teacher/mentor, King Arthur, who will bear witness to his battle with Gramoflanz.
8. Figuring out how to resolve the conflict of caring for his sister and honoring his father's memory without hurting either of them.
9. Reconciling those who have differences with each other.
10. Serving love in its pure form.
11. Responding with courtesy and delicacy to situations
12. Being at peace with himself.

The words that have to do with the transformation of feelings include those above—finding balance, controlling desires and speech, distinguishing, reconciling, loving, courtesy, delicacy, and peace. When the boy has gained a beginning mastery of these feelings, he has passed the first stage in the transforming of his feeling life and is ready to set out into the world. Granted, this is only the first stage, for he will return to these challenges on many different levels during his manhood.

Internalizing the Parzival character. Parzival represents the thinking part of the boy's development. He has to learn who he is, understand his background, and gain a vision of his destiny. He needs good teachers who enter his life at the right moment to teach him the skills he is ready to learn and use. Through these experiences he becomes a clear thinker who is able to direct his action with purpose. Finding, losing, and finding the Grail Castle is Parzival's rite of passage. Parzival's tasks are to:

1. Understand the meaning behind advice and not to get stuck in a literal interpretation.
2. Know why he does what he does. Think before doing.
3. Know when to hold his tongue and when to ask a question.
4. Know which battles to engage in and which to pass by.
5. Seek out true teachers and listen to their wisdom.

6. Reach out to others with compassion and interest.
7. Be faithful in love.
8. Set a goal and persevere until it is accomplished.
9. Listen to the voice of his higher self. Perceive the truth even when it is painful.
10. Be conscious of his actions rather than react to situations.
11. Find a connection with his parents, either in life or across the threshold of death.
12. Recognize and appreciate those who help him along the way, even when it doesn't feel good.

The task of the first stage of transforming his thinking includes the above words—understanding, knowing, seeking, reaching out, being faithful, setting goals, persevering, listening, being conscious, finding connections, and recognizing. If the boy has made an effort to start this process, he has the tools to set out on his journey toward manhood.

Internalizing the Feirefiz character. Feirefiz represents the will part of the boy's development. He has to keep an openness to those he meets, share his energy and strength with his companions along the way, be generous with his community, and trust his intuition. He is the true friend. Feirefiz's tasks are to:

1. Gain self-confidence and feel worthy enough to meet his father's expectations.
2. Be brave in battle and conquer many lands.
3. Be generous to his friends and enemies.
4. Be a good leader to his armies.
5. Be sharp of mind and know when to engage in battle and when to call a truce.
6. Overcome naïveté.
7. Temper impulsive action with thoughtfulness.
8. Commit to meaningful relationships.
9. Demonstrate forthrightness.
10. Support friends.
11. Give service to others.
12. Be gentle and loving to small children.

Let us look at the words connected with the transformation of the will—gaining self-confidence, feeling worthy, being brave, being generous, being a good leader, being discriminating, giving service, being gentle and loving. These are the means by which the boy learns proportion, balance, and equanimity in his actions. Then his actions can be of service to the world.

The boy's development is not complete without the feminine qualities he internalizes from the women in the story. Each character becomes part of his wholeness.

The Girl's Development through the Sacred Passage

The girl's journey is more horizontal. She gathers up qualities from many more characters in building her wholeness. In the legend of Parzival we don't follow one of the female characters in detail, but we experience the qualities that each represents. The girl's task are to:

1. Choose her boyfriends carefully, watching the situations she gets into when several boys are courting her favors. Although some good may come out of the relationship, she may find herself in a situation she didn't count on. (Belakane)
2. Be careful not to control people as a way of protecting herself and live out of herself, not through another person. (Herzeloyde)
3. Be loyal and supportive, knowing when to allow her partner to follow his own destiny. (Condwiramur)
4. Learn self-respect. She should not allow herself to be mistreated by the males in her life. (Jeschute)
5. Understand the spiritual meaning of a relationship. (Sigune)
6. Be patient and steadfast through hard times. (Sigune)
7. See beyond appearances to sense the nobility within another person. (Lady Cunneware)
8. Keep purity in her soul. (Repanse de Schoye)
9. Bring truth into relationships even though this is not wanted. In time her good intentions will be revealed. (Cundrie)

10. Not try to overcome past hurts by hurting other people. (Orgeluse)
11. Not allow arrogance to block openness and vulnerability. (Orgeluse)
12. Be gracious in actions and understand the man in her life. (Guinevere)

Let us look at the words that arise in connection with her journey—careful choosing, don't control people, live out of herself, learn self-respect, understand, be patient, see beyond appearances, be pure in soul, bring truth, do not hurt, don't be arrogant, be gracious.

In addition, she incorporates the masculine elements from the male journey. She is Parzival, seeking to understand her past, her present struggles, and her future destiny through clear thinking and deep understanding. She needs to be awake. She is Gawain, seeking to reconcile those who have had misunderstandings, free people from emotional quagmires, and learn to control her desires, her tongue, and to distinguish reality from fantasy. She is Feirefiz, a true companion, generous, open, and filled with goodwill. Incorporating these qualities represented by the various characters in the parzival legend is the challenge of maturity.

Conclusion

Dear Reader,

We have now completed parallel journeys—that of Parzival and his friends and that of modern adolescents. The journey or passage takes place during seven or eight fragile years that set the stage for the adult experience. Everything that happens along the way opens up new possibilities. Which path will the teenager choose at each crossroad? Some roads will lead to deep and difficult learning experiences; other roads will lead to profoundly meaningful relationships; some roads will lead to temptation; other roads will wind round and round before the end comes into view. One thing we can be sure of. Each choice provides opportunities in which adolescents can wake up to responsibility, to service, and to love—if they choose.

We adults cannot judge how the journey will go for each of the adolescents we know. But one thing is for sure. What we do during their adolescent years, how we support teenagers, how we make ourselves available, how we clean up our own acts and become authentic—will be gifts we can offer adolescents during these unstable and unclear years. The teenagers may not recognize our efforts or thank us at the time. That will come later. Now we just need to observe, relate, and act.

In the introduction, I referred to two poems. I will return to them now and look at them from the vantage point of having shared the journey of adolescence with you. William Blake's four lines capture the polarities of adolescence.

> *Joy and woe are woven fine*
> *A clothing for the Soul divine:*
> *Under every grief and pine*
> *Runs a joy with silken twine.*

One of the frustrations in working with teenagers is that they live in the tension of joy and woe. As their souls are expanding in this stage of life, they often seem as if they live in two states of consciousness at once. On one hand, they dream the impossible dreams, they have the highest hopes for humanity, they want to save the rain forests, they love animals, they love little children, they are gentle and caring, they want to protect the innocent. On the other hand, they can be thoughtless in regard to the environment, littering the ground with plastic lunch bags or Styrofoam cups, or revving up their cars sending clouds of pollution skyward. They often mistreat their bodies by gorging on junk food, smoking, using drugs, drinking alcohol, and tolerating loud pounding music piercing their eardrums. They fill their inner life with violent images from movies or video-games.

Yet the mystery is that in this duality of idealism and pain, of caring and misusing, of joy and woe, something breaks through, something that we can only call holy. But there is a risk. This generation of young people seems to need to confront darkness, violence, pain—to dip into it, face it, not run away from it. Through the thousands of images taken in from the television and movies or the zapping of the enemy in video games, they may become desensitized to the real pain of real people and not be able to respond caringly. They may damage their bodies and not be able to carry out their intentions or spend years in rehabilitation. However, if the core of their personality is strong and healthy, there will come a moment when they see what is happening, and out of their own individuality, they will decide to change their lives. They will say No to their habits and patterns of behaving, and they will reorient themselves. I have heard descriptions of this change over and over again in working with people in their twenties and thirties. In those moments, the divine shines through its covering of joy and woe, of grief and pain. They know it, and it sustains them through the next phase of the journey.

The other poem is by Rainer Maria Rilke. It offers specific ways in which teenagers can build the inner core of strength so that they can be able to move through the passage with health and purpose.

As once the winged energy of delight
Carried you over childhood's dark abysses,
Now beyond your own life build the great
Arch of unimagined bridges.
Wonders happen if we can succeed
In passing through the harshest danger;
But only in a bright and purely granted
Achievement can we realize the wonder.
To work with Things in the indescribable
Relationship is not too hard for us.
The pattern grows more intricate and subtle,
And being swept along is not enough.
Take your practiced powers and stretch them out
Until they span the chasm between two
Contradictions . . . For the god
Wants to know himself in you.

As I said above, adolescence is a big risk. It is a dangerous time, a turbulent time. Coming to terms with one's identity is a fragile experience. Who am I? What do I have to take me through this frightening venture? Where is the rudder in these perilous waters?

The first clue in this poem is the winged energy of delight. I don't want to put my own words into Rilke's imaginations, yet they come nevertheless. What experiences does the teenager carry from childhood that have the quality of winged energy of delight, delight that is so delicious he or she knows it comes from some other reality, and is held in the heart realm as a precious treasure, captured in memory, looked back to with a smile. It may have been the morning a brother or sister was born, an inner conversation with a beloved pet dog, the excitement of a thunderstorm, the comfort of sitting in a mother or father's lap, or being put to bed with a song. Those childhood treasures are the building blocks of a new consciousness. Without them, the teenager has nothing to hold in his or her heart. It is then a lonely world, indeed. Even one good memory can be a golden thread.

The second clue is that Rilke is speaking directly to the teenager.

Now beyond your own life build the great
Arch of unimagined bridges

Set yourself goals, way out beyond what seems possible. You do it! You build that great arch that you'll pass through. There's the road going under it. It's your road, the one you are building. Dream big!

> *But only in a bright and purely granted*
> *Achievement can we realize the wonder.*
> *To work with Things in the indescribable*
> *Relationship is not too hard for us.*

Dreaming isn't enough. Rilke adds the hard work to the dream. He adds the word But. You have to energize your will. You have to make achievements happen. You have to work with Things, not in a casual, even careless way. No, that won't work. You have to work in the indescribable relationship. You have to find the Other, the I-Thou relationship. It's not too hard. You can do it if you understand the power of it. How do you work with things? You have to have interest, pay attention, notice, commit yourself. This is a true high that doesn't come from drugs, but from the inner light of wonder.

> *The pattern grows more intricate and subtle,*
> *And being swept along is not enough.*

Once you realize the power that comes from this relationship, you begin to see subtlety in nature, in human relationships, in serving others, and you realize that it makes a difference what each person does in his or her life. Once you see that everything is interconnected, you no longer will just want to do whatever you've been doing in the past. Why? Because the actions of every person are important. What I do affects other people. What others do affects me. If I do nothing, that also has an effect. We all affect life on the planet. At this point, there is an inner change, and you cannot go back to your previous consciousness. Your ideals are becoming real and possible. Once this experience happens—and it doesn't happen to every teenager, at least not within the teen years—he or she has a skill, a practiced power that can be used.

What does Rilke suggest now?

> *Take your practiced powers and stretch them out*
> *Until they span the chasm between two*
> *Contradictions . . .*

Now we are back to the joy and woe, the pleasure and pain, the beautiful and the ugly. But they are no longer separate emotions. Through this new capacity, you can see that joy and woe are all part of the same experience of being human, the interconnectedness of all things spans the chasm between what used to be seen as contradictions, of hypocrisy, of the imperfection of the world.

And then comes the most powerful statement of all. Once you develop this capacity, the spiritual world speaks. It doesn't only speak. It becomes aware of itself through the efforts of you, a single human being.

> *For the god*
> *Wants to know himself in you.*

When that awareness comes, you are no longer alone. You are connected to everything. Furthermore, your life and your efforts actually help the spiritual world to become conscious of itself. The spiritual world needs you. You matter.

In Book Nine, Parzival had this experience when he was speaking with Trevrizent. Trevrizent was interested in Parzival. He saw the Other in the flawed young man. Parzival experienced this love and it awakened his own capacity to love the world, to love God, and to be able to take responsibility for his past deeds. He experienced the awakening capacity to be able to ask the grieving Anfortas, "Uncle, what ails you?"

This experience is a passage. Although it can occur at any time, it usually happens after the 16–17 year period. The teenager becomes a vessel for the incoming experience of "I," and the awareness of being an "I" makes it possible for the teenager to stand outside himself or herself and see the world in a new way.

It is powerful, it is frightening, and it is holy.

Bibliography

Albert, B., S. Brown, C. Flanigan, eds. *14 and Younger: The Sexual Behavior of Young Adolescents.* The National Campaign to Prevent Teen Pregnancy, 2003.

Bergh Kirsten. *She Would Draw Flowers: A Book of Poems.* Linda Bergh, Minneapolis, 1997.

Biddulph, Steve. *Manhood: An Action Plan for Changing Men's Lives.* Stroud, UK: Hawthorn Press, 1998.

Biddulph, Steve and Shaaron. *Raising Boys: Why Boys Are Different and How to Help Them Become Happy and Well-balanced Men.* Berkeley, CA: Celestial Arts, 1998.

Caron, A. *Don't Stop Loving Me: A Reassuring Guide for Mothers of Adolescent Daughters.* New York: HarperCollins, 1991.

Elium, D & J. *Raising a Teenager: Parents and the Nurturing of a Responsible Teen.* Berkeley, CA: Celestial Arts, 1999.

———. *Raising a Son: Parents and the Making of a Healthy Man.* Beyond Words Pub. Co., Oregon, 1992.

———. *Raising a Daughter: Parents and the Awakening of a Healthy Woman.* Berkeley, CA: Celestial Arts, 1994.

Elkind, David. *The Hurried Child: Growing Up Too Fast Too Soon.* Reading, MA: Addison-Wesley, 1981.

von Eschenbach, Wolfram. *Parzival: A Romance of the Middle Ages,* translated by Helen M. Mustard and Charles E. Passage. New York: Vintage Books, 1961.

Fryer, A., L. Knodle, and T. Slayton. *I Find My Star Curriculum: An Artful and Community Building Approach to the Inner and Outer Changes of Puberty and Adolescence.* Manuscript

Garbarino, J. *Lost Boys: Why Our Sons Turn Violent and How We Can Save Them.* New York: Anchor Books, 2000.

Gilligan, C. *In a Different Voice: Psychological Theory and Women's Development.* Cambridge, MA: Harvard U. Press, 1982.

Gilligan, C., N. Lyons, and T. Hanmer. *Making Connections: The Relational Worlds of Adolescent Girls at Emma Willard School.* Cambridge, MA: Harvard U. Press, 1990

Gurian, M. *Boys and Girls Learn Differently.* San Francisco: Jossey-Bass, 2001.

———. *A Fine Young Man.* New York: Jeremy Tarcher, 1998.

Hawley, R. *The Big Issues in the Adolescent Journey.* New York: Walker and Co., 1988.

Kindlon, D., and M. Thompson. *Raising Cain: Protecting the Emotional Life of Boys.* New York: Ballantine, 2000.

Klagsbrun, F. *Too Young to Die: Youth and Suicide.* New York: Pocket Books, 1976.

Luxford, M., ed. *Adolescence and its Significance for those with Special Needs.* Great Britain: Camphill Books, TWT Publications, 1995.

Mahdi, L., Christopher, N., and M. Meade, eds. *Crossroads: The Quest for Contemporary Rites of Passage.* Chicago: Carus Publishing Company, 1996.

Olivardia, Roberto, Katherine Phillips, and Harrison Pope, Jr. *The Adonis Complex: How to Identify, Treat and Prevent Body Obsession in Men and Boys.* New Jersey: Free Press, 2002.

Pipher, M. *Reviving Ophelia: Saving the Selves of Adolescent Girls.* New York: Ballantine Books, 1994.

Pollack, W. *Real Boys' Voices.* New York: Random House, 2000.

Pope, Harrison G., Katharine Phillips and Roberto Olivardia, *The Adonis Complex: The Secret Life of Obsession.* New York: Simon & Schuster, 2000.

Rideout, V., D. Roberts, and U. Foehr, eds. *Generation M: Media in the Lives of 8-18 Year-olds.* A Kaiser Family Foundation Study, March 2005.

Simpson, A. *Raising Teens: A Synthesis of Research and a Foundation for Action.* Center for Health Communication, Harvard School of Public Health, 2001

Sirommin, M. *Five Cries of Youth: Issues that Trouble Young People Today.* San Francisco: Harper, 1993.

Sleigh, J. *Thirteen to Nineteen, Discovering the Light: Conversations with Parents.* Edinburgh: Floris Books, 1990.

Staley, B. *Between Form and Freedom: A Practical Guide to the Teenage Years.* Stroud, Gloucestershire: Hawthorn Press, 1988.

Steiner, Rudolf. *Education for Adolescents.* Hudson, NY: Anthroposophic Press, 2001.

———. *Observations on Adolescence: The Third Phase of Human Development*, David Mitchell, ed. Fair Oaks, CA: Association of Waldorf Schools of North America, 2001.

Van den Berg, A. et al. *Rock Bottom: Beyond Drug Addiction.* Stroud, Gloucestershire: Hawthorn Press, 1987.

Wakerman, Elyce. *Fatherloss: Daughters Discuss the Man that Got Away.* New York: Henry Holt, 1987.

Sources on the Parzival legend

Godwin, M. *The Holy Grail: Its Origins, Secrets and meaning Revealed.* New York: Viking Penguin, 1994.

Hutchins, E. *Parzival: An Introduction.* London: Temple Lodge, 1979.

Kovacs, Charles. *Parsifal and the Search for the Grail.* Edinburgh: Floris Books, 2002.

Matthews, John. *Sources of the Grail.* Hudson, NY: Lindisfarne, 1996.

Polikoff, Daniel J., ed. and trans. *Parzival, Gawain: Two plays Drawn from Der Grahl by A.. M. Miller.* Fair Oaks, CA: Rudolf Steiner College Press, 2003.

Querido, René. *The Mystery of the Holy Grail: A Modern Path of Initiation.* Fair Oaks, CA: Rudolf Steiner College Press, 1991.

Stein, Walter Johannes. *History in Light of the Holy Grail: The Ninth Century.* Written in London 1948. English typescript; translation assisted by Mrs. I. Groves, Miss D. Lenn, and Mrs. V. Plincke.

Steiner, Rudolf. *The Holy Grail: The Quest for the Renewal of the Mysteries.* Forest Row, east Sussex: Sophia Book Rudolf Steiner Press, 2001.

Sussman, Linda. *Speech of the Grail: A Journey Toward Speaking that Heals and Transforms.* New York: Lindisfarne, 1995.

About the Author and Rudolf Steiner College

Betty Staley was born in 1938 in the Bronx, New York, attended City University of New York, graduating Phi Beta Kappa with a B.A. degree in psychology with a minor in history. She received her Waldorf teacher training at the Michael Hall Teacher Training Course, Sussex, England. She earned her M.A. in Education at St. Mary's College, Moraga, California. Ms. Staley began her Waldorf teaching at the Sacramento Waldorf School as kindergarten substitute and handwork teacher, then became a class teacher from 5th through 8th grade, and returned to take a 7th grade, which she then led to become the first high school class, which graduated in 1978. She guided the high school and taught in it full-time for nineteen years. Ms. Staley was one of the founders of Rudolf Steiner College, Fair Oaks, California where she is now directing the Foundation Year program and the Waldorf High School Teacher Education program.

She has been a consultant and guide to Waldorf teachers, both in independent Waldorf schools and in Waldorf methods public schools, and for teachers of at-risk students. A worldwide lecturer on child and adolescent development, multiculturalism, and Waldorf education, Ms. Staley is the author of five books including *Tapestries: Weaving Life's Journey; Soul Weaving; Between Form and Freedom: A practical Guide to the Teenage Years;* and *Hear the Voice of the Griot! A Guide to African Geography, History and Culture.*

Rudolf Steiner College is one of America's leading Waldorf teacher education colleges. It is also a center for anthroposophical studies and transformative adult education.

Programs at the College arise out of the work of Austrian philosopher, scientist and educator Rudolf Steiner (1861–1925) whose innovative ideas and discoveries have inspired a wide spectrum of practical activities worldwide—in the arts, banking, architecture, medicine, agriculture, and care of the disabled, as well as education.

Located on a beautiful thirteen acre campus in Fair Oaks, California, just outside of Sacramento, the College offers students a wide range of full-time and part-time educational opportunities including Waldorf teacher training, personal enrichment classes, workshops and cultural events. The campus includes a bookstore, publishing house, bio-dynamic garden and orchard, a performance hall, a student housing complex, and a LifeWays Children's Center. There are also two satellite locations—in San Francisco and Los Altos.

Waldorf education balances artistic, academic and practical work, educating the whole child, hand and heart as well as mind. Its innovative methodology and developmentally-oriented curriculum, permeated with the arts, address the child's changing consciousness as it unfolds, stage by stage. Imagination and creativity are cultivated as well as cognitive growth and a sense of responsibility for the earth and its inhabitants. Under the warm and active instruction of their teachers, children are provided with a creative and nurturing environment in which to develop, grow and learn.

Since its founding by Rudolf Steiner in 1919, the Waldorf school movement has grown to over 800 schools throughout the world, over 150 of them in the United States and Canada.

For further information, go to www.steinercollege.edu